NATIVES

Race and Class in the Ruins of Empire

AKALA

www.tworoadsbooks.com

First published in Great Britain in 2018 by Two Roads
An imprint of John Murray Press
An Hachette UK company

This paperback edition first published in 2019

4

A CIP catalogue record for this title is available from the British Library

Paperback ISBN 9781473661233
eBook ISBN 9781473661240
Audio Digital Download 9781473674400

Typeset in Sabon MT by Hewer Text UK Ltd, Edinburgh
Printed and bound in Great Britain by Clays Ltd, Elcograf S.p.A.

Hodder & Stoughton policy is to use papers that are natural, renewable
and recyclable products and made from wood grown in sustainable
forests. The logging and manufacturing processes are expected to
conform to the environmental regulations of the country of origin.

Hodder & Stoughton Ltd
Carmelite House
50 Victoria Embankment
London EC4Y 0DZ

To Uncle Offs

CONTENTS

1 – BORN IN THE 1980S

I was born in the 1980s and I grew up in the clichéd, single-parent working-class family. We often depended on state benefits, we lived in a council house, I ate free school meals. I am the child of a British-Caribbean father and a Scottish/English mother, my teenage parents were never married and they separated before I was born. My dad spent a portion of his childhood in and out of the care system and my mum was pretty much disowned by her father for getting with a 'nig nog'. The first time I saw someone being stabbed I was twelve, maybe thirteen, the same year I was searched by the police for the first time. I first smoked weed when I was nine and many of my 'uncles' – meaning biological uncles as well as family friends – went to prison. My upbringing was, on the face of it, typical of those of my peers who ended up meeting an early death or have spent much of their adult lives in and out of prison.

I was born in Crawley, West Sussex, but moved to Camden in north-west London before I had formed any concrete memories and I spent my childhood and teenage years living there. Camden is home to 130 languages and about as wide a divide between rich and poor as anywhere in the country. I went to school with the children of lords and ladies, millionaires, refugees, children clearly suffering from malnourishment and young boys selling drugs for their fathers. If there is anywhere in Britain that could serve as a petri dish for examining race, class and culture, Camden would be that place.

I was born in the 1980s in the 'mother country' of the British Commonwealth, the seat of the first truly global empire, the birthplace of 'the' industrial revolution and the epicentre of global finance. What does this mean? What are the social and historical forces that even allowed my parents to meet? My father is the British-born child of two African-Jamaican migrant workers who came to the mother country as part of the Windrush generation. My mother was an army child, born in Germany, spending her infant years in Hong Kong and moving to the small town in which I was born in her early teens. In my parents' meeting are untold histories of imperial conquest, macroeconomic change, slave revolts, decolonisation and workers' struggles. I was born poor, by Western standards at least. I was born poor and racialised as black – despite my 'white' mother – in perhaps the most tumultuous decade of Britain's domestic racial history.

I was born in the 1980s, before mixed-race children had become an acceptable fashion accessory. A nurse in the hospital promised to give my white mother 'nigger blood' when she needed a transfusion after giving birth; yeah, the 1980s was a decade bereft of political correctness.

The 1980s was also the decade of Thatcherite–Reaganite ascendency. The 'golden age of capitalism' had ended in 1973, and the 80s saw the start of the rollback of the post-war welfare state, increased sell-off of public assets and the embrace of an individualistic 'self-made' logic by the very generation that had become wealthy with the support of free universities and cheap council houses, and had literally been kept alive by the newly constructed National Health Service. The decade saw the most powerful military machine ever assembled spun into existential crisis by the enormous threat posed by the potential of a socialist revolution on the tiny little Caribbean island of Grenada, and the self-appointed captains of global democracy could be found backing genocidal regimes from Nicaragua to South Africa – though that could've been any decade, really. It was the decade Thomas Sankara was killed, the Berlin Wall fell, Michael Jackson started to turn white and the MOVE movement was bombed from the sky. The 1980s were fairly eventful, to say the least.

For black Britain, the decade began with the New Cross fire/massacre of 1981, a suspected racist arson attack at 439 New Cross Road, where Yvonne Ruddock was celebrating her sixteenth birthday party.[1] Thirteen of the partygoers burned to death, including the birthday girl, and one of the survivors also later committed suicide. Many of the families of the dead have maintained to this day that a) it was an arson attack and b) the police bungled the investigation and treated the families of the dead like suspects instead of victims. The community's suspicion that it was an arson attack was perfectly reasonable, given that it came in the wake of a string of such racist arson attacks in that area of south-east London.[2] The prime minister did not even bother to offer condolences to what were apparently British children and their families. Of course, Thatcher could not, in her heart of hearts, express sympathy for black British children while supporting an apartheid government rooted in the idea that black people were subhuman, so at least she was consistent. There certainly was not going to be a minute's silence and most of Britain is completely unaware it even happened, despite the New Cross fire being one of the largest single losses of life in post-war Britain.

The same year also saw the passing of the British Nationality Act, the last of a series of Acts that were passed from 1962 onwards and whose racialised motivations were barely disguised. British Caribbeans had come to learn that they were indeed second-class citizens – as many had long suspected – but they were not of a mood to be quiet and keep their heads down about it. New Cross led to the largest demonstration by black people in British history; 20,000 marched on parliament on a working weekday and foretold of the harsh realities of the decade to come: 'Blood a go run, if justice na come' was the chant. It was to prove prophetic.

The rest of the decade of my birth was punctuated by uprisings and disturbances in almost all of the Caribbean and 'Asian' areas of the country, as well as the miners' strikes of 1984–85 and the constant presence of the anti-apartheid struggle. These 'disturbances' included the infamous Brixton riots of 1981, set off by the sus laws – a resurrection of the 1824 Vagrancy Act, these laws allowed people to be arrested on the mere suspicion that they *intended* to commit a crime – and their manifestation in Swamp81, a racialised mass stop-and-search police campaign.

Brixton burned again in 1985, set aflame by the police shooting and paralysing Cherry Groce. Just a week later, the death of Cynthia Jarret after a police raid on her home sparked the Broadwater Farm riots, where a police officer was killed. I know members of both families personally, and grew up with the son of Smiley Culture, the reggae artist who died during a police raid on his home in 2011. I mention these connections only to point out that these people are not abstractions or mere news items, but members of a community, our community. Dalian Atkinson, the former Premier League footballer, was tasered to death by the police in 2016; it's hard to imagine a former pop star or a retired footballer from any other community in Britain dying after contact with the police.

These 1980s reactions to state violence, racism, poverty and class conflict were by no means limited to London; there was the St Paul's riot in Bristol in 1980, Moss Side and Toxteth in the north-west of England in 1981, Handsworth in the Midlands in 1981 and 1985 and Chapletown in Leeds in 1981 and 1987. How many millions of pounds of damage these outpourings of rage caused I don't know, but now that they are sufficiently distant from the present, very few academics would dispute that they had very real socio-political causes. Indeed, entire books have been written on them, and government policy and police behaviour and training were reformed in direct response to these events, though what lessons the British state has truly learned from the 1980s remains to be seen.

It's easy for people just slightly younger than myself, and born into a relative degree of multiculturalism, to forget just how recently basic public decency towards black folks was won in this country, but I was born in the 80s so I remember only too well. I was five years old when the infamous picture was taken of footballer John Barnes, kicking away the banana that had been thrown at him from the stands. I grew up routinely watching some of England's greatest ever football players suffer this type of humiliation in their workplace, in front of tens of thousands of people, who for the most part seemed to find it entirely acceptable, funny even. I knew Cyril Regis personally (rest in power, sir), I know about the bullets in the post and the death threats received by black players from their 'own' supporters and apparent countrymen because they wanted to play for England. No one asked in public discourse where that association with black people and monkeys came from, because if they did we might have to speak of historical origins, of savage myths and of literal human zoos.

I was not born with an opinion of the world but it clearly seemed that the world had an opinion of people like me. I did not know what race and class supposedly were but the world taught me very quickly, and the irrational manifestations of its prejudices forced me to search for answers. I did not particularly want to spend a portion of a lifetime studying these issues, it was not among my ambitions as a child, but I was compelled upon this path very early, as I stared at Barnsey kicking away that banana skin or when I sat in the dark and the freezing cold simply because my mum did not make enough money. I knew that these experiences were significant but I was not yet sure how to tease meaning from them.

I was born in the 1980s, when MPs in parliament could be found arguing that we – non-white Commonwealth citizens – should be sent back to where we came from. Now that where we came from had legally ceased to be part of Britain, our very existence here was seen as the problem. So, after our grandmothers had helped build the National Health Service and our grandfathers had staffed the public transport system, British MPs could openly talk about repatriation – we were no longer needed, excess labour, surplus to requirements, of no further use to capital. The entire management of 'race' – the media propaganda, the overstaffed mental institutions, the severe unemployment, the massively disproportionate incarceration rates and school expulsions – has to be understood in the context of why we were invited here in the first place. It was not so that we, en masse, could access the best of what British society had to offer, because that was not even on offer to the majority of the white population at the time. We were invited here to do the menial work that needed doing in the years immediately following the Second World War, and even in that very limited capacity, all post-war governments – including Attlee's spirit of 45 lot – were deeply concerned about the long-term effects of letting brown-skinned British citizens into the country.

The government and the education system failed to explain to white Britain that, as the academic Adam Elliot-Cooper puts it, we had not come to Britain, but 'rather that Britain had come to us'. They did not explain that the wealth of Britain, which made the welfare state and other class ameliorations possible, was derived in no small part from the coffee and tobacco, cotton and diamonds, gold and sweat and blood and death of the colonies. No one explained that our grandparents were not immigrants, that they were literally British citizens – many of them Second World War veterans – with British passports to match, moving from one of Britain's outposts to the metropole. Nobody told white Britain that, over there in the colonies, Caribbeans and Asians were being told that Britain was their mother country, that it was the home of peace and justice and prosperity and that they would be welcomed with open arms by their loving motherland. Similarly, no one told my grandparents and others over there in the colonies that most white Britons were actually poor, or that the UK had a history of brutal labour exploitation and class conflict at home. You see, out there in the colonies, whiteness implies aristocracy, whiteness is aspirational, and as the only white people my grandparents knew of in Jamaica were the ruling classes, this association was entirely rational. My uncle could not contain his shock when 'me come a England and me cyan believe say white man a sweep street'; the illusion was ruined the moment his four-year-old self got off the boat in the 1950s and saw poor white people. How preposterous – what is this place?

Within a week, my uncle also discovered that he was a black bastard – some adult let him know while he was in the sweet shop. You see, while the people in the colonies were being told Britain was their mother, much of white Britain had convinced itself that these undeserving niggers – Asians were niggers too, back then – had just got off their banana boats to come and freeload, to take 'their' jobs and steal 'their' women. Never mind that Britain has a German royal family, a Norman ruling elite, a Greek patron saint, a Roman/Middle Eastern religion, Indian food as its national cuisine, an Arabic/Indian numeral system, a Latin alphabet and an identity predicated on a multi-ethnic, globe-spanning empire – 'fuck the bloody foreigners'. Never mind that waves of migration have been a constant in

British history and that great many millions of 'white' Britons are themselves descendants of Jewish, Eastern European and Irish migrants of the nineteenth century,[3] nor that even in the post-war 'mass migration' years, Ireland and Europe were the largest source of immigrants.[4] And, of course, let's say nothing about the millions of British emigrants, settlers and colonists abroad – conveniently labelled 'expats'.

The reaction to our grandparents, and even more to their British-born children, was one of general and irrational revulsion, such that the mere mention of their treatment is sure to elicit rage and embarrassment today, now that the pioneering Windrush generation has officially become part of Britain's national story. These people who came to labour in post-war Britain were greeted by de facto segregation, verbal abuse, violent attacks and even murder, motivated by nothing more than their brown and black skin. Immigration acts put a stop to the British citizenship claims of the non-white Commonwealth, and hundreds of millions of British citizens were stripped of their citizenship and the freedom of movement that a British passport gave them, simply because they were not white. In a barely disguised move in the 1968 and 1971 immigration acts 'grandfather clauses' were placed into the legislation, which allowed the white citizens of the Commonwealth to continue to keep their freedom of movement without having to use explicitly racial language.[5]

Despite all this, my grandfather Brinsley worked hard, saved his pennies and moved out to the suburbs. Everything British capitalism says a good worker should do for the system to reward them – which, to be fair, it obviously did in his case. His neighbours all signed a petition to have the nigger removed from the street but my granddad, for reasons I could never quite understand, chose to stay put. As a homeowner surrounded by council tenants he could not be moved. My grandmother,

Millicent, also saved her pennies and bought a home, but she stayed in London. This was all back when a worker in London could have any hope at all of buying their home; soaring house prices have permanently put an end to that.

The 1980s drew to a close with the Hillsborough disaster, in which ninety-six people were crushed to death during an FA Cup semi-final game between Liverpool and Nottingham Forest. In the aftermath of the tragedy, the national press and police blamed the Liverpool fans for the disaster, relying on crude class stereotypes of them as drunk hooligans. The *Sun* went as far as claiming that some fans were pickpocketing the dead and that others had urinated on the police; to this day people in Liverpool boycott the paper as a result. After twenty-seven years of tireless family campaigning, an inquest finally reached a verdict of unlawful killing that laid the blame for the deaths at the doors of the police.

So where are we now? Has nothing at all changed since the decade I was born? While it's obviously true that aristocratic privilege and whiteness are among the basic assumptions of British ruling-class ideology, it's also obvious that Britain's inner cities – London in particular – are now some of the most successfully multi-ethnic experiments in the 'Western' world, despite what the right-wing press would like to pretend. Multi-ethnic Britain is a result of what scholar Paul Gilroy calls our 'convivial' culture, the normal everyday decency of ordinary people that for the most part keeps the peace in the face of enormous challenges.[6] Racism and anti-racism, complete contempt for the poor and Christian charity, home to the world's top universities and a strong disdain for learning, the pioneer of 'Anglo-globalisation' whose citizens constantly bemoan other peoples right to move freely without a hint of irony – Britain has long been a land of startling paradoxes. For example, why did Britain have an abolitionist movement on a far greater scale than any of the other major European slave-holding powers, even while Britain had become the premier slave trader? Why, two centuries later, was there such revulsion towards and organisation against apartheid by 'radical' groups here, even as 'our' government, British corporations and banks supported it? (Though the British struggle against apartheid in Britain was not without its own racial tensions, ironically.[7])

Britain has two competing traditions – one rooted in ideas of freedom, equality and democracy, and another that sees these words as mere rhetoric to be trotted out at will and violated whenever it serves the Machiavellian purposes of power preservation. This is how the UK can have the largest of the demonstrations against the invasion of Iraq and yet still have a government that entirely ignored its population on an issue with such globe-shifting implications.

Severe class inequalities persist, and while it's probably unrealistic to expect a society with which everyone can be satisfied, by European standards the British class system is still particularly pernicious. It's not that racism has disappeared from the UK since the 1980s, but without a doubt the resistance of black and Asian communities during the decade of my birth produced very significant reforms that have changed the way my generation experiences and understands 'race'. The gollywogs and banana skins are no longer a daily feature of black life here and neither is the Special Patrol Group, the notoriously abusive policing unit that gave almost all of the older men in my life a bloody good hiding, more than once. Though police brutality of course continues, few would deny things are far better in this respect than thirty years ago, for now at least.

The physical battles fought by our parents' generation have meant that 'nigger hunting' and 'Paki bashing' are far less common than they once were too. My father's and uncles' bodies are tattooed with scars from fighting the National Front

(NF), Teddy Boys and Skinheads; mine is not. We should not underestimate the newly emboldened bigots, though, and racist violence seems to be on the rise again.

This is partly because, despite much seeming and some very real progress, public discourse about racism is still as childish and supine as it ever was. Where we do discuss race in public, we have been trained to see racism – if we see it at all – as an issue of interpersonal morality. Good people are not racist, only bad people are. This neat binary is a great way of avoiding any real discussion at all. But without the structural violence of unequal treatment before the law and in education, and a history of racial exploitation by states, simple acts of personal prejudice would have significantly less meaning. In short, we are trained to recognise the kinds of racism that tend to be engaged in by poorer people. Thus even the most pro-empire of historians would probably admit that some football hooligan calling a Premier League player a 'black cunt' is a bad thing, even while they spend their entire academic careers explaining away, downplaying and essentially cheering for the mass-murdering white-supremacist piracy of the British Empire, which starved millions to death in India, enslaved and tortured millions more in countless locations and often used its power to crush, not enhance, popular democracy and economic development in its non-white colonies, especially when doing so suited larger aims.[8] Poor people racism, bad, rich people racism, good.

The kinds of racism still engaged in by the wealthy and the powerful – such as the theft of entire regions' resources under a thinly veiled update of 'the white man's burden' (basically 'the savages can't govern themselves'), or profiteering from a racially unjust legal and prison system – are far more egregious and damaging. Yet these forms of racism are given far less attention than racism as simple name-calling. John Terry calling Anton Ferdinand a 'black cunt' in front of millions of viewers may well be deplorable, but the Football Association's and England management's subsequent equivocation over whether to take him to the 2012 European Championships, over Anton's brother Rio, and for England as a nation to be happy and proud to be captained by a man who racially abuses his peers in the workplace, is the more interesting case study for any discussion about how race operates. Had the England team chosen to drop John Terry immediately and pick Rio instead, I'm sure there would have been uproar from much of the country, despite Rio's obvious abilities.

In the run-up to the 2017 general election, online racists told black MP Diane Abbott that they would 'hang her if they could find a tree strong enough for the fat black bitch' – just one message among the slew of racist and sexist abuse she regularly receives. It seems Britain's most honest racists emphasise the spiritual connection they feel for their American cousins quite well. Yet in reality, the hanging of black people was never a particular phenomenon in domestic Britain; ironically, the vast majority of people hung in British history were white, and they were often poor people hung by the state for not respecting rich people's property.[9] Oh the irony, oh the lack of respect for one's own ancestors!

All said and done, the idea of racial hierarchy and the attendant philosophy of innate white superiority were not invented by poor people, and while we are not excusing the central role that everyday racism has played in upholding racial hierarchies in the UK and elsewhere, our critique should not rest there.

While ethnic bigotry has been around for millennia and probably affects every known human community to some degree, the invention, or at least codification, of 'race' was an eighteenth and nineteenth century pan-Euro-American project, in which British intellectuals played a central role. Britain also had a pioneering role in making white supremacy a temporary political reality via its racialised global empire, yet to publicly discuss racism, much less have the gall to accurately name white supremacy as a strong current in Britain's history, is to be greeted with odium by some who claim to study that history, but it seems would rather be left to uncritically celebrate it in peace.

But what am *I* 'complaining' about, you might justifiably ask? Have I not, after all, had quite a good life so far, all things told? Yes, indeed, despite these historic forces and the kind of household I was born into, here I stand, a self-employed entrepreneur my entire adult life, an independent artist who has toured the world many times over and someone who barely went to college yet who has lectured at almost every university in the country. I come from one of the statistically least likely groups to attain five GCSE passes – white and 'mixed-race' boys on free school meals fail at an even greater rate than 'fully black' boys on free school meals do – but I got ten GCSEs, including multiple A* grades. I took my maths GCSE a year early and attended the Royal Institution's Mathematics master-classes as a schoolboy.

Am I unique? Do I have some special sauce that has made me different from so many of my peers? Surely my very existence proves Britain is meritocratic, and that if you just work hard you'll 'make it'? If there is a UK equivalent of the 'American Dream', aren't I one small example of its manifestation? Not only me, but my siblings too; my older sister is Ms. Dynamite, whom I'm sure you've heard of, one of my younger sisters is an award winning stuntwoman called Belle Williams who has worked on some of the biggest films ever made, my sixteen-year-old brother also just also got ten GCSEs and currently wants to be a neuroscientist. Isn't my successful, rags to half-way riches 'mixed race' family further living proof of the very social mobility that I am claiming is mostly fictional?

If only things were so simple. If only exceptions did not prove the rule.

The purpose of this book is to examine how these seemingly impersonal forces – race and class – have impacted and continue to shape our lives, and how easily I could now be telling you a very different but much more common story of cyclical violence, prison and part-time, insecure and low-paying work.

You see, alongside the familiar tropes and trappings of inner-city life, I also had many unusual things stacked in my favour: I went to a special pan-African Saturday school that made up for what my state schooling lacked; my stepdad was the stage manager of the Hackney Empire, thus I saw more theatre growing up than any rich child is likely to; I had politicised and militantly pro-education parents who were always willing to fight my corner against teachers, whenever and wherever necessary. Some of my happiest childhood memories were formed in the public library that was almost on the corner of our street, a facility that played no small part in inculcating in me an almost irrational love of books. I already own more books than I could ever read, yet I often still go to bookshops just to look at, browse and smell the pages of a freshly printed one – sadly nerdy, I know. Had I not had access to free public libraries courtesy of the taxpayer, and a mum willing and able to take me, this book you hold probably would never have been written. Yet, despite all of this, I still carried a knife out of fear and flirted with petty crime after I had left school.

Black consciousness did not save me from carrying a knife, and nor could it protect me in the streets, but it certainly shaped my sense of self-worth and imbued me with a community-oriented moral compass. It would be easy for me to ignore these factors and claim myself to be a 'self-made' man, but in reality there is no such thing.

Countless teachers and community activists gave me the tools for navigating life's roadmap; football coaches taught me to play and kept me out of trouble. I am not saying that my own hard work, discipline and sacrifice have played no role in my life's outcomes; that would be absurd. But I am saying that even these characteristics were nourished with help, support and encouragement from others, and that without this support – much of it from volunteers – it's inconceivable that I would be where I am today. When I say I could have been a statistic – another working-class black man dead or in prison – people who did not grow up how we grew up probably think it an exaggeration. But people that grew up like us know just how real this statement is, just how easily the scales could have been tipped.

Yes, I grew up without my father in the home, but we kept in contact and I went to stay with him and his new family many a school holiday. My stepdad was also a very positive influence in my life before he and my mother had a difficult split and, reflecting the unusual mix of cultures that is normal in Camden, I even had an 'uncle' from Cyprus called Andrew, who looked out for me all through my teenage years. But of all the men in my life, it is my godfather, 'Uncle Offs', the man to whom this book is dedicated, who made the biggest impact on my upbringing. While he was technically just a family friend, he has played a greater role in my life than many parents do in the lives of their own children. He was so close to my parents, and loved me and my siblings so much, that when my mum got cancer he agreed to let us live with him if she died, despite the fact that he had three children of his own and lived on a council estate in Hackney. I often wonder where men like my Uncle Offs fit in to the stereotype of the supposedly ubiquitously absent black father.

There were other benefits too that, while not exclusive to my family, are an inescapable part of our narrative. I got the measles aged five and I got treatment, for free. My mum got cancer when I was ten; she got treatment, also for free, and both courtesy of the NHS. I went on subsidised school trips to Rome and Barcelona that greatly expanded my horizons. In another time and space, someone born into my socio-economic bracket would have had to drop out of school and work to help feed the family; indeed, one of my best friends, the legendary Brazilian hip hop artist MC Marechal, had to do just that, as do countless children all across the world today through no fault of their own, just because of the lottery of birth. I am partly a product of Britain's injustices, of its history of class and race oppression, but also of its counter-narrative of struggle and the compromises made by those in power born of those struggles. I am a product of the empire, and also of the welfare state.

My age group, born in the early 1980s, find ourselves in a kind of black limbo; we are the last set of black Brits old enough to remember the old-school racism, though we only witnessed it as children as our parents comprehensively defeated it, in the major cities at least. While the generation born in 1981 is far poorer than those born in 1971 for the general population,[10] the narrative is more complicated for black people. Some of my generation, like me, have had opportunities afforded us that might have been far less likely had we been born just a decade earlier, and black British music in particular has a public international profile it has never had before. Millions of people from all communities right across the country care more about what Stormzy and Jme think about the world than their politicians, and the central role played by the Grime4Corbyn campaign in shifting the centre ground in British politics will no doubt inspire a slew of PhDs at some point in the future, if it hasn't already.

The changes brought by reform manifest in odd ways.

When I rented my first nice flat, I had a disagreement with the black man working at the estate agent after he told me, 'You should feel lucky, because coloured folks like us never usually get these kinds of opportunities.' Obviously it's an extreme example of self-hatred to think it is a privilege for black people to be able to give away thousands of pounds of their hard-earned money, but as more young black people in London and elsewhere become materially successful, it will complicate class–race dynamics and continue to challenge people's expectations.

I remember back in 2011 I was getting ready to interview a legendary black poet and activist for a programme I presented on Channel 4 called *Life of Rhyme* and, as myself and the crew finished setting up, he asked 'Where is the producer?' I pointed to the black woman with me. He then asked, 'Where is the director?' I pointed to the black man with me. The interviewee paused, then said 'Wow, in my day you would have never have gotten that' – an all-black film crew, that is. Of course, one only has to walk into the BBC, C4, or any major corporation to see that this is not a generalized trend; their staffs do not even close to accurately reflect the ethnic composition of the city in which they are situated. But nonetheless, if a poet whose entire career has been spent fighting racism can find himself looking for the 'white person in charge', it gives us a sense of the degree to which reality has conditioned our expectations, even in London. (To be fair to him, there *were* actually white people in charge of the production, as senior directors and producers, they just happened to not be with us that day.)

What both the poet and the confused estate agent were commenting on is the fact that there is a visible nascent black middle class on a scale that there just wasn't with our parents' generation. The trend is reflected in some of the occupations of my friend group – a classical composer, a university professor, a W10 bar owner, a trauma surgeon and a couple of lawyers, all second or third-generation black Brits. Though we should not wrap ourselves in joy just as yet, as the changing nature of my friends' occupations could also be seen to reflect the general closing of 'British' industry, and these exceptional cases sit alongside the ever-deepening reality of a black underclass that is in the process of permanently joining the much older white underclass. This process has been chronicled in the press obsession with gangs, and with making gangs synonymous with young black boys, despite the obvious fact that violent working-class youth gangs have been part of British history for well over a century, and despite the fact that they are still prevalent in areas of the country where there are hardly any black people, such as Glasgow, Durham, Cleveland, Belfast and most other decaying, post-industrial centres of deprivation.

Of course, a few successful black people also do very little to alter the race–class dynamics of the UK and can even help to cement it. These successes can and will be used – even sometimes by the 'middle class' respectable black people themselves – to beat other poor people that 'didn't make it' over the head. They can be used to pretend that the system is just and there are enough seats at the table – 'if you just work hard and pull your socks up you can be like me' – rather than simply being honest about the way things actually work. Most people, it seems to me at least, hate poor people more than they hate poverty.

This is classic, the old pull yourself up by the bootstraps trope. It ignores that people are not inherently good or bad, and that even 'bad' decisions are made in a context. For example, my aforementioned gangster uncles universally encouraged me to stay in school, paid me pocket money for reciting the theory of evolution to them as a child and even threatened to give me a bloody good hiding if I tried to be like them – i.e. a criminal. My good friend, a retired Premier League footballer from the notorious Stonebridge estate, was officially banned from the 'front line' by all the drug dealers in 'the ends' when he was growing up. They saw his potential, his chance for a life different to their own, and these 'bad' people – I am not denying that they were indeed hardened criminals – protected him and me.

Meanwhile, some of my white, middle-class teachers made my school life extremely difficult and penalised me for the very thing they were supposed to be nurturing; my intelligence. Law enforcement acted upon my body based on media-induced hysteria regardless of my school grades, my absolute geekiness and the fact that I wanted to be an astronaut when I grew up. We judge the street corner hustler or working-class criminal – from East Glasgow to East London – but we see a job as an investment banker, even in firms that launder the profits of drug cartels, fund terrorism, aid the global flow of arms, fuel war, oil spills, land grabs and generally fuck up the planet, as a perfectly legitimate, even aspirational occupation. I am not even necessarily passing judgment on those who are employed in that system, as I'm complicit in it to a degree because of my consumption, I am just pointing out that our evaluation of what constitutes 'crime' is not guided by morality, it is guided by the law; in other words, the rules set down by the powerful, not a universal barometer of justice – if such a thing even exists. We need not remind ourselves that slavery, apartheid, Jim Crow, a man's right to rape his wife and the chemical castration of gay people were all 'legal' at one stage of very recent history, as was most of what was done by Nazi Germany.

This 'if you just pull your socks up' trope also ignores the reality that many Britons (and people around the globe) are poor and getting poorer through no fault of their own under austerity – the technical term for class robbery. Can a nurse whose pay increases are capped at 1 per cent – below the rate of inflation – by politicians who have not capped their own pay, change the fact that he or she is literally getting poorer every passing year, despite doing the same bloody hard work?

So yes, in one sense we have come a long way since the 1980s. The much maligned 'political correctness' has made it far more difficult for bigots to just say as they please without consequence; there are fewer bullets in the post; we have even gotten used to an England football team that is consistently half full of black players and we even have a few black politicians and a Muslim mayor of London.

Yet despite these enormous changes, the essential problems are still with us and we look increasingly set for a re-run of the 1980s in twenty-first century clothes. The national riots of 2011, sparked by the police's failure to properly engage with the family and community of Mark Duggan after having shot him dead, bear obvious echoes of the past. The media's decision, in the crucial first forty-eight hours after the incident, to unquestioningly parrot the police's version of events that Mark had shot at them first showed that the workings of state power and mainstream media have altered very little in the intervening decades.

The horrendous Grenfell Tower fire in June 2017, which claimed at least seventy-one lives and was undeniably caused by systematic contempt for the lives of poor people, was perhaps the ultimate and most gruesome tribute to austerity yet seen. The state's reaction, or total lack of reaction, in the days after the fire versus the overwhelming outpouring of public support was one of the strangest things I have ever seen with my own eyes. The slew of racist abuse and virulent hate that can be found in any thread online discussing the Grenfell victims – who happened to be disproportionately Muslims – and the conceptual linking of the dead families to the terrorists at London Bridge and Manchester in the previous months speaks loudly of how 'Muslim' has become a racialised, culturally essentialist category in twenty-first century Britain. At the time of writing, seven months after the fire, most of the surviving families still have not been re-housed, even after the collection of millions of pounds of donations in their names and despite the fact that the local council is known to have £300 million in cash reserves. I lived on the same street as Grenfell for five years, but my building had sprinklers, working fire alarms, extinguishers and a maintenance man who came to check in every few months. Just a little bit of money can be the difference between life and death, even on the same London street.

There are other signs that the political 'logic' of the 1980s is returning. Despite the fact that Britain imprisons its population at double the rate the Germans do and 30–40 per cent higher than the French, we have a Metropolitan Police chief calling for tougher sentences for 'teenage thugs' and for a return of mass stop and search. Britain's prison population has already grown 82 per cent in three decades with 50 per cent more women in prison than in the 1990s, and there is no corresponding rise in serious crime to explain any of this.[11] If tougher sentences alone worked to reduce crime, the USA would surely be crime free by now? With 10 per cent of Britain's prisons now privatised and many more using prison labour, such seemingly illogical right-wing virtue signalling from the head of London's police starts to look like 'vested interests' and to signal tumultuous times ahead. We all know that black Brits – already seven times more likely to be imprisoned than their white counterparts, and already more harshly treated at every level of the justice system – are going to make up a disproportionate amount of any further increase in Britain's incarceration state.[12] Poor people of all ethnicities will make up most of the rest.

Other recent globe-shifting events in the Anglo-American empire – the recorded execution of Black Americans by the police, including women, children and the elderly; the election as US President of a man openly endorsed by Nazis, the KKK and white supremacist groups and his failure to condemn them even after they murder people; the same man's condemnation of the peaceful protest of Colin Kaepernick and other athletes; the ethnocentric and racist strains to the Brexit campaign rhetoric; the unjust deportations of Commonwealth migrants; the handling of and reporting on 'the migrant crisis' (without reference to Nato's destruction of Libya, of course) – make it pretty clear to any honest observer that the idea and practice of racism is not going anywhere anytime soon.

I was born into these currents, I did not create or invent them and I make no claims to objectivity. I find the whole idea that we can transcend our experiences; and take a totally unbiased look at the world to be totally ridiculous, yet that's what many historians and academics claim to do. We are all influenced by what we are exposed to and experience; the best we can hope for is to try and be as fair as possible from within the bias inherent in existence. The personal is the political, and this book is an attempt to give a personal face to the forces that you will often hear me speak of, if you hear me speak at all. This book is about how the British class system interacts with and feeds off a long and complex relationship with empire and white supremacy, and how those social forces can manifest in and shape the life experience of a random child, born to a father racialised as black and a mother racialised as white, in early 1980s England.

INTERLUDE: A GUIDE TO DENIAL

> . . . in a racially structured polity, the only people who
> can find it psychologically possible to deny the centrality
> of race are those who are racially privileged, for whom
> race is invisible precisely because the world is structured
> around them, whiteness as the ground against which the
> figures of other races – those who, unlike us, are raced
> – appear.
>
> Charles Mills, *The Racial Contract*

Before we go any further, I think I need to address the fact that
discussions about race in the UK are rather fascinating and
often coloured by what I am going to call 'A Very British Brand
of Racism'; polite denial, quiet amusement or outright outrage
that one could dare to suggest that the mother of liberty is not
a total meritocracy after all, that we too, like so many 'less civi-
lised' nations around the world, have a caste system. People
who can see so clearly the very real injustices in other nation
states, or even perceive how positive aspects of British history
have shaped the country's current reality, somehow become
unable to think when the lens of examination is turned inwards.
If you have ever attempted to discuss a social ill with a person
who is intensely invested in the order of things as they are, you
will have no doubt been met by some rather odd and profoundly
anti-intellectual responses. This phenomenon of self-induced
stupidity seems to be particularly pronounced and almost
laughably predictable when we attempt to discuss Britain's

racist history and reality with many people racialised as white. Here are a few of the likely 'counter arguments' that will be used in an attempt to silence you.

'If we just stop talking about it [racism] it will go away.'

Well, Morgan Freeman agrees with you,[1] you'll be happy to know, so you have your Blackman validation for ignorance, should you need to deploy it on any 'race-obsessed' idiot. But this idea that racism will vanish if we just refuse to discuss it is rather fascinating. Imagine for a moment if scientists and engineers thought in this way. Imagine they said 'Right, the best way to solve a problem is not to discuss, confront or challenge it, but to leave it alone completely and hope it just works itself out.' There would have been no political, moral, technological, medical, material or mental progress ever in the fragile history of our species if people hadn't decided to confront difficult problems with dialogue and then action.

'Stop playing the race card.'

Racism is apparently a card to be played; much like the joker, it's a very versatile card that can be used in any situation that might require it. Only non-white people ever play this card to excuse their own personal failings – even those of us that are materially successful. Humans racialised as white cannot play the race card – just like they cannot be terrorists – so European national empires colonising almost the entire globe and enacting centuries of unapologetically and openly racist legislation and practices, churning out an impressively large body of proudly racist justificatory literature and cinema and much else has had no impact on shaping human history, it has really just been black and brown people playing cards.

'Why can't you just get over it? It's all in the past.'

These two statements often run together. Apparently, history is not there to be learned from, rather it's a large boulder to be gotten over. It's fascinating, because in the hundreds of workshops I've taught on Shakespeare no one has ever told me to get over his writing because it's, you know, from the, erm, past. I'm still waiting for people to get over Plato, or Da Vinci or Bertrand Russell, or indeed the entirety of recorded history, but it seems they just won't. It is especially odd in a nation where much of the population is apparently proud of Britain's empire that critics of one of its most obvious legacies should be asked to get over it, the very same thing from the past that they are proud of. But anyway, let's imagine for a second that humanity did indeed 'get over' – which in this case means forget – the past. Well, we'd have to learn to walk and talk and cook and hunt and plant crops all over again, we'd have to undo all of human invention and start from . . . when? What period exactly is it we are allowed to start our memory from? Those that tell us to get over the past never seem to specify, but I'm eager to learn. In reality, of course, they just don't want to have any conversations that they find uncomfortable.

'You have a chip on your shoulder.'

This is one of my personal favourites. No one can quite define what a chip on a shoulder actually is, but we know that young black boys in particular seem to suffer from them. Even when these young black boys grow into materially successful men, you can watch the accompanying chip grow ever larger should they discuss any political issues of racial injustice. Examples of people with enormous shoulder chips include Muhammad Ali and Colin Kaepernick, men who gave up millions of dollars to protest injustice. In this materialistic world, even political opponents of Ali and Kaepernick should, in theory at least, admire their willingness to forgo personal comfort and even risk their lives for something so much bigger than themselves. They could easily have kept quiet and just continued being widely admired multi-millionaires. But hey, their political opponents were pro bombing 'gooks' thousands of miles away in one case, and are determined to ignore police brutality, even when police are caught on camera executing twelve-year-olds playing in the park, in the other. So not much hope for logic from them.

'Why don't you just go back to where you came from?'

This one is so unimaginative I hardly know how to respond. Their assumption is that anyone who is not racialised as white is not really a citizen, echoing the old white-supremacist adage 'Race and Nation are one' and the 'blood and soil' logic of the Nazis. When people say this to me I presume they mean Jamaica, as Scotland is still part of Britain – for now. Bless them. Their view of the so-called third world is so blinkered that they think they're insulting me when they say this. Yes, Jamaica has many problems with violence and poverty but, as elsewhere on the globe, the problems of Jamaican society predominantly affect those at the bottom of the social hierarchy.

As a member of the diaspora with some money I would be and am (I go back regularly) largely shielded from the worst aspects of Jamaican society – there I am one of the privileged, even in a 'racial' sense, as being light-skinned or 'mixed' carries with it the assumption of being from the upper-class in the Caribbean. None of my middle-class Jamaican friends experienced anything like the levels of violence and police harassment that I experienced growing up 'poor' in the UK. Many of them went to private school, never missed a meal and had parents who drove flash cars – unlike mine. Don't get me wrong, there are obviously opportunities, privileges and infrastructure that British citizens have access to that much of the world does not, but it is not as simple as many think. I can promise you that wealthy and middle-class Jamaicans – though few in number – have better material conditions of life than the poorest people in the UK. They are not living off food banks and, well, it's impossible to freeze to death in winter. Aside from that, the country is one of the most naturally beautiful places on the planet, with a strong and proud culture and community. There were many reasons our grandparents chose to migrate, but hatred of their home countries was not one of them.

'Well why don't you just go back to Africa then?' (Even if you are from the Caribbean)

Similar to the last one, those that say this believe in the idea of racial credit; they believe that all black people, regardless of class, nationality, political inclination or personal achievements, share racial credit for the shortcomings of the African continent's post-independence leadership. Conversely, they also believe that all those racialised as white, no matter how mediocre they may be in terms of personal intelligence and actual achievements, share some racial credit for the works of Russell, Da Vinci and Tesla, and for the prosperity of the modern 'West'

– even if they have personally played no role in creating this prosperity. Most interestingly, millions of European-Americans whose great-grandparents migrated to America only in the late nineteenth and early twentieth centuries from Germany, Italy, Russia and Ireland say this same thing to black Americans, whose ancestors arrived in the USA much earlier – not to mention the indigenous.

Again though, this is not an insult. I have travelled across much of the continent and I may well decide to move back to where my father's parents came from or to that country called 'Africa', but it will be because that's what I choose, not because some fools think that's where I belong. However unfair this statement is though, there is a degree of realism to it in that as long as African and Caribbean states are politically, economically and militarily weak, lingering ideas of black inferiority will still have an aura of credence, even for many liberals. Bigots here are helpfully suggesting to black people that the unfinished project of political pan-Africanism still awaits us.

'You should be grateful that you have free speech.'

There are a few interesting things implied by this one. First, the idea that 'free speech' is uniquely British – never mind that Britain shares with so many other states a long history of suppressing criticism at home and in its colonies – and therefore something I would not have if I lived elsewhere. Second, the implication that the degree to which Britain has free speech was a gift from enlightened leaders rather than a hard-won right. The Chartists might disagree, but much of Britain seems depressingly committed to forgetting its own radical history. Third, the idea that one should be grateful that your government does not kill, torture or imprison you for your criticisms is an extremely low bar of expectation coming from people who are apparently proud of their nation's democratic credentials.

Intriguingly, Jamaica regularly ranks in the top ten for press freedom globally, ranking eighth in 2017 for example, sandwiched in between Switzerland and Belgium, while Britain has slipped twelve places to fortieth in global rankings over the past five years. As you can see, Britain has been quite substantially behind its former colony in this respect for quite some time, despite Jamaica facing much graver political challenges. Furthermore, almost all of Jamaica's most prominent music artists have spent a good portion of their careers cussing the Jamaican government and, while general police brutality is a serious problem in Jamaica, the kidnap and torture of critical artists by the state have been virtually unheard of over the past three decades. If artistic free speech and press freedoms exist in the much more politically challenging terrains of Jamaica, Trinidad or Ghana (all three of these former colonies ranked above Britain last year) what is it exactly that we should be so grateful for here in the sixth richest nation on the planet?

'You just hate Britain, you are anti-British.'

This one is related to many of the others in that it implies that those of us that critique Britain's historic and current injustices are not real citizens of the country. Again, if we compare this with how critical artists are treated and viewed in some other nations the idiocy of the 'anti' label becomes apparent. For example, Fela Kuti is unquestionably Nigeria's most legendary musical icon, yet he was a constant opponent of the Nigerian government and critic of the failings of Nigerian society, to the point that the army killed his mother, yet still they could not shut him up. His sons continue that critical tradition today. Do Nigerians in general consider him anti-Nigerian and a hater of the country because of this? No, in fact quite the reverse – he is the country's greatest musical hero. The situation is much the same with Jamaica's Reggae musicians, who have had to struggle against poverty, endemic class snobbery and the Jamaican state's persecution of their predominant religion – Rasta – to become some of the most important and respected voices in Jamaican society and indeed the entire world of music.

Even if we return this idiocy to 'white' Britain, what would have happened if the Tolpuddle Martyrs, the suffragettes, Tom Paine, the Chartists, those that campaigned to end child labour and slavery had all shut up for fear of being called 'anti-British'? Put simply, many of the freedoms that people take for granted simply might not exist. What's more, this 'anti-British' label shows that the person using it conflates the interests of the British ruling class and their cronies in the House of Lords and the arms, oil and banking cabals with the interests of Britain's people as a whole. That said, I am not a nationalist, so to be accused of lacking sufficient patriotism does not fill me with indignation.

'But what about [INSERT ANY INJUSTICE HERE]?'

Yes, I am aware there is still a caste system and persecution of Sikhs in India, that the 'Islamic world' had several slave-holding waves of empire centuries before the rise of the modern West and that Islamic fascism, Hindu fascism in India and the persecution of Muslims in Burma all exist. I am aware that Kurds, Ainu, West Papuans, Palestinians, Indigenous Americans and Australians and a whole host of other people have far worse sufferings to speak of than black people in Britain. I am aware that no human community is perfect and that injustices exist everywhere. You have not made an insightful observation by distraction. Additionally, the idea that the spread of Euro-American imperialism has played no role in helping cement or prolong some of the above injustices is, well, rather quaint; but even if that were the case, we could deflect from any number of injustices with the 'what about?' clause. There are great studies on all of the above subjects, and this book does not negate any of them.

'You're obsessed with identity politics.'

This one is all the rage lately and 'identity politics' is spoken about as if it were something entirely new. Of course in reality Britain has a long history of crafting polities not around merit or even solely class distinctions but also around white identity.

Also, please explain to me how all politics is not in part 'identity' politics. Are 'working class' (especially in a post-industrial welfare state) 'Irish', 'Christian', 'Jewish' and 'Japanese' not all identities? Please explain how humans organised into any group identity can have an identity-less politics. Again, if you just don't want to hear from and engage with people from my identity or the experiences we've had as a result of that identity, no worries, put the book down, don't follow me on Twitter or watch me on YouTube. I am not stalking you, fam.

'You are trying to blame me for what my ancestors did.'

This one usually arises when discussing the particularly sensitive area of Britain's role in the transatlantic traffic in enslaved

Africans. 'I never owned slaves' or so the strawman logic goes. Well of course, everybody knows that no one alive in Britain today owned an African person, but that does very little to change how significant a role slavery played in Britain's history.[2] Also, as the writer Gary Younge once explained, people in Britain naturally take pride in positive national events they had no direct role in – 'we won the world cup', 'we won the war' – yet many seem less willing to confront the more negative aspects of our history. People seem rather happy to align themselves with the Dunkirk spirit but rather less interested in even acknowledging the 'Amritsar spirit'.

'Stop making excuses.'

If you were to ask why northern England is so much poorer than the south or why southern Italy is so much poorer than the north, why east London is poorer than west or why Glasgow and Belfast have been so much more violent than other UK cities, you will likely get an explanation grounded in history, politics and economics and not be told that those explanations are just 'making excuses' for the innate failings of the northern English, southern Italians or citizens of Belfast and Glasgow. The 'stop making excuses' clause is there to suggest that black people are not permitted to make use of the very same tools available to the rest of humanity to understand the shape of their communities today because their black skin and inferior culture are a sufficient explanation for any issues they might be having.

As people say this to me personally so often let's just recap on my family history and current position as briefly outlined in the last chapter to assess what I am supposed to be 'making excuses' for. Both of my mother's parents were alcoholics, my father grew up in and out of care, I grew up in a single-parent home on free school meals. As I'm sure you are aware most children eligible for free school meals do not achieve five GCSEs: all three of my mother's other children and I got ten GCSEs and lead very successful lives so I am unsure what exactly I am supposed to be 'making excuses for', as my life has panned out wonderfully well from a personal perspective. However. one of the main reasons me and my siblings were able to navigate life growing up was because we were made to understand very early that poorer children and poorer black children in particular would have to work twice as hard to get half as far. Apparently me passing on the useful knowledge of how racism and poverty are deliberately reproduced is 'making excuses' for poorer children to fail. Nonsense. I'm genuinely surprised that people do not get embarrassed looking at where I have come from and what I have done with my life when they try to hit me with the 'stop making excuses' clause, but that is the tone deaf nature of such persons.

'You just blame the west for all of the world's problems.'

This one is the geo-political equivalent of 'stop making excuses' and is usually aimed at anyone that dares to suggest that the disproportionate influence of Western power may still be having an impact on global human relations. If you ask the person saying this which African or Asian scholars' work do they think could usefully be described as 'blaming the west for everything' they will not be able to tell you of course, because such a body of scholarship simply does not exist. Post-colonial African, Asian and Caribbean scholarship takes as a basic assumption the obvious fact that non-white people are people and thus quite capable of oppressing one another without mighty whiteys' assistance. In fact this body of scholarship generally points out that the great challenges faced by the masses of Africa and large parts of Asia are caused precisely by the fact that they have two sets of oppressors' greed to satiate, their own domestic elites and the international corporations and foreign states their domestic oppressors often serve and collaborate with. But if you point out the simple and obvious fact that long after the official colonial period Western governments have been perfectly happy to install and support the most gruesome of dictatorial regimes and also overthrow democratically elected presidents as and when it suits them, this will be labelled 'blaming the west for everything'. You need not worry though as adjectives and slogans are not counter arguments of course.

'I don't see colour.'

This one does make me laugh and is grounded in the idea that colour itself is a negative, rather than the associations that have been forced upon it. It's so absurd to suggest that you don't see a person's colour that I can think of no better testament to the difficulties people have discussing race than this silly but often quoted one-liner.

'It's not about race.'

Nothing is ever about race; you should know this by now.

In reality, the idea of race has been one of the most important ideas in the modern world, it has underpinned centuries of enslavement, justified genocide and been used to decide the demarcation line between who lives and who dies, who gets to access rights of citizenship, property, migration and the vote. To not want to debate, discuss and deal with an idea that has been so impactful reveals a palpable lack of interest in humanity, or at least certain portions of it.

There are many variants on these non-arguments, you can't defeat them with common sense and you cannot – nor should you waste your time trying to – persuade everybody.

I returned home from primary school upset. My mum tried to figure out why but I was reluctant to tell her. After some coaxing, it emerged that a boy in the playground had called me a particularly nasty name. As I was finally about to spill the beans a strange thing occurred. I said 'Mum, the white boy . . .' and trailed off before I could complete the sentence. I looked to my mum as a profound realisation hit me. With a hint of terror and accusation, I said, 'But you're white, aren't you Mummy?' Before this moment my mum was just my mum, a flawless superhero like any loving parent is in a five-year-old's eyes, but I sensed that something about that image was changing in the moment, something we could never take back. I wanted to un-ask the question, I wished I had just pretended my day had been fine; I was mad at myself. My mother's expression was halfway between shock and resignation – she'd known this day would come but the directness of the question still took her aback.

She thought for a moment and then, using one of her brilliant, if perhaps unintentional, masterstrokes in psychology, she replied something to the effect of: 'Yes, I'm white, but I'm German and they're English.' It didn't matter that my mum was not really German – she was born in Germany and brought up in Hong Kong before returning to the UK, as my granddad was in the army – or that I was technically 'English': my mum had set up a mental safety valve for me so that I could feel comfortable reporting racist abuse to her without having to worry that I was hurting her feelings. Even at five, I had somehow figured out that there was a group known as 'white people' to whom it was now clear my mother belonged and that many of these people would get offended at the mere mention of their whiteness. I somehow knew instinctively that whiteness, like all systems of power, preferred not to be interrogated.

I told my mum that the boy had called me a 'Chinese black nigger bastard'. I felt naughty even saying the words back. My mum must have had to resist the urge to laugh before the anger set in. What a combination of words! We have to give the lad – or more probably his parents – ten out of ten for originality when it comes to racial abuse, for I have never before or since heard this particular racial epithet repeated among the predictable slew of clichés that peppered my childhood; coon, wog, darkie, coloured, nigger (obviously nigger) and even occasionally Paki – racists are notoriously imprecise with their insults. But as someone of mixed heritage with yellowish, light-brown skin, a round face and 'slanted' eyes, the insult was as close to an accurate description of my physiognomy as a five-year-old is ever likely to come up with. Looking at my great-grandmother and knowing the history of Jamaica, it is indeed quite likely that I have some Chinese ancestry, so even in this little boy's insult there was the trace of history, of empire and of the global movement of peoples.

This is my earliest memory of a racist insult directed at me; there were countless more to come, of course. The overriding feeling that I remember from the numerous instances of verbal racial abuse growing up was a sense of shame, a shame that was somehow incomparably deeper than a boy insulting your mum, the other taboo that, when broken, was almost sure to result in a fight. Racist insults leave you feeling dirty because, even at five years old, we already know on some level that, in this society at least, we are indeed lesser citizens with all the baggage of racialised history following us ghost-like about our days. We are conquered people living in the conquerors' land, and as such we are people without honour. At five years old we are already conscious of the offence caused by our black body turning up in the wrong space, and have begun to internalise the negative ideas about blackness so present in the culture.

For example, way back in the 1940s, African-American psychologists Mamie and Kenneth Clark came up with an experiment known as the 'doll test' to examine black American children's perceptions of race in the era of Jim Crow. The test involved giving children dolls that are exactly the same in every way except for colour and asking them questions about which doll is beautiful, which is bad etc. The results showed that black children had far more positive associations with the white doll, and the test eventually came to be used as part of the evidence for the negative effects of discrimination in the landmark 'Brown vs. Board of Education' case. The experiment has been repeated several times in the USA and even as far afield as Italy, right up until recent years, and you can watch many of the results in videos online. You will see that even now both black and white children generally understand very early that blackness is a synonym for bad and that whiteness is synonymous with wealth, power and beauty. The saddest part in the test comes when, after having identified the black doll as ugly and bad, the black children are asked which doll looks most like them, and you see the children hesitate as it dawns on them what that means. Children become race conscious very early despite what even well-meaning parents may want to believe.

For black children in Britain, our bodies commit the sin of reminding people racialised as white of an uncomfortable truth about part of how this nation became wealthy, and that the good old days when white power could roam the earth unchallenged are over. They now have to contend with one of their empire's many legacies; a multi-ethnic mother country. Those portions of white Britain that have bothered to get to know 'people of colour' or by simple fact of geography are located near them, like in Camden, seem for the most part to have adapted to and accepted this difference as an at least bearable fact of life. It's ironic that people living in the most ethnically homogenous parts of the country often fear the contamination of difference the most, but this irony holds true across the world. As James Baldwin famously observed, 'segregation has allowed white people to create only the Negro they wish to see.'

I was angry at the boy for his words, angry at the world for breaking my innocence, for making me aware so painfully early that my mum and I were not the same, and never would be again. Perhaps I already knew this before that day and was in denial; perhaps this day was just a confirmation rather than a revelation. Looking back now I feel shame for the other boy's parents – what kind of parent teaches their five-year-old child to think and act this way? The reproduction of such anti-human racist ideas is, to my mind at least, child abuse, but as racism is so endemic we tend not to see it that way.

As the racist insults continued to come, I learned to throw punches in response. This proved quite effective, but I was naturally a soft-hearted boy and would often cry when I got home even if I had won the fight because I didn't like hurting other people. We set up other defences; my primary school was very mixed ethnically and economically speaking, but the black children in my year group united against would-be bullies by pretending to be cousins (as all black children whose parents know each other do); we made up a secret language called 'African' (even though we were Caribbean), and other children got jealous.

From that day onwards, my relationship with my mother was not just the relationship of mother and son, but of a white mother to a black son. Race had intervened in our relationship and would be a mediator of it forever more, marking both our actions and attitudes, colouring our conversations and heightening the usual conflicts between mother and son, mapping onto them the loss and suffering of the black world at the hands of 'whitey' and the strange mix of guilt, fear and superiority that a great many white people feel every day as a result, but rarely talk about openly. It did not matter that my mother's family was piss poor by British standards, that they had their own history of being victims of horrendous institutional abuse or even that she was half Scottish and thus had her own quarrels with the English: race overrode those complicated nuances in our relationship because it more often than not also overrode them in British society.

My mother's reaction, to her credit, was not to run from the painful truths of the society we lived in and hope for the best, but to confront the fuckery head on. Another boy on another day called me a 'black bastard' (minus the Chinese and nigger parts) and my mum told me I should say 'yes, thanks' any time a racist came at me with that one, first because it would disarm them and second because it was true – I was black and my parents were not married when I was born, and neither of these things were anything to be ashamed of. She also told me I was black, not mixed race – she understood biological reality of course, but she also understood that race was social not scientific. She knew how I'd be treated when the time came, she knew the challenges I was facing were serious and that confusion would not help me.

My mother's understanding of race politics and even her general education were massively affected by her contact with British Caribbean ex-pats. Education was not particularly encouraged in my mother's household growing up, and certainly not for girls. My mum's father was an ignorant, violent, unapologetically racist man. He was also conditioned by the class and gender relationships of his day, thus when my mum got the highest exam grades of her siblings – she had three brothers – he told her she must have cheated. When my mum's teacher encouraged her to go to university her response was to laugh uncomfortably and say, 'No sir, that's for posh people'; it seems she had learned her place well. However, my mum had made friends with the only other black family (apart from my father's family) in the village, which was the family of my godfather, the man to whom this book is dedicated, Uncle Offs. Uncle Offs' father was a university-educated schoolteacher back in his native Guyana, he was heavily into radical politics and it was expected that his children would get a good education and ideally go to university. My mum was encouraged by Uncle Offs' family to attend university, and so she did, pursuing a degree in Caribbean history precisely because of this influence. Black Britons' refusal to accept the class impositions of this society are in no small part what has made our presence here so challenging both for us and for Britain as a whole. My mum's induction into a radical anti-colonial black politics fundamentally shaped how she raised her children.

It was her black mentors that had told her that I would be received and dealt with in this society as a black boy. My 'light skin' would not save me, this was not Jamaica or South Africa, I was not 'high coloured' here (colourism notwithstanding) but a black boy born of a white womb. Like so much else within racial theory, a biological fiction but a social and political reality. Out of principle and out of a recognition of this reality, I chose to identify with the black side of my heritage, not because black people are paragons of moral excellence who can do no wrong but simply because white supremacy is an unjust, idiotic and ultimately genocidal idea and because blackness can accommodate difference far more easily than whiteness can – because their historical and ontological origins are entirely different. I would be taught all about whiteness, I would know well its gravity and its weight, I would be taught to worship slave traders and imperialists and lionise philosophers and politicians who believed me to be less than human. This would all be mainstream, but if I wanted to learn anything about my other heritage or indeed the anti-establishment traditions of 'white' people, first my mum, and then I, would have to seek it out.

My mum had me and my siblings enrolled in the local pan-African Saturday school. At first the school was not sure, as we would be the first 'mixed' kids to attend. Other black parents fought for us and told the school that it was no use complaining about 'confused mixed-race youts' (a cliché in the black community, the tragic mulatto) if, on the occasion that a white woman did actually want her children to learn about their black heritage, the community refused to help. I'm pretty sure that had it been my dad trying to enrol me there would have been no issue. That said, I don't want to make it more serious than it was; we joined the school without much fuss in the end and had an incredible time there. A few other 'mixed' children even joined the school after us. The school was located in a few Portakabins in the south of Camden; despite the black community's best efforts to provide extracurricular education for their children and to keep them out of trouble, none of these institutions ever seemed to be close to as well funded as Britain's prisons were. Our school was called the Winnie Mandela School, out of solidarity with the struggle then being waged against apartheid in South Africa and to display the pan-African political orientation of our community. My mum still has a copy of an old black and white newsletter from the school with my picture on it and a quote from me saying 'we do better work here' – I was roughly seven at the time, yet I perceived the difference between my community school and mainstream schooling quite clearly.

Now race had made itself known to us, my mum did not hold back – she had me and my siblings watch films about the civil rights struggle, slavery and apartheid. She gave me a box of tapes of Malcolm X speeches for my tenth birthday and we watched Muhammad Ali documentaries together. In short, my mum did everything she could to make sure I 'knew myself' and to make sure that I would not become one of 'those' mixed-race kids, and in this endeavour she found ample support from the Black British pan-Africanist community.

Yet for all my mother's radical education and her long-standing political activity she was still white, she could never really 'get it'. She could never reach her black son in the way that other black people – even black women – could, and we both became painfully aware of this and mad at the world and perhaps each other as a result. As I grew into a young man, our conversations became tinged with racial difference and I became embarrassed about my mother's whiteness – no longer wanting her to accompany me to the very black spaces she had played such a role in introducing me to. Part of this was just the normal teenage desire to not want to hang out with your mum, but there was certainly an added racial something too.

I drifted deeper into a half-digested black nationalist politics that had been refracted to me through hip hop and the couple of books that I'd half-read, I radically simplified Garvey's position and thinking and made no real attempt to understand how different 1990s Britain was from 1920s America (I was a teenager after all). The only injustices I really knew about at that point in my life were those committed by white people; slavery, colonialism and apartheid. I did not yet have any knowledge of the Mongols, fascist Japan or the Abbasids; I did not know that the olive-skinned Romans often considered the people we now think of as white to be savages and had invaded their homes and enslaved them without much of a second thought; I did not know that Spain had been a Muslim country for hundreds of years; or that slavery had been a fairly global institution across cultures, not precluding the horrendous extremities of 'new world' slavery, of course. And so, when the Nation of Islam said the white man was the devil and I read about spectacle lynchings and the torture of enslaved Africans, it seemed entirely possible to my fifteen-year-old self that there might be something permanently, uniquely and irredeemably wrong with white people. Paradoxically as I looked at the centuries of slavery and colonialism, assessed the state of modern Africa and had daily encounters with the intense racial self-hatred of many black people I also wondered if there was something innately wrong with us, if 'we' were destined to be history's losers forever more or if we were just naturally more kind hearted than white people and this kind heartedness translated as weakness in the real world.

I saw the pain and uncertainty on my mother's face as I became a teenager and then a black man, her fears for and of my body; the six-foot-tall body, the scowling brown face that had once been a naive, smiling, sweet little five-year-old who didn't yet know that his mother was not a 'sister', but the oppressor. I saw my mum wish for the return of that boy that she had lost in the eyes of the teenager staring uncompromisingly and unfairly back at her, accusing her skin of all the crimes that the 'white race' had committed. When my mum tried to discipline me, it now felt like it was my white mum trying to discipline me as a 'black youth', like the bigoted teachers and the racist police and what felt like the whole world. I knew she had my back and she loved me and so it was different, but it didn't always feel different.

But wasn't it partly my mum's fault that I came to be this way? Wasn't she the one that gave me Malcolm X tapes for my birthday? Was Malcolm's assessment not a fair representation of his life and times in Jim Crow America? Wasn't it the case that my mum was raising black children in Britain at a time when black children could burn to death in their homes and the families of the dead would receive hate mail rather than sympathy, or grandmothers could be paralysed by police bullets and black people could still emerge from those tragedies as the criminals in public discourse?

Did my mum not enrol me in pan-African Saturday school and take me to the Hackney Empire to watch *Black Heroes in the Hall of Fame*? Wasn't it inevitable that this resentment would come? Weren't the facts of white people's crimes against Africa and its descendants more than enough cause for hate? A great many white people hated us and they had no historical reasons or motivations for doing so, just the blind prejudice against our skin. We are only human, why should we not hate in return?

In reality, black rage has never really morphed into the hatred of white people that white paranoia would like to believe it has, not even in the former slave states of the Americas. Not because black humans have some genetically inbuilt inability to be bigots – see for example the waves of xenophobic attacks against African migrants in South Africa in recent years – but because the brutality of the oppressor determined to hang on to privilege and power is always greater in any context than the resentment produced by resistance to oppression. Thus, my mother was largely embraced by the 'black community' and it was from them that she learned everything that she would need to arm her black children with for them to be able to survive and even thrive in this society. Though I'm sure some may have found her to be 'that annoying white lady', this was rarely if ever made clear in overt acts of prejudice.

Race had intervened in our relationship and for a long time it threatened to combine with the stresses of being poor and the more mundane familial resentments to wreck it, but we survived and even after many, many struggles, flourished. If racial difference opened a chasm between us that we could not bridge, it has also served as a common test of strength. To avoid confusion, my mum was far from perfect – she's human after all, and our childhood was in many other respects extremely difficult. My mum battled with mental health issues and our childhood home, despite all of its politics and pan-Africanism was also one of stress and anger compounded by poverty. My parents were damaged teenagers that had found one another and split up before I was born, and to say my father was not a great boyfriend to my mother would be somewhat of an understatement. My mother and stepfather's breakup was truly traumatic and left an emotional wreckage that it felt like we never recovered from as a family. During my mother's battle with cancer my sister and I, aged twelve and ten, had to assume all of the responsibilities of the household – cooking, cleaning, shopping and nursing our mother through chemotherapy, with very little external help. When she recovered my mum's attempts to re-assert parental control over her now essentially adult children played no small part in her clashes with us, particularly with my older sister to the point where she had to move out and live with our grandmother and then in a hostel. I would not want to give the reader a five-year-old's picture much less one of a white saviour. I love my mum deeply but she is flawed, just like me and just like all humanity, but it is her efforts in spite of these flaws and in spite of a truly horrendous childhood of her own that make her all the more remarkable. Seeing the personal transformation she has undergone in later life has been truly inspiring.

By the time I realised my mum was white she already knew only too well. She had already been called 'nigger lover' enough times herself, she had watched my dad fight the National Front and assorted bigots almost daily, and her own father had disowned her for 'getting with a nigger'. When she was pregnant with my older brother, people told her the baby would be a grey monstrosity and so she should get rid of it. This may sound stupid today but she was terrified; she had not seen any mixed children before and she genuinely didn't know what to think. People my mum had grown up with walked straight past her in the street when she pushed our prams; others refused to believe we were 'really' her children. My mum knew very well how deeply embedded anti-blackness was in the culture of the time.

All of my friends learned the meanings of race fairly early, and as far as introductions to racialisation go, my story is not exceptional or even particularly brutal by comparison. One of my best friends, a Sheffield-born, Jamaican-origin classical composer and entrepreneur, was introduced to the meaning of whiteness when his nursery teacher removed him and the only other two non-white children from the class and made them stand in the corner when it was time to give out the daily milk – the teacher was terrified that the undeserving 'immigrants' would benefit and was keen to preserve the unearned advantages that should properly accrue to white children, all things being well. She did this every day for a week until my friend lost his temper with the teacher in question and told her 'You want me to be down there' – he pointed to the ground – 'but I am going to be up there' – he pointed to the sky. His CV now stands as testimony to his five-year-old self's proclamation.

My own father was assaulted and called nigger by the police and by the people supposed to educate him more times than he would care to remember. If you want to hear some real child-hood horror stories talk to black people brought up in the care system, as my father was for a portion of his childhood. It does not matter how many of these stories black and Asian people in the UK can muster, how consistently we tell the world these experiences are fairly 'normal', the reaction of white society to such revelations is more often than not one of (perhaps feigned?) shock. How could noble England sully itself with widespread racist abuse of mere children? Surely this grade of behaviour is for less green pastures?

In reality, of course, both my Scottish/English and Jamaican families had their own internal histories of abuse, and many of my parents' experiences would be mirrored in 'white' communities right across the country, albeit without the added racial baggage. Remember the tens of thousands of white parents – often stigmatised single mothers – from poor areas of the UK who were coerced by the state into sending their children to Australia right up until the 1970s? These children were frequently victims of sexual abuse, hard labour and even flog-ging. We would call this child trafficking if it had been done by a non-Western state.[1] British Prime Minister Gordon Brown apologised for the programme in 2010, as did Australian PM Kevin Rudd the year before, though naturally the widespread abuse of black children in the care system, prisons, police cells and mental asylums of this country occurring at the exact same time will have to wait for some more years before it is officially recognised and atoned for, if ever.

By affirming my blackness my mum and, more importantly, the black community around us were not only giving me strength and a sense of self, they were preparing me for combat, for the lived experience of blackness in the UK that they knew would find me as surely as night follows day. The police harass-ment, the confrontations with teachers, the violence and frustration of my soon-to-be teenage peer group, the perils of avoiding the prison that I was likely destined for. That was all to come. My real awakening to race began that random day in 1988, when I realised, or rather learned, that my mum was white. Tellingly, I never had a similar moment with my father or any of the men in my life where I realised suddenly that they were black and I was not, which speaks to the way in which whiteness and blackness have been defined and understood in Britain.

However, it was not until over a decade later that I started to really think about what whiteness actually means. Like most people, I had just accepted that white people were actually white without much further thought. Only in my late teens did I start questioning what whiteness is, and how Celts, Saxons, Corsicans and Nordic people had come to be defined as 'white'. Had people of European heritage always seen themselves as white and doled out political and economic privileges upon that basis? Had racism always existed? Was Europe always economically and militarily the most dominant region of the world? Had slavery always been an institution run by white people that black people were the exclusive victims of? So what is whiteness?

'Whiteness is a metaphor for power,' James Baldwin tells us. 'Money whitens,' say the Brazilians. South Africans can be found calling rich black people 'white man' and they mean this as a compliment, as in 'now you have money, you are so success- ful that you are an honorary white man' – the very definition of prosperity, even in an African country. Or, as Frantz Fanon tells us, 'you are rich because you are white, because you are white you are rich.'

It is often assumed that race can only be understood through the eyes of people of colour; however, this idea assumes white people to be the normal 'raceless' group, which of course could not be further from the truth. Led by seminal African-American thinkers such as W. E. B. Dubois and James Baldwin, scholars, thinkers and anti-racist activists have gradually turned the anthropological lens the other way. Even discussing whiteness can be uncomfortable for people who have taken their white identity for granted, who think of themselves as unaffected by all that race stuff, but there is now a good body of work on the history of 'whiteness' that we ignore at our peril.

So, if whiteness really is a metaphor for power, how is that power actually exercised? Theodore W. Allen's meticulous study *The Invention of the White Race*, which took over a decade to produce, observes that in the first two generations of census data in the Virginia colonies there were no humans defined as white; the people we now think of as white were at that point still predominantly defined by other factors, such as the region of Europe from which they came. He argues that the ancestors of European Americans started to be defined as 'white' in response to labour solidarity between African- and European-American bondservants, especially after Bacon's Rebellion of 1696, a multi-racial rebellion against British governor William Berkely. European ruling elites began doling out privileges, like the right to bear arms or certain privileged positions within the plantation economy, based on skin colour, or rather on 'whiteness' such as the Virginia slave codes of 1705 that made it illegal to whip a white Christian slave naked or for a black person to employ or own a white person. The act also fined white women for having bastard children with negroes or mulattoes, made racial intermarriage punishable by imprisonment and made it legal for a master to kill his slave.[2] As indentured servitude turned to chattel slavery and slavery came to be reserved strictly for people of African heritage, this white privilege became all the more important, as it literally became the difference between still being a human being and becoming a piece of property.

Closer to home, Allen also contrasts the management of racial dominance in British-occupied Ireland with racial oppression in Anglo-America; there are many striking parallels between the way the Irish were treated and the way later racialised groups would be.[3]

The idea that the Irish were essentially savages still lingered with us in England until the 1960s, with the infamous 'No Irish, no blacks, no dogs' sign being just one example. Yet in the Americas, Irish immigrants became big supporters of black slavery, the confederacy and white supremacy, and ended up as a significant portion of slave owners throughout the Americas – though still far less than the English or Scots. My surname, Daley, is of Irish origin and possibly reflects the origins of the man that owned my grandfather's great-, great-grandparents. Despite their own very real experience of oppression in Ireland, once in the Americas, particularly during the nineteenth century, the Irish came to understand very well the benefits of learning to be white, and learn quickly they did.[4]

Even if we look at the differences between the racial regimes of the continental United States, where European settlers were the majority, and the Caribbean, where people of European heritage were a minority, we still see whiteness functioning as a fulcrum of power. In the USA, especially after slavery was 'abolished', there was a tendency toward the 'one drop' rule, which defined a person containing any vestige of 'black blood' as a negro and thus subject to Jim Crow discrimination. In the Caribbean plantations, there was a greater likelihood of 'whites' recognising their mixed-race offspring and even using these offspring as a buffer class in the plantation system. These different systems of race management have legacies that are with us until this very day; in the USA I am without a doubt a black person, yet the same light-brown skin that makes me a black person in America or even Britain, with all the stereotypes and issues that come with 'blackness', makes me a person of 'high colour' in the Caribbean. In the Caribbean, my complexion is associated with being middle class, with privilege and wealth and snobbery. Very few people of my complexion live in Jamaica's ghettoes for example, which is part of what made Bob Marley's story so unusual.

To understand just how flexible the boundaries of whiteness have been, even in America, we can look at the case of just one state. In the early twentieth century, Virginians made the first change in their definition of 'mulatto' in 125 years. From the Act of 1785 to 1910, a mulatto, or 'coloured' person, was someone who had a quarter or more negro blood. In 1910, that category expanded to include anyone with one sixteenth or more negro blood, and many people previously classified as white became legally coloured. Then in 1924, in a statute entitled 'Preservation of Racial Integrity', legislators for the first time defined 'white' rather than just 'mulatto' or 'coloured'. The statute, which forbade a white person to marry any non-white, defined a 'white' as someone who had 'no trace whatsoever of any blood other than Caucasian' or no more than one sixteenth American-Indian blood. In 1930, the Virginia legislature defined 'coloured' in a similar, though slightly less restrictive way, as any person 'in whom there is ascertainable any negro blood.'[5]

Despite pretending to be permanent, fixed and scientific, racial classifications have always been bent to the perceived needs or wills of ruling groups. For example, in colonial Spanish America mixed people could buy a certificate of 'whiteness'[6] and at a certain point under very specific circumstances in eighteenth century Georgia, when the frontier 'needed protecting' from Native Americans and the Spanish, even a black person could become white.[7]

At various points in history, Hindus, Arabs and even the Japanese could find themselves defined as honorary whites; racial theory was never as precise as we may assume it to have been today, it was always amenable to utility.[8] In Brazil, where racial slavery lasted the longest, and where by far the largest number of Africans were taken, there emerged an incredible number of racial categories dividing the different portions of a person's ancestry. Below are just a few of the possible 500 variations.

> Branco, preto, Moreno claro, Moreno escuro, mulato, Moreno, mulato claro, mulato escuro, negro, caboclo, escuro, cabo verde, claro, aracuaba, roxo, amarelo, sarara escuro, cor de canela, preto claro, roxo claro, cor de cinza, vermelho, caboclo escuro, pardo, branco sarara, mambebe, branco caboclado, moreno escuro, mulato sarara, gazula, cor de cinza clara, creolo, louro, Moreno claro, caboclado, mulato bem claro, branco mulato, roxo de cabelo bom, preto escuro, pele.[9]

Regardless of how many terms there were to define people racially, Brazil, like all of the other former slave colonies of the Americas, worked to extend and maintain white supremacy long after slavery had ended, despite all its claims to being a racial democracy.[10] From trying to import as many people from Europe as possible, expressly to lighten the population and get rid of what was often called 'the black stain', to becoming a home for fleeing European fascists, Brazil's maintenance of horrendous racism can be seen very clearly today. I have visited Brazil many times and I can say confidently that you will struggle to see Afro Brazilians in the wealthy areas of Rio or even Salvador, and if you do find them there they are likely to be homeless or on their way back to the favela from doing some kind of menial work. This despite the fact that the majority of Brazil's population is black and that Brazil has the largest population of black people in any country on earth, aside from Nigeria.

During one of my trips there, I got a very real personal taste of the Brazilian authorities' attitudes to race. I was shooting a video for a song called 'Yours and My Children', which touches on police brutality in Brazil as one of its themes. We had been shooting all day in the Rocinha favela in Rio, which is said to be the largest slum in South America. We packed the equipment into the car and left, quite satisfied with our day's work; my director and cameraman, both 'white' Brazilians, were in the front of the car, and I was in the back. As we left the favela one of the cars from the massive police blockade that seems to permanently surround the neighbourhood followed us and pulled us over.

Rather than demand to speak to the driver or see his licence, as one would assume the police would do when stopping a vehicle, they demanded that I get out of the back of the car. No sooner had I got out of the car than one of the policemen pointed his huge machine gun in my face and started shouting something at me, but unfortunately for me I had done the typical British thing and learned barely any Portuguese. The officer got more irate and seemed to take his gun off safety; I kept my hands in the air where they had been the whole time and said nothing. It is very strange; I have been in life-threatening situations a few times in my life and while you assume that fear will consume you, your reactions are often just odd, not out of bravery or heroism but just simply as a reaction to the absurdity of it all. In the moment, I knew I was so powerless that I actually just felt rather resigned. I had come to make a video for a song that was partly about Brazil's horrendous police brutality, so I knew very well how often their police shoot people, even children.[11] How ironic would it be if I get shot by the police while making this video? I thought, as I stared down the barrel of the officer's gun. I think I even let out an awkward chuckle at the thought.

Then, in a flash, the director of the video ran over to me and pulled up my top to reveal my waist to the officer, and I immediately understood. The director and the officer exchanged a few more words and the relieved policeman lowered his gun, got back in his car and drove off. As we drove back to our destination the director and cameraman explained what had happened, even though we all already knew. The officer had been shouting at me to pull up my top and show that I did not have a gun on me; he had obviously assumed that I was a favela drug dealer accompanying my two rich clients somewhere – because why else would an Afro Brazilian be in a car with two rich kids? – and that I was likely to be strapped. The director claimed that the policeman had genuinely been getting ready to shoot me, as he assumed I was Brazilian and just being difficult by not pulling my top up. Once the fracas was over and the officer put his gun down, the director got to explain to him that I was not 'one of those people', i.e. not from the favela but actually from the UK. The officer, like most Brazilians, just looked bemused at the idea that I was not a Brazilian.

My director and cameraman felt so palpably uncomfortable at having to confront such an obvious example of white privilege that I practically had to counsel them for the rest of trip to assuage their guilt. It wasn't their fault, but they nonetheless knew that they lived in a society where tens of thousands of poor people – overwhelmingly darker skinned – were murdered every year, thousands of them by police. By being descendants of later migrants to Brazil from Italy and Germany, brought in to whiten the country, they would likely never face what is a daily reality for most of their fellow citizens. This vast difference in opportunity and outcome exists through no direct fault or merit of either party, but rather through the traces of history and the random luck of birth. Still, while whiteness can usually be taken for granted by those it protects, the absence of whiteness can literally be the difference between life and death even in an ostensibly colour-blind country like Brazil.

In all of the former slave colonies of the Americas where whiteness was pioneered as a tool of social control, it pretty much worked a treat. For all the centuries slavery went on – with just a few notable exceptions like the Polish in Haiti, John Brown's raid on Harpers Ferry and the multi-ethnic working-class rebellion that almost took over New York in 1741[12] – no matter how deplorable the conditions for poor whites may have been, they rarely joined the side of the enslaved in the scores, perhaps hundreds of rebellions against slavery throughout those years. Indeed, free blacks and mulattoes, often property owners and sometimes even slave owners themselves, were far more likely to join and even lead slave rebellions out of racial nationalism alone. This was also because even free blacks and mulattoes were subject to intense discrimination. For example, in Saint-Domingue (now Haiti) in the late eighteenth century, the unusually large and wealthy group of free people of colour were not permitted to become doctors or lawyers, to eat, pray or be buried with whites, nor to dress like whites. They even needed a permit for dancing and were forbidden from taking their French fathers' surnames.[13]

To greater or lesser degrees this discrimination against free communities of colour existed right across the Americas, but after slavery was reformed or ended race became even more important, as 'free people of colour' ceased to mean anything, seeing as all black people were now technically 'free'. New systems of slavery were invented, particularly in America, and even more sadistic ways of publicly killing and torturing black people than had existed during slavery became common.[14] Ironically at least during slavery a black person's status as property sometimes acted as a barrier to killing them or damaging them beyond repair (though I do stress, only sometimes). During slavery, white and black Americans had lived in the closest proximity imaginable, with black women often wet nursing and raising white children, and of course 'sexual relations' and rape were entirely normal. But once black people ceased to be white people's property, proximity became a problem, so segregation was enforced along with anti-miscegenation laws that made what was common during slavery – sex between the races – a crime after it. Having defined themselves as superior and marked themselves out as racially distinct for the purposes of being able to own other human beings and profit from their labour, whites understood that they had made themselves a potential target for racial revenge now that black people were free. The entire history of the USA since 1865, particularly in the southern states, has been indelibly shaped by this fear.

When we think of white supremacy and segregation (if we think about them at all), we tend to think of the American south before 1965 or of South Africa before 1990, but virtually all European colonies were ruled by white-supremacist legislation of one form or another, though to massively varying degrees. In British-ruled Hong Kong, for example, the Chinese had to carry night passes, were banned from attending certain schools and going to the theatre at certain hours and had to travel in separate rail carriages from 'Europeans'. The rat-infested Chinese slum 'below the peak' of Hong Kong had much in common with other racialised slums across the 'third world'.[15]

Back in Europe itself, whiteness had long been associated with beauty and divine light and blackness with evil and demons. However, sixteenth century writers and thinkers were still able to recognise that their standards of beauty were only relative, as evidenced in many writers' works, including Shakespeare's series of sonnets to a female love interest of his that he repeatedly describes as black, usually referred to by others as the 'Dark Lady'. However, during the eighteenth century thinkers like Voltaire, Kant and Hume started to espouse an openly white-supremacist philosophy.

While it's absolutely obvious that white people have no monopoly on ethnic hatreds or dominating and brutalising other human beings, in my personal opinion – and I do believe it's somewhat grounded in the evidence – the idea of race and white supremacy pioneered in eighteenth-century Europe, combined with newly formed nation states and industrial technology, took the human capacity for and practice of barbarity to levels rarely if ever before seen in history. It was Europe's capacity for and mobilisation of greater organised violence that colonised the planet, not liberal ideas, Enlightenment Humanism or the Protestant work ethic. And the dehumanisation of the racial other made mass killing particularly permissible and thus was central to Western dominance. The Second World War is often seen as the peak of this brutality in world history, and what the Nazis did as an aberration. But however much some try to divorce Nazi Germany from this earlier history, the reality is they were very much inspired by American race laws when crafting laws to govern 'the Jews', as well as drawing on the much wider and longer pan-Euro-American dialogue about race and eugenics. The practice of what came to be known as genocide apparently seemed perfectly acceptable, even admirable to mainstream Western political figures – including Winston Churchill – when its victims were a 'lower-grade race'.[16] The Nazi genocides sprang from a much longer history of articulating white supremacy that had been developed on the plantations of the Americas, practised in colonising the globe and then codified into a respected philosophy during the Enlightenment and the long nineteenth century. We will return to the specifics of the idea of 'race' as opposed to just white supremacy later, though the two are inextricably linked.

The sole non-'Western' nation to successfully adopt and apply 'Western' ideas in the nineteenth century was Japan. Imperial Japan quickly and consciously adopted European technological innovations during a period known as the Meiji Restoration, and went on to have its own brutal nationalist empire. Imperial Japan's capacity for extreme brutality was one of the main things that actually undermined the idea of white supremacy in the early part of the twentieth century.[17] All of the pleading and protesting or even attempts to valiantly fight back with obviously inferior weaponry by non-white colonised people around the globe did very little to dent European imperialists' self-confidence and their appetite for brutality; if anything it only further convinced imperialists of the innate inferiority of the savages. Only once Japan showed that 'Asiatics' could beat or at least equal white people at their own game did mainstream Western thought seriously start to entertain what the few radical critics of imperialism had long been saying; that imperial expansion could not go on unchecked and that white people were not, in fact, supreme – even in the capacity for cruelty.

Had Japan come to dominate the modern world we may now be discussing the prejudices of the Japanese. In fact, despite the collapse of the Japanese empire, the brutality of imperial Japan is still a sore point in much of South East Asia and China, quite rightly and understandably. I'm sure the same Brits that think critics of the British Empire should just 'get over it' would not think or say the same when talking to a Korean or Filipino about being occupied, enslaved and tortured by the Japanese, though I'm not entirely convinced they'd feel much empathy either. Revealingly, even the *Daily Mail* turned into a 'left-wing snowflake' that bemoaned Japan's refusal to apologise for the brutality they inflicted on Brits during the battle of Hong Kong, when remembering the seventy-fifth anniversary of the British defeat there.[18]

But while white people have no monopoly on oppression, and hierarchies run by people other than 'whites' may well share many of the same features, it does not change the fact that whiteness from its very inception in the slave colonies of the New World was a supremacist identity, an identity aggressively predicated on what it is not. Thus whiteness has always functioned as a tool of domination, as Charles Mills puts it: 'Whiteness is a phenomenon unthinkable in a context where white does not equal power at some structural level.'[19]

The concept of whiteness goes hand in hand with the concept of white supremacy – hence why the progress against white supremacy that has been made so far feels, to some white people, like an attack on their identity. This is obviously not white genocide; in fact if white people were experiencing anything remotely resembling a genocide white nationalists would not throw the term around so lightly. But when a given group is used to having all of the political power, and virtually unlimited privilege to define and name the world, any power sharing, any obligation to hear the opinions of formerly 'subject races' – who would have once been called uppity niggers and lynched accordingly – can feel like oppression. However, while whiteness seeks to create a monolith, in that it aims to mask significant class oppression and ethnic conflict between people who are all supposedly white, people racialised as white are obviously not a monolith, and intra-European ethnic, class and national conflicts may well again override any fragile sense of white unity, as they have so many times before in history.

Many of the most celebrated intellectual icons of the last few centuries, from Jefferson, Roosevelt and Wilson to Lincoln, Kant, Hume, Churchill, Hugo, Hegel and many more otherwise intelligent and in some cases very brilliant people, openly espoused their belief in innate white supremacy, so it is rather odd that we are so squeamish about the phrase now. Even stranger that we are trained to think of white supremacy as the invention of some supposedly obscure hooded lunatics in the American South. This belies reality, first in that the KKK at their height had many millions of members, and second because, as shown above, white supremacy was a mainstream and openly espoused legal, political and moral imperative until the latter half of the twentieth century, so hardly ancient or remote history.

The picture is nevertheless complicated in Britain – at home, if not in its former empire – and *might* provide some of the reasons why white people here sometimes find terms like 'white supremacy' and 'white privilege' either inapplicable to Britain or hard to understand. First, Britain never practised open white supremacy on domestic soil as it did in the colonies, so those of us who hail from the colonies have a different understanding of British racial governance, even if we were born here. Second, the most deprived and violent regions of Britain remain areas that are almost exclusively white, such as the rough parts of Glasgow, Belfast and north-east England, a subject to which we will return later. Can the white people who burned to death in Grenfell Tower along with the 'ethnics', or were crushed to death at Hillsborough and then demonised in the press as thieves, or the dead at Aberfan, be said to have had 'white privilege'? I can totally see why this might at first seem absurd to some people. Especially in relation to Kensington and Chelsea, where the working-class Muslim population in the north of the borough so visible during the Grenfell fire contrasts sharply with another large population of Muslims in the south of the borough who hail from the Gulf states, and are rich enough for the paupers to know not to aim their hatred of Muslims at them as they drive up Kensington High Street in their Louis Vuitton-patterned Lamborghinis.

Class affects everything, even racism, but in complex ways, and a phrase like 'white privilege' is not an absolute but a trend, a verifiable factor in human history produced by the philosophy and practice of institutionalised white supremacy. The idea that millions of white people still being relatively poor somehow proves that white privilege does not exist is such a juvenile and historically illiterate argument I'm surprised it is taken at all seriously. There were poor whites in the Jim Crow south, apartheid south Africa and the slave colonies of the Caribbean yet no one would be silly enough with the benefit of historical distance to claim that white privilege did not exist back then. But at the time poor whites in Saint-Domingue for example felt and claimed to be oppressed because they were too poor to own slaves! The practice of legally privileging all people racialised as white literally came about so ruling groups could buy the racial loyalty of poor whites, not to entirely eradicate their poverty. Thus you will hear people talk about 'the white working class' in Britain as if whiteness infers indigeneity even though most immigrants to Britain, even before we joined the EU, have been 'white' people.

This is why, in spite of all the sufferings of poor people in Britain, there was a 'Keep Britain White' campaign and not a 'Keep Britain Celtic, Norman and Saxon' one. These people understood very well what whiteness meant to them emotionally and psychologically, even if its material benefits were meagre.

The mental and emotional benefits of whiteness are why my granddad – working class, a soldier who had been tortured in battle, an uneducated alcoholic with few serious accomplishments to speak of – could still say 'well at least I am not a nigger' as frequently as he did. What did my grandfather understand about whiteness that so many pretend they cannot?

And it's also why, though my mum was far from rich and had a great many sufferings of her own to speak of, she still shared a degree of racial discomfort when faced by the questioning eyes of her five-year-old son. But she sought and led him to answers, and did her best to rise to the challenge staring at her from the little person she had created.

My schooling, like everything else in my life it seemed, was an entanglement of contradictions. My primary school was not as 'mixed' as my secondary, where the ratio of children hailing from around the globe seemed to be at least half of the student body, but there were still a fair few black and brown children in every class and the economic differences between the families in the school were vast. Like my house, my primary school sat in the nexus between Highgate, a leafy, very wealthy, over-whelmingly white London semi-suburb, and Archway, an area not quite as rough as nearby Tottenham but still nonetheless an area of concentrated council estates packed with the children of Irish, Caribbean and Cypriot immigrants. My primary school was probably one of the better ones in the area and so attracted slightly more of the Highgate crowd than the Archway lot, but that seemed to only highlight how differently we were treated by some of the teachers.

From my first year I encountered what can only be described as bullying, not from other students as one might expect – the odd racist insult and normal fights aside – but from some of my teachers. My very first teacher felt I had too much to say for myself; he was annoyed that I was a 'know it all', apparently. He was so irritated by my self-confidence, my willingness to speak, to offer opinions and even to know the answers to questions asked – all traits that schools are apparently supposed to encourage – that he told me that I was not allowed to speak in class at all unless he pushed my 'magic button'. My magic button was an invisible spot on my chest that he would poke, thus allowing me to speak. His poke was hard and painful enough that this device had its intended outcome; I stopped asking to speak or to answer questions in class at all. I was five years old.

Yet it was only during my final year of infants that I really started to appreciate how much an adult, even a teacher, could find a child's intelligence a reason to be pissed off. I'd been on a trip to Jamaica during the summer holidays before returning to start the new school year. I had the same teacher that I had at the tail end of the year before for some reason. Knowing how talkative I was and what I had just experienced, my mum asked my teacher if she would allow me to take story time that week and tell the rest of the class about everything I had seen in Jamaica – that way I would get it out of my system and not get into trouble for talking in class. The teacher reluctantly agreed, until I actually started to tell my stories, that is. During one of my tales, I told the class that Jamaica was thousands and thousands of miles away and my teacher, clearly annoyed by having to give me this platform, interjected sarcastically with 'and I wish you were still there.' I was crushed by the comment and my stories stopped that day.

The second incident I remember occurred when my mother asked to bring some books from class home for the Christmas holidays and my teacher refused because I had previously lost one behind the apparatus at the play centre. My mum said she would pay for the book if it was not found, but still the teacher refused. I'm not quite sure whether my mum came back into the school another day when my teacher was not there or if it was the same day, but somehow we were left alone in the classroom and my mum decided to 'steal' a whole set of books, so I could read over Christmas anyway. I pleaded with my mum, 'No, you can't do that Mum, you'll get me into trouble', but she said, 'Don't worry son, we'll bring them back after the holidays.' So off we went, with a whole set of the top level books available for my age group. Despite my teacher's insistence that she was reading with me regularly, my mum was convinced I was not being pushed hard enough to reach my potential, and was determined to properly assess my reading level for herself. Over that holiday period, my mum made me read the whole set and it became very clear that the books I was being given in class were well below my level. Then the tension finally reached a head.

I'm not sure precisely how it occurred, but at some point during the course of the year I had ended up in a 'special needs' group outside of regular schooling; these groups were for children with learning difficulties and those for whom English was a second language. It is both necessary and admirable that schools make such provisions for those in need of them, but how did I come to end up in such a group? I was born in England and, shamefully, to this day the only language I speak is English; at home I was already reading books for young adults by this age, so clearly neither learning difficulties nor linguistic challenges could explain my being there. I knew at the time that something was amiss about me being in the group but as they gave us hot chocolate and biscuits every session, I was in no rush to leave. In the group we did work that was well below what I was intellectually accustomed to and thus I started to fall behind, to become lazy, bored and even resent the lack of challenges now inherent in my day's schooling, but I also got the chance to get away from my teacher. On some level I also thought I had done something wrong and that the group was some form of punishment, so I don't think I quite communicated to my mother that I had been taken out of formal classes.

Which brings us to the crux of the matter – if I genuinely had learning difficulties my mother and stepfather would surely have been consulted beforehand or at least informed that I was to be placed into this group, but they were not. For reasons best known only to my teacher, she had decided to put me in this group without informing my parents. I'm not sure exactly how long I stayed there, perhaps a month or two, then by total chance one of the staff from my pan-African Saturday school happened to be visiting my 'normal' school and noticed that I was in the special needs group. My Saturday school had already been telling my mum that something was up with my behaviour and attitude and now they knew what it was. They immediately informed my mum about me being in the special needs group and she was, of course, furious.

Now that my mum had found out, she quizzed me about the group and I revealed just how deeply the problems ran. I did not like this teacher at all, I thought she hated me; I offered my mum a litany of reasons for why I was actually glad to be out of her class. She had told me she wished I had stayed in Jamaica; she always overlooked me to answer questions in the class and even got annoyed by me being a 'know it all' (that one again); she was generally horrible to me; sent me out of class for little to no reason and had even hit me with a ruler and a book, on separate occasions. My mum could not believe what she was hearing, that a teacher had hit me and I had not told her – she was livid with me and with the situation, but most of all with the teacher in question.

Needless to say, the very next day my mum marched up to the school and demanded a meeting with my teacher. I sat there uncomfortably, wanting the ground to swallow me as my mum quizzed her, demanding answers about why I had been placed into the group, why she sent me out so frequently and why she shouted in my face. My mum then dropped the bombshell 'and why did you hit my son, with a ruler on one occasion and with a book on the other?' or words to that effect. The teacher had already seemed uncomfortable but now she lost her composure entirely. 'I admit to tapping him,' she said, 'but it's not because he is . . .' She trailed off and stuttered, looking at me and then at my mum, trying to find the right word to describe me. I imagine she wanted to say 'coloured' but knew that was an outdated expression; she perhaps then mulled over calling me black, but looking at my white mother made that seem inaccurate, so she blurted out 'it's not because he is brown'. My mother had not mentioned race up to this point but it had been an unspoken subtext hanging in the air, and now the teacher, of her own volition, had made it central.

The mix of relief at having finally spoken her mind, embarrassment, shame and indignation on the teacher's face has stayed with me until now. I can still see her sat back on her chair, I remember the exact classroom at the end of the corridor on the first floor next to the headmistress's office, the door that I had stood outside of so many times, the large scary windows that let in an unbearable amount of light on the odd days that it was sunny and the tiny little chairs for the future adults. It was now clear to us all that whatever abuses I had had to deal with from this woman were entirely a result of her discomfort at having to teach little brown children, particularly those with a little too much brains and a little too much to say for themselves.

I was removed from the group and I re-entered formal schooling, but the rest of that year was fraught with difficulties and I started to hate school, resentful at having to obey someone that I knew did not like me simply because I was brown. I remember a supply teacher came in for a week, to my relief. When reading time came I picked *The Man with the Golden Gun* by Ian Fleming and she told me I could not possibly read that and gave me something 'more suitable'. It may have just been honest disbelief that a seven-year-old could read such a book, but I took it to be disbelief that *I* could possibly read such a book, and so the incident has stayed with me. Real-life racism makes you paranoid, even in children it creates the dilemma of not knowing if someone is just being horrible in the 'normal' way, as people so often are, or if you are being 'blacked off' – as me and my friends call it.

My mum became extra diligent in observing my relations with the teacher; she saw my enthusiasm and behaviour deteriorate and stressed herself out trying to find possible solutions. She spoke to my black Saturday school and they confirmed that, despite their best efforts, I was still misbehaving and my grades were slipping. My mum toyed with changing my school, she even considered sending me to private school knowing that I was probably 'bright enough' to get a scholarship of some kind, but I was entirely against the idea. I was excited at the prospect of a more challenging education but I complained to my mum that I would be surrounded by 'posh white kids' at private school and therefore it was an absolute no-go. As hard as state education was proving, I'd take my chances with my multicultural inner-city school over and above the cultural isolation of being the only poor child among rich kids and the only brown child among white ones. By seven, I had understood my 'social location' already and was not willing to venture into such spaces of alienation.

By the end of the year my near depression over school life had become so acute that when it became time for us to enter a new school year, the first year of 'juniors', my mum pre-emptively had a row with my new teacher. Clearly stressed, she – in retrospect unfairly – scolded him, 'If you're not going to bother to fucking teach my son just let me know now and I'll just pull him out of the bloody school altogether.' To the teacher's credit, he was not put off by my mother's swearing but actually rather impressed by her passion for her son's education. He sat her down and they had a proper talk about the problems I'd been having; a conversation that ended with my mum agreeing to volunteer to come into the class on selected days to help children with their reading so she could keep an eye on me and be of use to the school as well. The effects on me were dramatic. While I was not overjoyed at the prospect of having my mother in my class – what child would be? – my new teacher took such an active role in trying to unpick some of the damage done to my self-esteem and my attitude to school that I could safely say he changed the entire course of my relationship with formal education.

It helped that I admired him; he was a mountain of a man, an amateur body builder with a passion for American football and a very smart bloke too. What young boy would not want to be like him? I had not yet fallen in love with normal football and so under his influence I gravitated towards American football, persuading my mum to get me a ball and my friends to play this most un-English of sports with me. As you can imagine, young boys did not take that much persuading to throw themselves and each other to the ground; knees and elbows were cut and grazed on the concrete more times than I care to remember during this year-long obsession. My reading and attitude started to improve and I even got used to my mum being in class; in fact, I was proud that she was helping other children with their reading skills and one of my best childhood friends swears to this day that it was my mum who taught her to read.

My relationship with this teacher became so close that he even gave me several American football books, expensive hardbacks that could not have been easy to replace. I am pretty sure I cried at the end of the year when I had to leave his class, but he would go on to look out for me for the rest of my primary school years. This would even bring him into conflict with my future teachers, those who did not have my interests so close at heart. He was of Polish origin but I think British born, and in retrospect I do wonder if his own experience of being an immigrant or the child of immigrants may have helped him to better cope with the challenges that such a diverse classroom presents. I never got to ask him about his upbringing during my school years and I have not seen him since, unfortunately.

The next year of junior school was another major step backwards with a teacher that I clashed with, someone my older sister had already experienced and had not got along with, to say the least. She made my sister cry once by shouting at her and insisting that she was lying about having forgotten her homework at the house – to this day my sister swears that she had actually done the work. It's only looking back now I realise how strange it actually is to shout in an eight-year-old's face and call them a liar. My relationship with this teacher is best exemplified by two incidents, the first of which I will recount here. The other I'll come back to later.

It's fascinating how impressionable a child is and how one seemingly insignificant experience can shape your life profoundly. For example, I nearly drowned twice as a child and had to be saved by a vigilant adult both times. As a result of these bad experiences it took me until I was thirty years old to actually become a decent swimmer. Something similar has occurred with drawing and handwriting. My handwriting is almost illegible and, spookily, it is almost identical to my father's and grandfather's writing, and I draw like a below-average five-year-old. I love visual art but, much like swimming, an early negative experience very much discouraged me from pursuing drawing throughout my childhood.

In the run up to Christmas my new teacher – the one that followed our English-Polish body builder – had tasked all the students with drawing festive things, and I chose to draw a snowman. I was already quite insecure about my drawing, well aware that the 'natural' talent I had with numbers and words did not extend to art. However, with this snowman I was determined to prove myself and so I did – or at least I thought I did. I drew what to my mind was the best picture I had ever drawn, a round and believable snowman, complete with a Christmas hat and surrounded by falling snowflakes. Perhaps it was not all that good in comparison with the more artistic children but I was immensely proud of the piece and I turned it in to my teacher with great satisfaction. She never seemed to be satisfied with my work, but I was sure she would be this time. I was mistaken. She told me the drawing was rubbish, or words to that effect, then ripped it up and commanded that I re-draw it. I was devastated, but this was only the start. This process of re-drawing my unsatisfactory snowman continued for the next couple of days while the rest of the class had moved on to other pursuits. I was totally humiliated.

Of course, I have no idea if the snowman incident had anything to do with race and class in a direct sense, and I'm sure there are plenty of horrible teachers at private boarding schools too, but as you will see in Chapter Five, this particular teacher was an odd kind of liberal and seemed to have a real issue with me and my friend from Indonesia in particular, and my older sister before that. It may just have been she was in a bad mood that day, did not like children generally or just did not like me. Perhaps she genuinely thought I was being lazy with the drawing, who knows? I retell this story in this context, however, to reflect on how a relatively simple action from an adult, in this case the tearing of a drawing, can affect a child's self-esteem quite dramatically, though I am aware it hardly ranks highly on the list of cosmic injustices.

If there is a silver lining, perhaps this and other experiences like it have given me a degree of humility – a knowledge that whatever talents I have are only relative. As a child, I could remember dates and facts with relative ease and I was very good at mathematics – though I am crap at maths now through lack of practice. I was an archetypal nerd in my tastes, often preferring to watch wildlife documentaries than cartoons, and I could be found at many a family party engaged in philosophical discussions with the adults over and above running around with the other children. I wanted to be a scientist of some kind and/or an astronaut. When my school took us to the Planetarium and the Science Museum it blew my mind to think about how vast the universe was and how much humans had come to know about it through curiosity and hard work. I was being shown the very best of British achievements – Newtonian physics, the theory of evolution, the steam engine – yet being led away from my natural desire to pursue these interests by the outdated bigotry and class conditioning of some of my educators. I was being encouraged to admire men – and they mostly were men, for obvious reasons – who had changed the course of history and expanded the scope of human knowledge, and at the same time being told to know my place. I was being exposed to genius but being rewarded for not trying to aspire to it myself.

This gives us pause for thought about formal education as a whole and the dynamics contained within it: whether education should be a site of power, a place to reproduce the social, societal norms, or a place to be encouraged to question and thus attempt to transcend them and be an active participant in remaking them. Is state education designed to encourage more Darwins and Newtons, or to create middle-management civil servants and workers? What tensions are brought into being when a child's natural proclivity to question everything in their own unique way comes into contact with a one-size-fits-all mode of education?

State schooling in Britain both today and when I was a child seems stuck in a Victorian-era paradigm, guided by notions of discipline, obedience and deference to ones betters, of becoming a good worker and getting a good job. The idea that we go to school to find our passions, our calling, to learn to be happy, to 'draw out that which is within', as the root meaning of the word 'educate' commands, is almost entirely absent. Let alone any sense that we plebs should contemplate participating in the governing of the country.

We can become so enthralled with officialdom that it's easy to forget that curricula are not the result of some universal abstract truth but rather the designs of actual human beings like you and me. Despite the fact that I got almost straight As, at no point in my formal schooling was I ever taught to think in terms of class or race, even though those two concepts have obviously shaped the world and my reality so profoundly – though in full fairness I did not take sociology as a GCSE option. I left school without knowing what capitalism was, much less a mortgage, interest rates, central banking, fiat currency or quantitative easing. The word imperialism had never been used in the classroom, much less 'class struggle'. What history I did learn can be seen as little more than aristocratic nationalist propaganda; Henry VIII and his marital dramas; how Britain and America defeated the Nazis – minus the Commonwealth and with a very vague mention of the Soviet contribution; how Britain had basically invented democracy and all that was good and wonderful.

No one in my classes was given any understanding at all of why their classroom contained people whose parents hailed from all over the world; when the British Empire did come up it was as this plucky railway-building and sugar-exporting exercise devoid of any human victims. The fact that Britain has almost constantly been at war for the last century, even during the entire 'post-war' era, was of course not mentioned even once.[1] I understand that managing a national curriculum is no mean feat but I am not sure that children being taught that their state is essentially benevolent, if a little rough round the edges, is the best way to breed adults who actually respect the limited freedoms their ancestors have attained. Thus it can be said that even though I left school with almost straight As, I had learned very little critical thinking in formal schooling. What remnants of disobedience I had left were learned outside of school, or taught by the few renegade teachers that encouraged us to go beyond the curriculum.

I am aware that it's cliché to look to the Nordic countries as ideal models and I'm sure their systems have their own deficiencies, but my experiences teaching in Scandinavia still shocked me. I saw children waltz into school to loud house music blaring from the school speakers, I went into classrooms where no one calls their teachers 'Miss' or 'Sir', and yet this lack of formality does not seem to be affecting the quality of their educational outcomes. In just one example, in Copenhagen I worked with a school group in a rough 'suburb' (what we call a housing estate) where many of the kids were migrants from the Afghanistan and Iraq wars and other areas of conflict. To my complete shock, within five years of being in Denmark all of these children – a mix of refugees, asylum seekers and immigrants – had learned to speak Danish fluently and English to a standard that the poems they created compared favourably with any written by an average group of British sixteen-year-olds.

While it's always dangerous to extrapolate from an isolated experience, this did send me into a philosophical examination of British educational attitudes and practices and I concluded that our schools do indeed, for the most part, kill creativity as writer and internationally renowned educator Ken Robinson asserts,[2] and I would argue that they do this by design. This led me to do some more research and stumble across the 'perplexing' case of Finland, where students have no uniforms, are not banded into sets by ability, are not regularly tested or ranked and yet are as high-achieving as any in the world, and the gap between their 'strongest' and 'weakest' pupils is the smallest.[3]

My friend, the classical composer and entrepreneur I mentioned in the previous chapter, had a similar 'know it all' experience in school, except all subtleties were suspended. He comes from a very formal and strictly religious Caribbean family, so when his mother was called into his primary school one day it was taken very seriously at home. The teacher went on to tell his mother that her son was too smart, he knew all the answers and that he was 'not giving the white kids a chance'. If she could just get him to be quiet, that would be wonderful. His mum is a fairly reserved person, but even she could hardly contain her indignation at something so ridiculous.

But is it so ridiculous? Well, on the one hand it's totally absurd for a teacher to feel this was an issue worth calling a parent into school for, on the other hand I actually understand where the teacher is coming from, and can usually empathise if given the opportunity to have an open, adult conversation about things. British identity, despite all of the liberal rhetoric to the contrary, is obviously seen as synonymous with whiteness; modern British identity grew with and was shaped by the fundamentally and undeniably racist British Empire. The domination of 'subject races' is one part of that identity and for many teachers – in this case a woman born in the 1930s – it's entirely understandable, though still unacceptable, that within that frame of reference she would feel like a traitor to her race, to her culture and to her nation if she was to encourage colonial migrants – members of the subject races – to reach their full potential for excellence. To blame individual teachers or write this phenomenon off as just a few bad apples is not only to completely ignore decades of studies, but also to refuse to confront one of the key contradictions of British modernity.[4]

When large numbers of British-born black children started to attend British schools in the 1960s, the establishment was presented with a serious problem. How to educate – or under-educate – a group of people it had never intended to have full citizenship rights and did not really see as British. This problem must also be placed within the context of an already heavily class-stratified society and the history of education more broadly. During the 1960s, remnants of eugenics-inspired assumptions about students' natural abilities were still all the rage – schools for the 'Mentally Subnormal' (MSN) had simply been rebranded with the slightly more palatable title of schools for the 'Educationally Sub Normal' (ESN). These were schools outside of the official system where apparently difficult students, those with 'special needs' or those with learning difficulties, were dumped. Unsurprisingly, black children were found to be massively over-represented in these ESN schools in relation to the percentage they made up of the population as a whole.

As a response to this reality, Grenadian scholar Bernard Coard set about publishing the now legendary 'How the West Indian Child is Made Educationally Subnormal in the British School System' to expose the scandal of systemic discrimination in British schools.[5] The pamphlet was published by a small independent black publishing company and sold all 10,000 copies of its initial run and actually received generally favourable press at the time of publication in 1971. The reaction of the establishment was of course to deny the truths set out by Coard – before eventually admitting he was in fact correct – but more shockingly to tap his phone and have the police threaten his nephew, such is the weaponised history of black education in Britain.[6]

The response of the British Caribbean community and progressive teaching staff was to attempt to try to tackle what they knew was an endemically and unfairly racist system. In every major Caribbean community, black supplementary schools were set up, like the one I went to during my childhood. The first of these supplementary schools had already been set up three years before the publication of Coard's pamphlet, by Professor Gus John, and Coard estimates that as many as 150 of them existed at the peak of the movement. Parent–teacher conferences and initiatives were launched, and scholars and black professionals lent their voices to a mass campaign to ensure that black children were given a fairer deal in Britain's school system.

It is a very odd community indeed that simultaneously takes their meagre resources – remember most British Caribbeans are working class even now – and uses them to set up extra schools for their children, that manages to find volunteers willing to staff these schools every weekend for decades and is at the same time 'anti-education', as black people have so often been represented.

How have things progressed since the 1970s, and since I was in school? Are black children being treated fairly in British schools these days? Sadly and predictably, the answer is no. For example in the year 2000, David Gillborn – David is white by the way, for all those who need white references – and his colleague Heidi Safia Mizra were commissioned by Ofsted to examine the links between race, ethnicity and educational attainment as part of the legacy of the Stephen Lawrence Inquiry.[7] They examined the data from six local authorities' 'baseline assessments', which use a mix of written tests and teacher assessment to measure pupils' intelligence when they enter the school system aged five. They found several unsurprising things that fly in the face of all the eugenics-based bullshit, most notably:

- There was significant variation in the levels of attainment among the same ethnic groups in different parts of the country
- There was at least one Local Education Agency (LEA) where each of the major ethnic groups was the most likely to achieve five or more GCSE passes
- In one particular LEA, black children had the highest assessment scores of all ethnic groups when they entered school aged five
- In all six LEAs, the educational attainment of black students fell relative to the LEA average as they moved through the school system
- In the largest LEA in their sample, one of the largest in the country, black students entered the school twenty points above the national average as the highest performing ethnic group and in that very same LEA they left school as the lowest performing of all groups, twenty-one points below the national average

This report was widely cited in the left-wing media at the time, and you would perhaps think that showing such an obviously racialised pattern of educational disenfranchisement across all six LEAs would have caused a sea change in policy for the better, if indeed the intention was to remedy said institutional racism. Such change did not happen, and national policy changed instead to assess children entering school using the Foundation Stage Profile, or FSP method, a method that is entirely down to the individual teacher's judgment – that is to say, non-empirical.

Unsurprisingly, the outcome of FSP, teacher-assessed tests has been to conclude that white children are actually the smartest of all ethnic groups, despite the fact that Indian students have been dramatically outperforming them on average for many years. Why the state would make a form of non-empirical assessment compulsory in Britain's schools when it so obviously leaves room for whim and even unintended bias one can only ponder. We *can* be sure that if the FSP assessments had dramatically changed the picture to the detriment of white students they would have been changed by now. No special treatment is needed or being asked for, just a fair test that removes the margin for human error or misperception to influence the results. That's if we must test five-year-olds at all.

We know for certain that this trend of underestimating black children's intelligence continues right throughout schooling, which tallies with my experience and makes sense of the LEA data quoted above, where black children fall further behind the longer they stay in school. It is not complex; if a fair portion of your teachers or even just a couple of them constantly assume you are way less clever than you actually are simply because you are black, and treat you accordingly, you are going to resent them and it will naturally affect your self-esteem and grades.

In the final year of primary school in England and Wales, all pupils must take external examinations, which are blind marked by someone who does not know the child, thus eliminating any potential for racial bias. At the same time, teachers also assess the children in their class. According to a national study by Bristol University, between 2001–02 and 2004–05 teacher assessments of black Caribbean students were 5.6 points below their 'blind' SATs results.[8] This figure was 6.4 points for black African students, almost double that of the difference between teacher assessments and SATs for white students, which stood at 3.3 points. The study proved beyond any doubt that British teachers assess black pupils' academic ability as being far lower than their actual academic ability, and underestimate their intelligence twice as much as they do for white children. Intriguingly, teachers underestimate black British students of African origin by an even greater degree than those whose great-grandparents came from the Caribbean, despite the fact that British-African students have generally performed better academically. It is only with the blind marking of Key Stage 2 SATs, in which an external marker does not know the child they are assessing, that we can see the huge discrepancy between teacher assessments and blind test results.

The same study also concluded that Indian and Chinese students tended to be over-assessed by their teachers in comparison to their actual academic performance, again confirming the widespread stereotype that they are all super-smart, and white students from poorer areas tended to be more underestimated than white students from more expensive postcodes. In short, the study confirmed that teachers are human beings and that they project their biases and those of our society onto children. The DfE is as aware of these studies and this data as I am – or at least we would hope so – and technically they have a legal duty to eliminate racial bias from within Britain's education system, but as you will see in a later chapter it is increasingly unlikely that they are going to do so without serious parental, community and teacher pressure.

When understood in its historical context, then, my being siphoned off into a special needs group starts to make much more sense. What's fascinating is that the British state, apparently committed to a quality education for all, has rarely and barely supported these massive community-led efforts to make sure black Brits attain a quality education, and in the decades since the initial sympathy to Coard's work and the issues it raised, the British media has in fact been happy to feed the image of young black people as little more than thugs, muggers and drug dealers with little to offer British society.

Nonetheless, my generation of British Caribbeans experienced schooling quite differently from our parents in a number of ways. First, I don't think it an overly harsh generalisation to say that our colonially educated grandparents generally had more faith in the British authorities than our parents came to have, and this often led them to refuse to hear the legitimate complaints of their own children against 'authority'. Tales of being unjustly beaten – corporal punishment in school was not made illegal until 1986 – or otherwise punished by teachers, and then returning home to complain to parents who would then beat you again – often far worse than the teachers had, it must be admitted – and insist that 'you must a do something wrong if dem beat you' and 'if you na hear u mus feel' are typical of our parents' age group. Our British-born parents therefore well understood the racialised challenges their children would inevitably face in school and thus, while their strategies to combat such things were not always perfect, they certainly were far less likely to side with the authorities against their own children.

My father's and my uncles' experiences at school were so horrendous that they viewed school as a cultural and intellectual war zone, where victory in battle was won by every black student that emerged with As from a fundamentally racist, classist institution. So when, in my last year of primary school, I complained to my dad about another teacher psychologically bullying me in vindictive ways that only an acute observer would see, he did not respond as his parents would have done, by beating me and telling me to 'just listen to your teachers'.

Instead, he came up to my school from West Sussex and met with the headmistress. When the headmistress tried to dismiss his claims that the teacher was patronising me and generally being intimidating and bullying, my father, six foot two and fifteen stone, got up and stood over the seated headmistress. Speaking in his softest, most patronising voice, he said: 'Now look, I'm speaking softly and being nice, aren't I? Yet we both know you are intimidated, don't we?'

The headmistress told my dad that he had made his point and that she would speak to the teacher in question, which to her credit she did. The teacher's response was a characteristic mix of sarcasm, total dismissal and feigned concern. She declared to the whole class that we were having an official 'be nice to Kingslee day' or 'BNTK day' – yes, she did abbreviate it and even wrote it on the board in big capital letters – and that Kingslee would today be able to do and say anything he wanted without anyone speaking back in response. Of course, I understood what was happening and tried to stay silent that day, but she directed every question at me, insisting to the class that Kingslee had to be given the chance to answer first, as it was BNTK day today after all. I was ten years old.

Had my parents told me that my negative experiences in school were a result of my own behaviour entirely, or had they not had the intellectual equipment to adequately challenge my mistreatment, like so many of their class and generation, I would have likely dropped out of school entirely. But luckily they took an active interest in my schooling and had no problem coming to my defence against 'the system'. My mum understood that white children in general and rich white children in particular would be given the benefit of the doubt and that I would not; my dad and all of my uncles knew how threatened many in British society, even some 'liberal' white women, felt by educated black children, especially boys, and how hard they would work against my educational attainments, even if sometimes only subconsciously. Were it not for their understanding and support, and that of a few radical teachers (of all ethnicities), ironically my intellectual aptitude, my willingness to read and question beyond the syllabus, may well have led me away from formal education entirely.

Even as an adult, the shock some people still have at a 'smart black guy' often provides me and my friends with priceless moments of comedy. Of course, I can tell the difference between someone genuinely complimenting my public speaking as they would any other speaker and someone shocked that I 'speak so well' – for a cockney-sounding darkie. When I'm on a television programme or a panel and the opposing person feels the need to patronisingly let me know that 'you actually made quite a good point' as if they are still processing the fact of it, one wonders whether race, accent (a class indicator) and dress code are all factors. It's hard to imagine them feeling the need to let a RP-speaking white Cambridge professor of my age know that he *actually* makes a good point, though perhaps some of these types are just that patronising. I'm sure many northerners or 'scousers' have felt similarly patronised based on the stigmas attached to their accents, and my friend who is a professional writer of Cypriot origin, whose father 'came up' in Hackney, often talks about his early jobs working in various companies where his colleagues and bosses could not believe that 'you read Hermann Hesse? You?' So as always there is much crossover between assumptions based on class indicators and race (race itself being one of the biggest and most obvious class indicators).

It's also interesting how class norms can be a disability going into certain spaces, like televised debates, because the truth is that working-class people often don't have time for all the poncey doublespeak, and when someone is openly patronising and rude our natural response is to tell them to fuck off or, if they are rude enough, to offer them a trip outside for a good old dust-up. I cannot tell you how many times I have had to fight that urge.

My composer friend and I often joke about the look of shock on some white people's faces when they're introduced to him as the composer of the music they just heard the orchestra play; and when they try to politely hide their shock and/or resist the urge to ask who helped him do it. No, I am not joking, the question 'who helped you do it?' has been asked of him many times. What's most funny is that my composer friend confuses and confounds the racial stereotypes of everybody. He is very traditionally 'well spoken' – even posh – and a classical composer. He is also one of the best-dressed men going and manages to pull off 'out there' fashions that most brothers would never try, such as tweed suits and ponchos. Black people sometimes hear the accent, see the clothes and assume 'he wants to be white', because they have sadly internalised the idea that there are only certain types of authentic ways to be black. I've seen their shock too, when they realise how 'black' his politics are despite the suits, the piano and the RP. He actually knows far more about African history and culture than the vast majority of dashiki-wearing Afrocentrists. White people often make the same mistake and say the strangest of things to him, again thinking that he is not one of 'those' black people – you know, the ones that respect and love themselves.

The threat posed to some people's entire sense of identity by an exhibition of human excellence inside a black body is an amount of fear, sideways admiration and contempt for another group of humans that I can't even imagine being constantly burdened by. These seemingly odd responses to black excellence did not pop out of a vacuum, but rather stem from centuries of anti-black marketing in European literature, thought, philosophy and historiography. Take the 'historians' that claimed that Africans, unlike the rest of humanity, had no history, and thus when they found evidence of this supposedly absent history from 'pre-colonial' Africa – from the ruins of great Zimbabwe, to the manuscripts of Timbuktu, to the sublime metal art of Ile Ife and Benin – set about trying to look for a non-African source for these works. In some cases, scholars were more willing to entertain the idea that aliens were responsible for African history than Africans! This 'intellectual' trend was pioneered by those who took the conditions of enslaved people – that is people physically prevented from attaining an education – and decided that their perceptions of the intellectual aptitude of slaves represented the permanent and genetically pre-determined state of all black people. To smarter and more humane European thinkers, even during the nineteenth century, it was obvious that an enslaved person had very good and obvious motivations for hiding and/or playing down their intelligence, and that any technological gaps between Europe and West Africa were no more likely to be due to skin colour than the technological gaps that existed for centuries between the olive-skinned Romans and the 'white' people to the north and west of them, or indeed between Song China and tenth-century Britain.

Euro-America's ability to dominate black people has not been read as one more chapter in a long history of human exploitation and domination, but rather as permanent racial superiority and inferiority. Thus, as late as the 1990s, 'top' academics could argue that racialised differentials in IQ scores in the USA had absolutely nothing to do with the material history of that nation, but rather that black people were just genetically inferior. Of course, the obvious parallel argument that white people are genetically inferior to South East Asians, now that people from that region score higher on the Western – eugenics inspired – IQ test, has certainly been far more muted.

While I am not suggesting that people who are shocked at my friend being a classical composer or by my other homie who is a trauma surgeon would publicly admit or even honestly believe that black humans are genetically inferior, this is never-theless the historical propaganda they are responding to and have been influenced by. Britain, it seems, is trapped by its own history and the conflict with its own liberal rhetoric. Are we really trying to encourage and normalise black academic excel-lence in the UK? Or would we prefer the extra cost of imprison-ment and crime that comes further down the line after neglect, just so one can still feel superior? What are the long term demo-graphic and political consequences of creating a prosperous and thus potentially politically powerful black middle class? Let's just be honest. If we want to fix the racial and economic disparities in the criminal justice system or at least reduce them, combat teenage gang violence, produce better educated chil-dren and create a generally better society, then the work starts in the primary school, not in the prison.

4 – LINFORD'S LUNCHBOX

'The Negro is an example of animal man in all his
savagery and lawlessness, and if we wish to understand
him at all, we must put aside all our European
attitudes . . .'

G. M. F. Hegel

'[Africans are] the most degraded of human races, whose
form approaches that of the beast and whose intelligence
is nowhere great enough to arrive at regular government'

Georges Cuvier

'One is no longer aware of the Negro but only of a penis;
the Negro is eclipsed. He is turned into a penis. He is a
penis.'

Frantz Fanon

On 1 August 1992 I sat down to watch the final of the men's
100-metre sprint at the Barcelona Olympics. I was just nine
years old but athletics and football had by now become a virtual
religion for me, though I never quite inherited the obsession
with cricket from the older generation of Caribbeans. The
whole family fell silent as the men took their starting positions;
we were all rooting for Linford Christie, the British champion
and one of the foremost black British figures of a generation.
Along with Ian Wright, Soul2Soul, Lenny Henry and Lennox
Lewis, Linford was part of the strange phenomenon of black

Brits winning an informal and unspoken access to a contingent 'Britishness' through sports, culture and entertainment.

Black excellence in sport and entertainment has been a particularly contradictory feature of Anglo-America; on the one hand it echoes old stereotypes about natural rhythm, brawn over brains and 'natural' animal athleticism, and on the other hand it creates a noticeable schizophrenia: how could black people remain second-class citizens when some of the greatest representatives of 'British' (or American) excellence to the world were black? How could England fans keep throwing bananas at black football players now that half the national team was black? How could white America keep claiming the niggers were inferior post Jesse Owens, Jack Johnson and Muhammad Ali? The contradiction was glaring.

This dichotomy, and the way people handled it, came to life for me in that first week of August 1992. Linford won the Olympic gold medal in the 100 metres that night, one of only two British athletes to do so since Harold Abrahams in 1924. My house went wild. We were so happy for Linford, yet as we watched him drape himself in the Union Jack we felt the discomfort, joy and confusion of black households up and down the country: happy for Linford, but resentful of the flag that to us represented the National Front, colonialism, police brutality and the Babylon system.

Many of our grandparents proudly saw themselves as British subjects and had no real issue with the flag, indeed many thousands of them had fought under it. However, by the time of Linford's victory we had become so disheartened by decades of institutional racism that most of us accepted we probably would never really be 'British' in the way white people could be, even the millions of 'White British' people whose immigrant grandparents arrived at the exact same time as ours. Norman Tebbit's infamous 1990 'cricket test', in which black Britons were invited to pick a side when England played the West Indies, showed both how exclusive some people's concept of national belonging was and exposed the area of sport as a key site of national and racial anxieties, loyalties and frictions.

As Linford ran back around the track, close to tears, draped in the Union Jack, with thousands of adoring fans cheering and millions watching at home, I doubt he had any idea how the tabloid press would convey his victory in the coming days. Watching at the time, I certainly had no idea.

I walked into the newsagent's in the days after Linford's win and, oddly for a nine-year-old, was browsing through one of the tabloids – maybe taking a sneaky peek at page three, to be honest – when I stumbled upon the strangest cartoon. There had been a hosepipe ban that summer, and this cartoon featured a caricature of Linford Christie with a huge bulge in his trousers. The 'hose pipe inspector' was pointing to the bulge and informing Linford that 'there is a hosepipe ban you know', or words to that effect. I knew this was very strange and that there was something significant in this story being run just after the highlight of Linford's career, but of course I get the significance a little better now.

In the days and weeks after Linford's historic victory, the press was not focused on his contribution to British sport but instead full of stories about 'Linford's Lunchbox', a less than subtle euphemism for his apparently huge penis. Presumably Linford had the exact same penis for his entire career and did not get a transplant on the night of 31 July 1992, so why had the press chosen this moment, the moment of the greatest glory in an athlete's career, to objectify Linford in such a way?

The obsession with Linford's Lunchbox was said to have been begun by the *Sun*, who on the 6 August 1992 ran a feature entitled '10 ways to pack your lunchbox like Linford'. In this feature, they got a black model to pack his shorts full of goodies to achieve 'that look'. Other newspapers, including some of the broadsheets, ran their own stories about 'Linford's Lunchbox', and it became a sort of cultural cliché. If you ask any person of my age or older about 'Linford's Lunchbox' they are likely to know what you mean and to remember that particular race at the Barcelona Olympics. Prior to that night, I'm not sure much thought had been given to Linford's penis in particular, as all of the male athletes wore similar Lycra shorts. The question is, would Linford's penis ever have become a story if he had not won?

Linford made his feelings about the distasteful nature and poor timing of the comments pretty clear, which only damaged his already rocky relationship with the British media. Linford's concerns were generally brushed off or dismissed as him being oversensitive, even by some black journalists like Tony Sewell at the *Voice*, who accused Linford of being a 'big girl's blouse' and claimed that 'celeb guys' – like Linford – made him ashamed to be a black man. Rather odd, to say the least.

The lunchbox 'scandal' reached its iconic peak when Linford appeared on ITV's *Sport in Question* with Jimmy Greaves, Chris Eubank, Ian St John and a journalist from the *Mail on Sunday* called Patrick Collins. After a question from an audience member about the media treatment of him, Linford Christie again made it quite clear that he felt the media had treated him unfairly and overlooked his achievements in favour of an obsession with his 'Lunchbox'. This *Sport in Question* episode then descended into a row that will be – and has been – written about for decades because of what it said about race, sexuality, culture and British politics. Patrick Collins defended the press and accused Linford of 'seizing' on some negative comments and making generalisations about the media, despite Linford pointing out that even the broadsheets had carried the 'Lunchbox' story in the wake of his Olympic gold. Jimmy

Greaves told Linford he should wear something more appropriate if he was so offended, and let him know that 'he has never offended me with it [his penis], I can tell you' and that 'a lot of women are fascinated by it'.

Unsurprisingly, Chris Eubank then took the side of Linford and entered into an argument with Jimmy Greaves, where Mr Greaves revealingly told Eubank that he should not have entered the ring to the song 'Simply the Best' – essentially that he should have been more humble and known his place. Why were these thoughts on the tip of his tongue? By the end of the dialogue, Linford wound up crying and the mood entirely changed once Greaves realised Linford was actually seriously offended.

It is an iconic moment in British television and I felt an enormous sympathy for Linford and actually feel that his tears, far from making him a 'big girl's blouse' as Tony Sewell said, showed a fragile and human side of black masculinity that is rarely if ever seen on British television. It's fairly clear to all that Linford could snap Jimmy Greaves' neck in two if he chose to, but instead of raging and becoming 'the angry black man' – though there is certainly a place for that – Linford cried, a perfectly valid response to the rage that a person might feel when their spectacular achievements have been overlooked in favour of their genitalia. Stuart Pearce, Paul Gascoigne and many other British footballers have publicly cried at iconic moments in their careers and received sympathy and support, so it's rather a shame that a writer at Britain's main black newspaper took this moment as a chance to have a dig at Linford for not being man enough, rather than to examine the dynamics that were really at play.

Linford did further complicate the picture and invite justifiable accusations of hypocrisy by later making adverts that overtly played on his Lunchbox; one for Kleenex featured a topless Linford with the slogan 'I've got a small packet'. He also became the face of underwear campaigns, which again invited a certain criticism.

However, the issue here for me is not really about the personal decisions of an individual black athlete but rather how this story fits into the larger narratives around black athleticism. In one of his brilliant essays looking at black British athletes, Ben Carrington contrasts the rocky relationship between the British media and Linford Christie to the almost unconditional love offered to Frank Bruno by that very same press in the exact same period of history.[1] Bruno and Linford are in many ways symbolic of the differing cultural attitudes, desires and understandings of blackness between Britain's black population and the white mainstream. For most black people old enough to remember, Bruno has always been a problematic character and certainly not an icon or hero, often seen as an ignorant stereotype that makes 'us' look bad. This is of course totally unfair to Frank, as he should not have to be a representative of his race.

That said, while Mr Bruno seemed to mean no harm, his unapologetic royalism, Thatcherite politics and even his refusal to respect the cultural boycott of South Africa at the height of the apartheid struggle make him a more problematic proposition than the simple-Frank persona might suggest. Despite enormous pressure from anti-apartheid groups, Bruno fought the South African Gerrie Coetzee in 1986 and justified this with the Thatcherite politics of 'every man for himself' and 'I gotta feed my family', he even went as far as to say that his promoter Mickey Duff had told him that Coetzee was 'anti-apartheid and that he has dozens of black friends'.

For all of these reasons, Bruno came to be seen by most black people I knew as white people's black guy, despite his achievements in the ring. Growing up, I remember hearing uncles and community members regularly 'diss' Frank and most would cheer for the black American over him, unlike with Lennox

Lewis or Nigel Benn, both of whom were more loved. For the most part, the deference, the solely individualistic concerns and the failure to see the way he was being used in Thatcherite Britain made Frank Bruno at best an ambiguous figure to black Britain, and at worst a very disliked one. Frank was obviously well aware of this and it eventually took its toll on him.

In 1995 Frank Bruno fought Oliver McCall for the WBC heavyweight championship of the world. I tuned in as always – boxing was very much part of that aforementioned sporting religion. The fight was titled 'The Empire Strikes Back', with copious use of the Union Jack on the flyers and posters and in the press. Bruno's earlier fight with Lennox Lewis had been marketed as 'The Battle of Britain', so the nationalist, imperial themes were not new. After twelve hard-fought rounds Bruno won on points to become one of just nine Britons to enter the elite category of world heavyweight champion, seven of whom are black.

The post-fight interview contrasts very interestingly with Linford's television breakdown. Sat at ringside, still sweating and with tears in his eyes, Frank Bruno repeatedly asserted to the interviewer that 'I'm not an Uncle Tom, I'm not Uncle Tom', perhaps seven or eight times across the interview, even though the questions he was asked bore no relevance to that issue at all.

Here we have two black athletes at the height of their careers breaking down on television for reasons entirely to do with the dynamics of racism, but with very little mainstream public analysis in the aftermath. In the pre-fight hype, McCall had indeed called Bruno an Uncle Tom, as had Lennox Lewis in the run up to their fight. Bruno had claimed repeatedly to not see colour, a sentiment guaranteed to win applause from much of the white British public. He also claimed that racism was just a few ignorant people and he may well have sincerely believed that, but watching the big man cry at ringside and repeat over and over again that he was not a sell-out or an Uncle Tom you really get a sense that Frank, despite himself, really did understand that something was majorly amiss, that there was a part of his identity or credibility with his community that was missing. Something that he felt he needed to vindicate right then and there, at the most important moment of his career.

You see, black adults I knew growing up did not hate Frank Bruno, they actually loved him, perhaps felt a little sorry for him, and for that reason it pained them to see people that did not really respect Frank's humanity claim to love him while sneering behind his back. Had Frank ever asserted himself, problematised the obvious racism that existed in Britain at that time or chosen to boycott fighting the South African in a basic recognition of black South African humanity, large portions of Frank's 'fans' would certainly have turned on him. This we knew, so in a sense we wanted to protect Frank from exactly the kind of desperate outrage and cry for help that he displayed in that post-fight interview.

As Carrington points out, unlike Linford's Lunchbox, Bruno's 'Uncle Tom' breakdown went largely uncommented on by the mainstream media, perhaps because the British press at the time would not have had the political vocabulary and knowledge of history to even deal with the significance of the event. To deal with it would have meant many white journalists asking why their favourite son, a black heavyweight champion and presumably a multi-millionaire, still felt somewhat like a failure because he did not have the love of his own people. Frank was admitting with this breakdown that the money and the admiration of white Britain was not enough; that he knew in fact that it was not genuine and that he craved to be loved by black people in the way that other athletes and public figures had been. Tone deaf British journalists who have kept themselves functionally ignorant of Britain's racial history simply could not grapple with all of this.

Fast forward to 9 August 2012; I sat down to watch the men's 200 metres final at the London Olympics. Usain Bolt had already won the 100 metres a few days earlier and it looked set to be another year of dominance for him and for Jamaica; like all British Jamaicans and sprint fans everywhere, I was very excited. Then something very strange happened. For who knows what reason, the BBC decided to play a weird eugenics film just before the final. The commentator who was sat next to a trio of black track legends, Colin Jackson, Michael Johnson and Denise Lewis, introduced the film in the following way:

> As we build up to the 200 metres, and this is a subject that doesn't get raised very often, because it just doesn't, but the fact is that not a single white athlete has contested the men's 100 metres final in the Olympics for thirty-two years. Eighty-two people have broken ten seconds for 100 metres and eighty-one of them have been black; the only one who is white is Christophe Lemaitre of France, who is running tonight in the 200 metres final. In fact, only four white men have ever gone under twenty seconds for 200 metres. So it brings the whole issue of nature or nurture into very sharp focus.

There are a number of obvious problems and lapses in basic logic within this statement. First, almost 40 per cent of the men on Earth are from India and China – not to mention the rest of the non-white but not-black world – yet whoever wrote this script seems entirely unconcerned with their lack of presence in Olympic sprint finals. A very clear white nationalist statement is being made, the issue is that white men are not winning, which should apparently be the norm, and to make matters worse it is black men defeating them – as if there is a permanent competition between black and white athletes. The viewer and society are being told that if black people are beating white people at anything there must be some kind of explanation. After that introduction, a short film played beginning with a discussion of Darwin's *On the Origin of Species*, the eugenics movement and Nazi genocide. This was then linked to black athletic performance, as the voiceover informed us that all of the great sprinters could trace their ancestry to Africa, 'that is to slaves', then the voice asked: 'Who was it that survived being put in shackles, packed into slave ships and taken across the ocean, who was it that survived the life of forced labour on the cotton and sugar plantations, the fittest, only the fittest could survive.'

The film stopped and Colin Jackson was asked for his opinion. After Colin refuted the nonsense with a scientific study – which he was actually a part of – that found that both black and white athletes have the 'fast twitch' muscle that is apparently the 'key' to sprinting, the commentator's response was: 'But are we at the point now where if you are a very talented athlete at fourteen/fifteen/sixteen, and you are white, you are almost institutionally programmed to think that you won't be able to compete at the highest level in the sprint?'

This is a very revealing question from a white public figure, because when black people assert that representation is important, that having role models you can relate to and who look like you is helpful, they are often accused of making excuses, playing the race card or wanting special treatment. Yet here, before the 200 metres final, was a public service broadcaster asserting that, actually, it does matter, and that seeing black people win, in a competition that no white people have ever been barred by law from entering, or in any way discriminated from participating in, could still discourage white teenagers from bothering to even try. Wow.

Michael Johnson who – sadly – also did a whole documentary investigating the 'possible link' between slavery and sprinting also refuted this suggestion, saying that culture, training and the national popularity of a given sport are all more important factors than some mystery gene, which is obvious enough even to a non-scientist.

The fact that the question is even asked, the fact that black excellence in a particular field needs 'explaining', tells its own story. I can't recall any documentaries trying to discover an organisational gene left over from fascism that explains why Germany and Italy have consistently been Europe's best performing football teams. Spain's brief spell as the best team in the world, with a generation of players born in the years immediately after Franco's death, would seem to confirm my fascism-meets-football thesis, right? Clearly this would be a ridiculous investigation – or who knows maybe I am on to something – but the question would never be asked because German, Italian and Spanish brilliance don't really need explaining, or at least not in such negative ways.

When I was young, I vividly remember watching a BBC doc called *Dreaming of Ajax* which investigated why one Dutch club, Ajax Amsterdam, was able to produce better football players than the whole of England. It was a fantastic documentary that looked with great admiration at the obviously superior coaching systems of Ajax, which became so visible in their home-grown players' performances. But it did not look for some mystery Dutch gene left over from some horrendous episode in European history. Nor did white dominance in tennis or golf – until Tiger and the Williams sisters, anyway – need to be explained by their ancestors having so much practice whipping people for so long, and ending up with strong shoulders and great technique as a result!

To get to the root of just how ridiculous the slave–sprint 'correlation' is, let's look at some basic, common-sense facts. Before Usain Bolt's victory in Beijing in 2008, Jamaica had produced not one single male 100-metre gold medallist, yet we are apparently being asked to believe some latent super-slave gene suddenly manifested itself 148 years after the abolition of slavery at the birth of one Usain St Leo Bolt. Brazil has roughly forty times as many black people as Jamaica and was the last country in the western hemisphere to abolish slavery, yet not a single Brazilian has won even so much as a bronze at the 100 metres. Brazil's sole individual sprinting medal was a bronze in the 200 metres in 1988, won by Robson Da Silva. Frankie Fredricks from Namibia – so not a descendant of an Afro-American 'slave' – has won four Olympic silvers in sprinting, so that is four more than all 80 million plus black Brazilians put together.

What is one to do with such lack of common sense? The inability of whoever commissioned that film to accept that the hard work, sacrifice and years of vomit-inducing training it took eighty-one black men to run 100 metres in under ten seconds are hardly representative of the other hundreds of millions of black men is a little odd. To air such anti-intellectual nonsense right before one of the most watched sporting events in British television history is odder still. The idea that black athletes owe their achievements to the sideways gift of benevolent slave masters rather than to greater hard work, the cultural importance of sprinting in a given country, the quality of the coaching and better organisation and preparation is just fantastical. What's more, it's an even greater insult given that the real institutional legacies of slavery that can be so clearly seen in Jamaica and throughout the Americas are ignored or played down, while this nebulous 'link' between slavery and sprinting is given prime-time coverage.

Cuba's phenomenal record of achievement in Olympic boxing, like Jamaica's recent one in sprinting, or New Zealand's in rugby union, or the USA's in basketball, might have something to do with these same institutional and cultural factors. Yet, for whoever commissioned this film, the rather easily traceable nature of Jamaica's athletic excellence – youth athletic meets fill the national stadium – just cannot be. It's not possible that mere Jamaicans are like the Dutch of Ajax; better prepared, more dedicated, disciplined and more organised than their competitors. It's not as if any of the other Caribbean islands, all of which also had plenty of slavery, have come close to replicating Jamaica's success in this area; Usain Bolt has won 3 times as many 100 metre gold medals as all of the other islands combined. Lastly, the vast majority of enslaved Africans were not taken to the continental United States and there is good evidence that the slave regimes of the Caribbean were far harsher, so if the 'survival of the fittest slave' theory held true, the Caribbean nations would always be the leaders in this arena. Yet it is the United States that has traditionally dominated sprinting, by quite some distance.

Yet as the commentator frankly admitted, for racist people who have convinced themselves of innate white superiority, consciously or unconsciously, watching black men dominate the two supreme sporting tests of 'masculine virility' – the 100 metre final and heavyweight boxing – must feel quite disheartening. It's notable that East African domination of long-distance running seems not to evoke similar insecurities, though it has also invoked its own plethora of 'explanations' and stereotypes.

My own relationship with sport is an interesting one; being of Jamaican heritage, sprinting was always popular among my community and friends. Despite being primarily interested in football as a teenager, I ended up competing in the London youth games in the 100-metre sprint, where I defeated the seven 'fully black' boys in the final and went on to compete in the all-England games. Of course, you could not help but notice how disproportionately represented black youngsters were at the games, but I was knocked out of my competition in the semi-final, and the only white boy in our entire competition came first. The truth is, we did find this weird, and on the way back on the coach people made jokes about 'getting beat by a white boy'. My mum being white didn't count in the conversation. It seems even we had internalised this idea about black people being naturally athletic rather than seeing what was obvious; that sports and entertainment are two of the only fields where black success has been clear and visible in post Second World War Britain, and so it's hardly a surprise that young black men pine after the only two fields they see as open to them. When I go to schools here and ask young black boys what they want to be when they are older, footballer and rapper are the two most commonly repeated aspirations. I have asked this same question in schools in Zimbabwe, South Sudan and Ethiopia, and the answers were vastly different and much more varied.

Like the typical black yout from the ends, I played football at various levels; school, district and Sunday league. However, I went that little bit further than normal and eventually played for the youth team of West Ham United during the golden years when the club produced future England internationals Joe Cole, Michael Carrick, Rio Ferdinand, Glen Johnson and Jermain Defoe.

Race was an ever-present theme in football, though it often went unacknowledged. Black players were expected to accept racial 'banter' without having a 'chip on their shoulder' about it. So when my coach asked us to go and get the 'wog box' – the stereo – I was the one who could not 'take a joke' and got irritated. Maybe my white coaches had watched Spike Lee's legendary film *Do The Right Thing* and remembered Radio Raheem, but I doubt it very much. The sport vs. academia struggle was a strong current in my teenage years and it always contained racial undertones. I was good at football and played for West Ham schoolboys, but I also went to the Royal Institution of Mathematics' masterclasses. My black Saturday school and my Uncle Offs were pushing me toward my first love, science. My uncle always told me I was smart enough to pursue a career in quantum physics from an age when I did not even know what quantum physics was. Years later when I took up football, he was secretly disappointed and told my mum that he feared football would ruin me. He, like many others in 'the black community', essentially viewed black sportsmen mostly as fools who did very little for their community and rarely if ever used their platforms to speak out about injustices once they personally had made it, with obvious notable exceptions. People like my Uncle Offs were far more impressed by black academics like Walter Rodney and C. L. R. James than they ever would be by a footballer.

When I started secondary school, my mum said in passing to Mr Muhammad (a famous black teacher at my secondary) that I could not wait to join the football team, and his response was to say, 'I hope he is as keen on his studies.' I now find myself saying the exact same thing to classes full of black boys who all want to be football players. I know Britain has spent quite some time convincing itself that black people in general and Caribbeans in particular are naturally great at sport and inimical to education, but all this shows is how little they actually know us. Quite aside from the tradition of community self-education that I was a beneficiary of, you could just venture into any Caribbean barber shop or takeaway – the only two businesses we run in the hood – and see who is on the wall, who it is that we choose to venerate. Is it drug dealers? Never. Is it athletes? Sometimes, but rarely. More often than not the faces on the wall will be Marcus Garvey, Malcolm X, Bob Marley, Muhammad Ali and, in the case of my barber in Harlesden, a poster of black scientists and inventors.

So why have so many white people and publications been upset by black sporting achievement? I mean, I can't imagine watching Russian or Chinese dominance in gymnastics and thinking I'm never going to try that because I am not Russian or Chinese, much less feeling ethnically inadequate. I can't imagine watching *Lord of the Rings* and thinking, *Oh, white people being excellent again, what a bummer*. This brings us to one of the least spoken about aspects of Western racial mythologies over the past few centuries: the insanity it inflicts on many of its intended beneficiaries. An identity predicated on supremacy is not healthy or stable. An identity that says 'I am, because you are not' is what Hegel was talking about when he wrote his master–slave dialectic, even if he did not realise this himself. The long and short of it is that the master makes himself a slave to his slave by needing that domination to define him.

White supremacists, as much as they don't want to admit it, make themselves slaves to black excellence when they allow its existence to unbalance their entire sense of self. This racialised fragility is what caused the racist mob attacks in Britain in 1919 and 1958, the fire bombings of the 1980s and the now-famous case of Stephen Lawrence. Humans kill for a whole host of strange reasons, yet we rarely think about how strange it is for the colour of another person's skin to provoke a strong enough reaction to want to murder them. We talk about white privilege but we rarely talk about the white burden, the burden of being tethered to a false identity, a parasitic self-definition that can only define itself in relation to blacks' or others' inferiority.

This is the mentality that made lynching a form of light entertainment and made it illegal for black and white people to get married or even be seen together in the street in apartheid South Africa, the mentality that crafted the Nuremberg Laws and gave birth to theories of vast Jewish conspiracies behind every movement in history – from the ultra-capitalist banker to the Bolshevik revolutionary, those evil crafty Jews were apparently behind it all. It takes work to fear another people that much and while black people should be right to fear and even resent the history of white racial dominance, they should also feel, in a strange way, quite flattered by it. Despite what white supremacists claim, going to such extents as they have to prevent black excellence is really a rather huge compliment. For Jack Johnson's success to lead to the search for a great white hope is, frankly, rather pathetic; for Jesse Owens to be able to spoil the worldview of an entire nation is, again, pretty sad. Dangerous as racism is, it also makes victims out of white people – like those of my school teachers that felt threatened by a child's intelligence.

I know some black and brown folk reading this will think I have gone crazy, but hear me out. As much as racism might piss me off, I'd never want to have been born anyone other than myself in this culture at this time. Why? Because in spite of whatever challenges I might face, I love my people, history and culture and I don't need Chinese people or Indians or Spaniards to not reach their full human potential to feel good about myself; that is far too much power to give to another group. I can be inspired by the brilliance of Shakespeare or Stephen Hawking or Lao Tzu and it's totally fine that they are not black. I'm sure people racialised as white but not aggressively tethered to a supremacist identity feel similarly. So while we are often encouraged to spill our hearts about how bad racism is as if we were its sole victims, and as if white people can't even comprehend what is going on, I'd never want to swap roles and be the one spitting on children because they look different and want to go to school, or be ready to beat a child to death because they apparently whistled at a woman of my 'race'.

Granted these are American examples and the US is pretty extreme in all ways – positive and negative – but the UK has not been totally free of these insanities, even domestically. So when news anchors ask about race, why not turn the anthropological lens around? Let's ask white people about whiteness on occasion and not allow the dominant identity to remain invisible, thus retaining its mystical power. Some activists would argue this would only 'centre' whiteness again and is thus problematic; I am not so convinced. It would have been great had Denise Lewis or Colin Jackson asked the commentator why he felt white people could not be inspired by Usain Bolt's achievements the way that generations of writers who are not white men have been inspired by Shakespeare, Dickens, Steinbeck and Herbert. The way that all football fans, whatever their country of origin, have been inspired by Maradona and Messi. The way that the millions of us, including myself, who practise Asian martial arts have been inspired by Bruce Lee and Buakaw and the monks of Shaolin. What is it this man feels about white identity that makes him opine that white people are incapable of being inspired by the excellence of people that happen to be black, and is he correct? Why does he think so little of white people and why did his saying this in front of millions provoke little to no reaction?

Whether it's Linford's Lunchbox, Jack Johnson's unforgivable blackness in defeating the great white hopes, or Jesse Owens embarrassing Hitler on his own soil, the black athlete has had and continues to have a strange relationship with the white public imagination. In the 1960s and 1970s, Muhammad Ali occupied an iconic place in British popular culture, his legendary interview on *Parkinson* in 1971 exhibited such charisma and intelligence that it won him the admiration of audiences everywhere, even while he told white people that he'd frankly had enough of them.

On the one hand, the black athlete has totally destroyed the myth of white genetic superiority time and again, yet for many this has served not as an example of black excellence, discipline and achievement in one of the only obvious routes out of poverty for working class black youth, but rather as conformation for the existence of some deviant mystery nigger gene. Today, black athletes representing Britain is a norm – there are no more banana skins and no more bullets in the post for black footballers playing for their country. The nation has just had to get used to an England football team that is half black, and if current youth-team trends are anything to go by, set to get 'blacker and blacker' into the future. The Premier League, much like the NBA and NFL in the USA, would simply not be the brilliant spectacle it is without black athletes, yet the same institutional controversies surround them; a palpable lack of black managers and coaching staff and, of course, no owners at all in a field so disproportionately dominated by people of African heritage.

Yet there have still been scandals surrounding football and racism, even in these now golden post-banana-skin years, most famously former Aston Villa manager Ron Atkinson calling Marcel Desailly 'a fucking lazy thick nigger' in 2004. Atkinson was working as a commentator for ITV at the time and did not realise his mic was still recording – the comment was actually broadcast in some parts of the world. Atkinson had to resign from ITV in shame, but had the comment been made off air, we can have strong doubts whether that would have been the case. As his defence, Atkinson claimed that he was 'one of the first managers to give black players a chance'. He obviously thought this made him sound less racist, when of course what it suggests is that he thinks black players need to be 'given' a chance, i.e. they do not work hard and automatically deserve their places like others based on merit, they are 'given' their chances by the inevitably white 'authority' figures like him. You would never hear a manager claim he was one of the first to give white players a chance. There were several puzzling things about the episode, not least Big Ron's claim that it was just a mistake to have such a vitriolic phrase as 'lazy thick nigger' ready for one apparently bad game by a footballing legend such as Marcel Desailly. Also, and predictably, a crew of black ex-players lined up around the block to defend Big Ron and let the world know that he was not really a racist – yes, those black people do exist, those that would rush to defend someone calling their colleague a 'lazy thick nigger' but are totally silent about issues the rest of the time. At the time of writing two separate stories around racism in football have recently broken, one involving a number of former Chelsea youth team players accusing two former coaches Graham Rix and Gwyn Williams of inflicting regular racist abuse during their years at the club. It is alleged that Rix and Williams routinely referred to black children at the club as monkeys, coons, niggers, wogs, spear chuckers, even telling one of them that 'if his heart was a big as their cock he might be a great player that ran more'.[2] The other story was a confessional from England under-17 World Cup winner Rhian Brewster about the regular racist abuse he has had to deal with whilst playing for Liverpool and England and his dismay at a lack of action from the authorities.[3]

Which brings us onto the bigger question: what is blackness? And what is it about blackness in the bigots' mind that could provoke an adult to feel so threatened by young boys in their care who dream of one day playing in the Premier League? Or provoke sexual insecurities so deep that a lynching could ensue at the mere thought of sexual intercourse between a black man and a white woman in the Jim Crow south?

What I want to look at here is the construction of blackness in the racist imagination and the specific form of historical prejudice meted out to people on the grounds of having black skin or being defined as black. That hatred for darker-skinned people is a global issue can be glimpsed from the beatings and discrimination meted out to African students in India, or the monkey chants aimed at black footballers in Eastern Europe – Eastern Europeans were major victims of slavery, historically speaking, and never embarked on racialised globe-trotting empires like their Western neighbours – or the strange mix of fear, revulsion and intrigue that greets black people in many parts of south-east Asia – which stopped me from getting a taxi on one of the busiest streets in South Korea for almost an hour. I asked my Korean friends if I was being paranoid, and they just laughed and said of course not.

Despite this global pattern, blackness is defined very differently from place to place. One of the reasons that I know that white people are being obtuse when they pretend to not understand something as basic as white privilege is because, being 'half white', I have myself been treated entirely differently based on the perception of my blackness in a given society. In Britain and the USA I am racialised as black, in South Africa I am coloured, in Brazil I am a Carioca, a person from Rio, across the Caribbean I am 'high coloured' as previously mentioned – and in all places I am treated accordingly. In northern Africa, where I pass for a brown-skinned Amazigh local, darker-skinned black people are regularly referred to as Abeed, meaning slave, and I am not because I am light enough to 'pass'.

It is interesting to note that even a disproportionate number of black America's revolutionary icons are lighter skinned;

Malcolm, Martin, Muhammad, Angela Davis and Huey Newton – partly reflective of the history of the 'one drop rule' in America in that if any of those people who are very 'light' had been born in the Caribbean, their skin tone and the history behind it would have almost certainly meant that they would have been born middle class or aristocracy or at least be perceived as such. If mixed-race-looking Malcolm X or Angela Davis were born in Jamaica, they would have been 'uptown people', and thus had an entirely different life experience than the one they had in America, based simply on the different perceptions of the very same colours in different places. On the other hand, if you moved them to Brazil they would again be associated with those from the bottom of the society. Was part of Bob Marley's 'marketability' his light skin? Would Obama have been elected if he had two black parents and jet-black skin? We'll never know, but I personally doubt it.

But perhaps the most unusual way of setting the boundaries of blackness I have ever encountered has to be in Australia. I have toured in Australia twice and gone there to do Hip-Hop Shakespeare Company work on a separate occasion. I have appeared on panels there with activists and thinkers and done workshops with school and youth groups. In Australia I met many people that to me looked white and certainly would be perceived as such in any country I have ever visited apart from Australia, yet they swore they were blackfellas – as Aboriginal people often call themselves – and the intensity with which they spoke about their blackness let me know they had really seen and been through some things, that they were not trying to be cool, that they really had lived blackness in the harshest sense Australia could possibly muster. How could this occur that people that literally have a 'white' complexion (but Aboriginal features) came to be seen as black? The root of this seeming oddity of course has to be sought in history. From 1910 to 1970 between one in three and one in ten Aboriginal children were forcibly removed from their families to be raised either by white families or in children's homes across the country. This was a policy of forced assimilation designed to get Aboriginal Australians to forget and forgo their traditional culture and language. Physical and sexual abuse were rampant, the children were functionally undereducated and were often taught that their families and community had willingly forsaken them. These victims of this process are today referred to as the stolen generations. The 'white'-looking Aboriginal people I encountered along with all the other gradations of mixed-looking Aboriginal blackfellas are one of the legacies of this insane and genocidal process. No wonder they so fiercely defend their blackness when Australia had literally physically stolen their grandparents and tried to erase every aspect of their black identity. There is little doubt that today blackfellas in Australia, even the nearly white-looking ones, are treated and viewed more harshly than a relatively well-off black British visitor such as myself is, showing again how race and class can adapt and change depending on time and place. Australia attempted to reconcile with this history – to a degree – during the 1990s with the 'Bringing them Home' report and expressions of regret from the then prime minister John Howard, but terrible treatment of Australia's indigenous population and the resentment that results from this treatment continue to pose a serious challenge to the country.[4]

That even black people can seriously internalise anti-black sentiment can be seen in the massive trend for skin bleaching across black communities, and old Caribbean sayings such as 'anything too black cyan good'. As long as whiteness is a metaphor for power, blackness must of course function as a metaphor for powerlessness, and as long as money whitens, poverty must blacken.

If anti-black prejudice is global, to massively varying degrees of course, has this always been the case and, if not, how did it become the case? This is what I will try to answer below; however, I would like to note that I am not going to address the caste system in India here for the simple reason that I don't know enough of that history to do it any real justice. What we are looking at then is the development of anti-black prejudice in the cultures of the Middle East, North Africa, Europe and the Americas.

Interestingly, while the Bible and the Koran are both free of anti-black prejudice, in some ways the story of anti-blackness is rooted in the history of the Abrahamic faiths and sort of begins with a random Bible verse that does not even mention colour at all. Genesis 9:18–25 talks about the sons of Noah; Ham, Shem and Japeth. Ham and all his children were cursed to be slaves because according to this verse, Ham did not cover his naked father.

Despite the actual verse not mentioning Ham's colour at all, from this passage a whole mythology developed around black people being the cursed sons of Ham and therefore eternally suited for slavery, well over a thousand years before the invention of 'race' as we think of it. While the colour symbolism of black as bad and white as good has existed for thousands of years, across many cultures including in Africa, there is no reason that this esoteric colour symbolism should have been applied to human beings' skins, and social structures designed accordingly.

That is something that came about more through slavery. Slavery is a common and ancient institution. It has existed right across the planet from the largest empires to the smallest tribal groups. It has underpinned the most admired periods of European history; Ancient Greece, Imperial Rome, the Florentine renaissance, the (European) Enlightenment and the Industrial Revolution. For most of history, the people doing the enslaving came from similar(ish) regions of the world to those being enslaved. The very word slave comes from Slav, meaning Slavic, because so many 'white' Eastern Europeans were enslaved by other 'Europeans' and even sold to Muslims by them for centuries. Slavery in medieval Europe, the Mediterranean and the ancient world, though common, never came to be racial in a white–black binary sense. Even in the quintessential ancient 'European' empire, Rome, a society partly built by plantation-style slaves, blackness and slavery never came to be widely associated, yet when we think of 'slaves' today it tends to conjure images of black Africans enslaved in the Americas. The process by which this became the case has its roots in the ancient and medieval world.

While a certain degree of cultural chauvinism is near universal, with the expansion of Arab Islam from the seventh century and European Christianity – first Roman from the fourth century then western from the fifteenth – that chauvinism came to be linked to the spread of a written monotheistic theology claiming to be a universal truth. While Muslim jurists, unlike their Christian counterparts, continually upheld the idea of racial equality in theory, in reality most of the enslaved in the empires of the Islamic world came to be black, and though lighter-skinned and even 'white' people were enslaved by the Ottoman, Abbasid, Fatamid and Moroccan empires, black slaves were particularly devalued, costing less, given the lowest jobs and in general prevented from attaining more sought-after roles as 'easily' as their lighter skinned counterparts. As for the women – who made up most of the enslaved in these regions, unlike later in the Americas – they were seen as less beautiful than their white European fellow slaves, with the notable exception of the Abyssinians.

Slavery in the 'Islamic world' then, perhaps more than any other region, meant many and vastly differing states of exploitation. In the classical Islamic societies, this included conditions ranging from the Devshirme of the Ottomans – who were European Christian slaves educated for administrative service, some of whom rose through the ranks of Ottoman society to be grand viziers – to widespread use of military slaves, household servants, women of the harem, eunuchs and, at the very bottom, black plantation slaves, such as in the Egyptian cotton boom of the 1860s, the clove plantations of Oman in the nineteenth century or the salt flats of Basra in the ninth century, where the famous revolt of the Zanj (blacks) occurred.

Many of the early Islamic world's greatest thinkers – Ibn Khaldun, Al Idrisi, Ibn Sina, to name but a few – can be found exhibiting a similar kind of anti-black prejudice that we would see in European Christendom and the Enlightenment. Ibn Khaldun, for example, opined that 'Blacks are dumb animals naturally suited to slavery'.

It must also be said that in the Greco-Roman world and in early Islamic societies, black people can be seen occupying all kinds of social and professional roles, and the Ancient Greeks – Aristotle, Herodotus, Diodorus etc. – seemed to think that the Ancient Egyptians, who they saw with their own eyes, were black people. Within early Europe we see images of famous black saints like Maurice, and even black Madonnas. In the 'Islamic world' there were black scholars, revered generals and even powerful dynasties in northern Africa and Muslim Spain. And of course several West African societies and empires adopted and 'Africanised' Islam. Yet from the second century onwards, 'Ethiopians' (a generic term for black people that has no relationship to the country that today bears the name) fairly consistently came to be represented as living in 'the dark', as in sin, and as representative of evil demons and even the devil itself. In the fifteenth century, Mediterranean and Iberian slavery was still common and, while slavery in the Iberian peninsula of the fifteenth century was not of the exclusively racial type, we find in Seville in the 1470s the 'Casa Negra' – the house of the Blacks – which appears to be a kind of charity set up by black people to buy the freedom of their enslaved 'kinsmen'.[5] I use quote marks in this way because there is no reason to assume that they all came from the same ethnic group, but their shared sense of 'blackness', as expressed by their 'charities' title and the common experience of slavery, had bound them together, much as it would for other black people in the new world over the coming centuries, yet it would seem that black people were still a minority of the enslaved population in southern Spain at this time.

As the states of Iberian Europe, and particularly Portugal, started to trade down the West African coast from the mid fifteenth century, Europeans did not find entirely backward or savage cultures that they were universally revolted by; in fact, some observers compared African towns and cities of the period with those of Europe, and explicitly thought their African business partners to be civilized and cultured.[6] Prejudice, stereotype and a sense of difference there certainly was, but systemic racism was not even possible before the technological gap between Africa and Europe – and the slavery, massacres and domination that technology gap made possible – became a chasm.

Meanwhile, in the Americas, the Curse of Ham was applied and linked to a philosophy based on Plato and Aristotle's ideas about 'natural slaves' to inform the largest and most intense experiments with industrial-scale slavery in human history. After the indigenous people of the Caribbean had been all but wiped out by Spanish brutality and European diseases, Africans began to be brought in as slaves. The earliest black people brought to labour in the Caribbean actually came from Spain, reflecting the earlier Mediterranean and trans-Saharan slave routes, and the earliest plantation labour in the Caribbean and America was, for a brief period at least, multi-racial. But for a whole host of reasons, such as a reluctance to enslave 'Indians' on their own land (decimation would do just fine), Ottoman suzerainty in the Mediterranean cutting off the supply of white Slavs to the Iberian peninsula, the strength of state formations in western Europe eradicating the possibility of enslaving the populations of rival European nations, the comparative military and economic weaknesses of West African states and of course hatred and fear of black people, slavery in the Americas came to be an exclusively 'black' affair. The European prejudices about blackness and evil were by no means fixed or without contradiction, but by now they were over a millennium old and could be redeployed to serve a purpose, in the process clearly violating a professed Christian ethic of universal brotherhood.

Black slavery in the Americas, then, was by no means inevitable. Indeed, the first Spanish governor of Hispaniola, a man named Ovando, requested that his king outlaw the enslavement of blacks, as they were apparently too troublesome and caused white indentured servants and the natives to rebel, and it seems for a brief while that the Spanish monarchs obliged.[7] The myth of the docile African, as you will see in later chapters, has no basis in history, and 'African' resistance both in Africa and across the Americas limited the scale of the traffic significantly, just as 'African' collaborators and slave traders fed it.

Once slavery in the Americas was exclusively reserved for humans of African origin, black skin became a signal of merchandise rather than humanity, property rather than personhood and thus anti-blackness became one of the bedrocks of the emergent capitalist economies of western Europe and North America. The decimation of indigenous

Americans and the theft of their land, combined with the literal working to death of millions of Africans and access to New World metals, are no small part in the history of Western development, however much committed ideologues may try to pretend otherwise. Cotton, sugar, tobacco, coffee – the primary commodities of their days – were produced by human commodities with black skin, under what Sven Beckert rightly calls 'war capitalism'.[8] It wasn't free trade or open markets, but military rule, forced servitude, national monopolies and absolutely no semblance of democracy that helped modern Europe and America to develop. Racism gave slave owners the justification for an unprecedented experiment in the denial of liberty and forced servitude and thus racism, far from being marginal or just a side effect, has been absolutely central to developing Euro-American prosperity.

An estimated 12 million Africans at the very least were transported in floating dungeons across the Atlantic from the mid-fifteenth to nineteenth centuries; countless numbers of them died en route to the African coast, and also during the horrendous middle passage. The idea that black Africans were savage heathens, and thus slavery was a good and necessary stage in preparing them for civilisation, became so embedded in Euro-Christian thought that even some abolitionists accepted and parroted the idea. However, even as late as the mid-eighteenth century, it was still rare for a European observer, even those heavily involved with slavery on the African coast, to assert that black people were not human.[9] Inferior perhaps, heathens for sure, but up until this point the humanity of Africans had rarely been questioned. This may seem strange given the inhumane treatment intrinsic to enslavement, but again we must realise that inhumane treatment of the lower orders was the norm in Europe at this time; in Britain, for example, poor people were still regularly hanged for small property theft, or transported to Australia in horrendous conditions and violently ejected from their lands so that those lands could be enclosed in a manner that would be repeated in the settler colonies of the future. Though, of course, the dehumanisation of anti-black racism gave transatlantic chattel slavery a particular sadism. The turning point towards a 'scientific' and systematic racism came when writers like Edward Long, a British-Jamaican slave owner, started to justify the plantation regime on the grounds that black people were not just inferior but that they were not even human.[10]

'An orangutan husband would not disgrace a negro woman,' Long opined, an early example of the obsession with comparing black Africans to monkeys. Mr Long's work would seem so silly to any rational person today that it is hard to believe that some of the brightest minds of the eighteenth century took it extremely seriously, but they did, and an entire corpus of supposedly scientific racism was spawned that sorted humanity into gradations of race and even excluded some groups from the ranks of humanity altogether. These theories could be used to justify what we would now call genocide,[11] with the dehumanisation made legally explicit in Britain with cases such as that of the infamous slave ship *Zong*, where 133 Africans were thrown overboard when the ship got into difficulty. Disposing of the enslaved people in this way meant that their 'owners' could claim insurance on their property, but the insurance company refused to pay up, solely on the grounds that the goods had been discarded deliberately. Only when the legal dispute rumbled on did abolitionists argue that the crew should be charged with murder, but both cases were fought on the grounds that the drowned peoples represented goods, not humans, and the judge concluded that 'so far from the guilt of anything like a murderous act, so far from any show or suggestion of cruelty, there was not even a surmise of impropriety and that to bring a charge of murder would argue nothing less than madness.'[12]

In all fairness to those who investigated race 'scientifically', they were not all of Mr Long's level of bigotry (or Kant's or Hume's or Voltaire's, for that matter) and they certainly were not all slave owners, and the process by which 'fully racist' ideas – if I can call them that – caught on was long and complex. For example, in 1813 Dr James Cowles Prichard, perhaps the top British student of race science at the time, could be found saying quite the opposite of Mr Long:

> On the whole it appears that we may with a high degree of probability draw the inference, that all the different races into which the human species is divided originated from one family.

Dr Prichard was part of a school of scientists known as mono-genesists, who were guided by Christian ideas about the brotherhood of man and concluded that all humanity descended from Adam, and thus were branches of the same family. But later in the nineteenth century, ironically in the years following the abolition of slavery, ideas like Mr Long's, ideas that some groups of people, particularly black people, were not really human, started to hold sway.[13] These ideas were generally promoted by the polygenesists, who believed in several separate origins for the different races of man.[14] The legacy of 'scientific' thinking about race included the human zoos in Paris, London, New York and Brussels, that still existed in some form as late as the 1950s, as well as the banana skins and monkey chants for black football players that I grew up watching.

While some scholars have taken to locating the origins of anti-black racism in the plantation economies of the Americas or as a simple by-product of capitalist greed, it seems more accurate to say that the prejudices that made New World slavery's exclusively anti-black nature possible had much deeper roots in European history and culture, and had long precedents in other regions of the world, most notably the Middle East and North Africa.[15] As slavery continues in northern Africa today and as barely disguised semi-slavery continues in the prisons of the United States, the legacies of the invention of blackness are all too apparent and alive, from the Brazilian favela to the Johannesburg slum.

The collection of prejudices attached to black people invariably involved a fear of the supposed hyper-potency and special sexual endowment of black men, rather ironic given their alleged inferiority, and the variants of these ideas applied to black women. Even though the obsession with Linford's Lunchbox, eugenics-based slavery-sprint films and the odd relationship between white audiences and black heavyweight champions may seem rather unconnected, a study of the history of scientific racism quickly reveals the glue that binds these episodes and issues.

But blackness also had another trajectory, an alternative origin and a very different set of definitions. Prior to colonialism, black Africans seem to have found their blackness perfectly beautiful and normal, unsurprisingly.[16] But also, by making whiteness the colour of oppression, the colour that defined a person's right to own other human beings, to rape and kill and steal with impunity, white supremacists had paradoxically opened up the way for blackness to become the colour of freedom, of revolution and of humanity.[17] This is why it's absurd to compare black nationalism and white nationalism; not because black people are inherently moral, but because the projects of the two nationalisms were entirely different. This difference is why the black nationalist Muhammad Ali could still risk his life, give up the prime years of his career and lose millions of dollars in solidarity with the non-black, non-American people of Vietnam. It's also why Ali could show as much sympathy as he did to the white people of Ireland in their quarrels with Britain, despite him saying, somewhat rhetorically, that 'the white man is the devil'.

The most dramatic example of the revolutionary human capacities of black nationalism comes very early in its history in Haiti where, after the only successful slave revolution in human history, the independent black government made the white Polish and Germans who aided the revolution legally 'black' in 1804.[18] The revolutionary and oppositional nature of black identity is also part of why so many millions of people racialised as white are inspired by black culture, music and art in spite of all the racist propaganda that they have been exposed to asserting that these people – and thus their culture – are inferior. It's why John Lennon – great as he was – can never be a symbol of freedom for black people in the way that Bob Marley, Nina Simone or Muhammad Ali are for so many white people.

These visions and understanding of blackness are why, in spite of living in a world indelibly shaped by white supremacy, the most recognised icons of freedom in the English speaking world in the twentieth century (Ali, Malcolm, Marley, Martin) were disproportionately black, apart from Che Guevara. Indeed the two most famous black nationalists of all time – Bob Marley and Muhammad Ali – are loved by countless millions of people of all ethnicities all over the world. The fact that such outspoken uncompromisingly anti-white supremacist political figures as Ali and Marley are also global humanist icons shows quite clearly the innate difference between black nationalism and white nationalism as political imperatives. For mainstream white society to deal with this obvious fact journalists, media and fans would have to acknowledge that white supremacy is an obviously anti-human idea, so instead Marley is more often reduced to little more than a weed-smoking hippy whose only song and political sentiment was apparently 'One Love'. But the idea that different nationalisms are different in intent and content depending on their historical origins is not a difficult concept to understand. For example the SNP and the BNP whilst both made up of 'white British' people could not be more different; whilst there are plenty of bigots in Scotland, Scottish nationalism in our times is rooted in a rejection of English superiority and a refusal to be dictated to by Westminster rather than in the same racist imperial fantasies that nourish so much British nationalism. Whilst I have a million criticisms of the SNP, if I lived in Scotland I might well vote for them; I could obviously never vote for the BNP. Anyway, I digress.

Blackness continues to represent traditions of resistance and rebellion such that even today, when young people in Britain who are not black wish to participate in an oppositional culture they flock to hip hop and grime, and before that Reggae, in a way that black youngsters never did and never will to punk or grunge – much as we may personally like both genres. The culture and music of African-Caribbean migrants to Britain and our American cousins has invariably been the one culture that has brought young people of all walks of life together; blackness is both despised and highly valued. It's rarely acknowledged by any of the parties involved that the roots of this contradiction are both the prison whiteness has created for its adherents and the revolutionary power of blackness. However, the almost universal failure of white music artists, apart from Eminem, to even attempt to address the contradictions of white identity, alongside black artists' constant willingness to put blackness front and centre, suggests that all parties understand the racial dynamics at play much better than they seem willing to admit.

5 – EMPIRE AND SLAVERY IN THE BRITISH MEMORY

'I think he would be very proud of the continuing legacy of Britain in those places around the world, and particularly I think he would be amazed at India, the world's largest democracy – a stark contrast, of course, with other less fortunate countries that haven't had the benefit of British rule. If I can say this on the record – why not? It's true, it's true.'

> Boris Johnson of Winston Churchill, on whom he has just finished writing a book

'I am strongly in favour of using poison gas against uncivilized tribes. It would spread a lively terror.'

'I hate Indians. They are a beastly people with a beastly religion.'

> Winston Churchill

'Come over here, Kingslee,' my teacher's Canadian voice called excitedly, as she beckoned me towards her. She was never usually nice to me, so I was a bit suspicious about her calling me over with such enthusiasm. When I got close enough, she put her hand on the shoulder of my seven-year-old self with just the right weight of touch to communicate the monumental solemnity of the occasion.

Pointing to the painting on the wall, she said, 'Kingslee,' and then drew in a dramatic breath to add power to the punchline, 'this man stopped slavery.' She managed to pull her eyes away from the picture and turned them in my direction, her gaze instructing me to be thankful.

She expected me to share in her joy, but I was just thoroughly confused. 'What, all by himself, miss?' I asked. 'Don't you mean he helped?'

Her face distorted and she took the exact same flustered breath that liberals everywhere would take in 2008, right before they were about to lecture any black person who had the gall to declare themselves a non-supporter of Barack Obama. (I was there in 2008, I was one such sinner, I know that face of 'you can't possibly know what is good for you and how could you be so ungrateful' very well.) 'No Kingslee, he stopped slavery,' she retorted, clearly annoyed at my refusal to blindly accept what I was being told.

We were on a school visit to the National Portrait Gallery and the painting on the wall was of one Mr William – patron saint of black emancipation – Wilberforce. I did not have the strength or wherewithal to argue back with my teacher, I was only seven after all, but I knew her statement was absurd, hence the memory staying put. By what force of magic could an educated adult be compelled to believe that one man, all by himself, could put an end to a few centuries of tri-continental multi-million-pound business enterprise – and genocide – by the sheer force of his moral convictions? What's more, why would this teacher try to convince me, of all the students in our class, of such an absurdity? I was not the only child of Caribbean origin in our class, so it could not have been a 'let's just pick out the black kid' scenario, but I was the only one who went to pan-African Saturday school, and thus had demonstrated a particular penchant for challenging what I was being taught. Courtesy of that community schooling, by the time this teacher was telling me that Wilberforce had set Africans free I already had some knowledge of the rebel slaves known as 'Maroons' across the Caribbean, and of the Haitian Revolution, so I had some idea that the enslaved had not just sat around waiting for Wilberforce, or anyone else for that matter, to come and save them.

While it's certainly true that Britain had a popular abolitionist movement to a far greater degree than the other major slave-holding powers in Europe at the time, and this is in its own way interesting and remarkable, generations of Brits have been brought up to believe what amount to little more than fairy tales with regard to the abolition of slavery. If you learn only three things during your education in Britain about transatlantic slavery they will be:

1 Wilberforce set Africans free
2 Britain was the first country to abolish slavery (and it did so primarily for moral reasons)
3 Africans sold their own people.

The first two of these statements are total nonsense, the third is a serious oversimplification. What does it say about this society that, after two centuries of being one of the most successful human traffickers in history, the only historical figure to emerge from this entire episode as a household name is a parliamentary abolitionist? Even though the names of many of these human traffickers surround us on the streets and buildings bearing their names, stare back at us through the opulence of their country estates still standing as monuments to king sugar, and live on in the institutions and infrastructure built partly from their profits – insurance, modern banking, railways – none of their names have entered the national memory to anything like the degree that Wilberforce has.

In fact, I sincerely doubt that most Brits could name a single soul involved with transatlantic slavery other than Wilberforce himself. The ability for collective, selective amnesia in the service of easing a nation's cognitive dissonance is nowhere better exemplified than in the manner that much of Britain has chosen to remember transatlantic slavery in particular, and the British Empire more generally.

My Wilberforce moment was not unique or isolated, but springs from this larger tradition of extremely selective recall that Brits tend to call propagandistic when it occurs in other nations. For example in 2007, on the bicentenary of the Abolition of the Slave Trade Act, the government and media organised a season of celebration and commemoration. Tony Blair expressed his deep sorrow and regret about Britain's involvement with slavery but stopped short of an apology, and a glut of articles appeared across the press asking if Britain should apologise, most of which inevitably regurgitated the 'we were the first to abolish, why can't you just get over it' line. The only major film to emerge from these festivities was, of course, one about Wilberforce, predictably titled *Amazing Grace* – after the redemptive hymn written by the English slave trader John Newton.[1] The film depicts a simple, Hollywood-style narrative of one brave and visionary soul who challenges the dominant and powerful interests of his day and in the end wins them over with his plucky righteousness. There were some other voices during this abolition season, including my sister, who presented a documentary about the Jamaican Maroons on BBC Two, but those voices were extremely faint in comparison to the Wilberforce chorus that echoed across the nation.

Black activists and scholars were offended by the Wilberforce-centric narrative, so much so that community activist and founder of legali.org Toyin Agbetu was compelled to make an entire independent documentary calling into question what was dubbed the 'Wilberfest'.[2] Agbetu and others were responding not just to the 2007 celebration but to the longer tradition of miseducation, and to programmes such as the 2005 BBC doc *The Slavery Business*, where the presenter tells the viewer that 'in 1807, Britain did something remarkable; it ended the slave trade and turned its back on its enormous profits. This was largely down to one man'. This childishly idyllic – and completely inaccurate – sentence is largely representative of mainstream narratives around abolition. A couple more examples will suffice to make the point. In the conclusion to his 900-page tome *The Atlantic Slave Trade*, the historian Hugh Thomas fails to even mention slave resistance as a factor in abolition at all, lists a number of European abolitionists and of course positions Britain as the abolitionist in chief, apparently motivated by pangs of conscience and nothing more. Thomas also asserts that the slave trade went on as long as it did because Africans – apart from the Muslim ones, apparently – were 'good natured and usually docile'.[3]

In recent years, three separate schools in different parts of the country have made headlines because of their teaching and remembrance of slavery; two of the schools gave their students worksheets that were essentially business plans for buying and selling African people as slaves, and a teacher at another school thought it would be a good idea to get children to come in dressed as slaves for black history month![4]

Even Bob Geldof, our very own latter-day Wilberforce, this generation's chief white saviour in command, is not above this kind of reductionist rhetoric when it comes to Africans. In his series *Geldof in Africa* we see him strolling along the shores of a West African beach, telling the viewer that Europeans came to Africa in search of gold, 'but, to their eternal shame, what the Africans had to sell was their own people.' Geldof may well not have written the script, but he said the words.

So what are the facts then? Did Wilberforce do it all by

himself? Was Britain the first nation to abolish slavery and were Africans queuing up on the shores of the Atlantic to sell their own children to the highest bidder? No, no and nope.

Britain quite simply was not the first nation to abolish trans-atlantic slavery; Denmark did so in 1792 and France briefly abolished slavery during the height of the French revolution in 1794. What was 'abolitionist' Britain's response to these abolitions? Was it to quickly follow suit? No. The British government's response was to send its armies to the Caribbean to invade French-held islands and to try and reinstall slavery everywhere the French had abolished it. This conflict with France included imprisoning some 2000 black French fighters in Porchester Castle, among them some of the most prominent black abolitionists of the era, and this at a time when the entire black British population was somewhere between 10–15,000.[5]

The British invasion of the French Caribbean included an invasion of Haiti, which is particularly significant given Haiti's place in the history of the period; during the 1780s Haiti was by far the most profitable slave colony in the Americas, exporting as much sugar as Brazil, Cuba and Jamaica combined,[6] producing half the world's coffee and generating more revenue than the entire thirteen colonies of what had just become America. Haiti, or Saint-Domingue as it was then known, was the pearl of the Antilles, the cash cow that allowed the French Empire to still compete with the British. To capture such a prize would have been a massive boost for both the British Empire and for the continuation of industrial-scale, racialised slavery.

As it panned out, formerly enslaved Africans fighting under the French flag were able to defeat the British armies and retake the portions of the island Britain had won – reinstalling slavery as they went, remember. This mass campaign for re-enslave-ment in the Caribbean was undertaken by none other than Prime Minister William Pitt, the very same man who would encourage Wilberforce to front the abolitionist campaign in parliament just a few years later. In fact, Pitt himself raised the question of abolition of the slave 'trade' in parliament before even Wilberforce.[7]

The Caribbean campaigns of the 1790s proved to be one of the greatest military disasters in British imperial history with defeats, setbacks and unwanted treaties undertaken right across the Caribbean. British troop losses are estimated to have been at least 50,000, by some estimates quite substantially more. It is absolutely inconceivable that Britain would have suddenly had a moral epiphany in 1807 if they had won Haiti from the French, making them undisputed masters of the Caribbean by holding the two most important Caribbean colonies of the time, Haiti and Jamaica. Remember, at this point America had only just won its independence, a fact about which Britain was less than happy – see the war of 1812 – and was not yet a global power like Britain and France.

Just a few short years later, France would renege on its temporary abolitionist principles and attempt to re-enslave the people of Haiti, the same people who had fought and defeated the Spanish and the British and kept the island for France. Toussaint L'Ouverture had proved his willingness to accommodate the French planters even to the point of letting them keep their plantations and forcing former slaves to continue to work for them – albeit with meagre pay – but Napoleon just could not bring himself to work on anything resembling equal terms with a negro; legend has it that on his deathbed, Napoleon said 'I should have recognised Toussaint'.

Britain helpfully removed the naval blockade it had previously had in place in the English Channel during the years of war with France to allow French troops, headed up by Napoleon's brother-in-law, to travel to Haiti and try to put the 'gilded negroes' back in their rightful place. The latest British prime minister, Henry Addington, said 'we must destroy Jacobinism, especially that of the blacks.'[8] The British Governor of Jamaica sent weapons and assistance to the French mission in Haiti; like Addington, he understood that the preservation of slavery and white supremacy, even that of their French rivals, was preferable to empowering abolitionist-minded rebel negroes.

Once the French realised, as predicted at the time by British abolitionist James Stephen (and by the Haitians themselves), that the Haitians could not be re-enslaved, the French plan was to exterminate them all and start over again with newly enslaved people brought from Africa. The war that ensued became an explicitly genocidal one, in which the French troops were instructed to exterminate all of the blacks on the island.[9] This extermination attempt included the massacre of families and surrendered soldiers, the elderly and the sick, but the French also excelled themselves in the range of human barbarities they introduced with this war. These included turning ships into gas chambers, mass drowning – Toussaint L'Ouverture's brother and his family died this way – and importing thousands of dogs from Cuba that had been trained to eat people. None of this savagery cowed the Haitians, rather it appears to have only emboldened them; French soldiers and observers have left many terrified records from the period.

The formerly enslaved African and Creole (Haitian-born) 'slaves' and their allies – the Maroons, the free people of colour and the Polish defectors – defeated the French just as they had defeated Spain and Britain before them, and Haiti declared itself independent in 1804. This was the first and only successful slave revolution in human history, and only the second colony in the Americas to be free of European rule. Haiti abolished slavery immediately upon independence – thirty years before Britain would do so in its Caribbean possessions – and became the first state in the world to outlaw racism in its constitution, despite everything done in the name and practice of white supremacy on the island over the preceding centuries. As alluded to earlier, the Haitians in fact went one step further than merely outlawing racism and declared that the 'whites' – in reality Polish and some Germans – that had fought with the revolution were now officially black; honorary blacks, if you will.

Britain and the other major Atlantic powers (France and the USA) refused to recognise the independent black republic despite its abolition of slavery (in fact because of this very abolition), and despite their willingness to recognise the newly created nations that would rebel against Spanish rule in the coming decades. To add bitterness to this irony, it was the newly independent black state of Haiti that aided Simón Bolívar in his attempts to liberate South America from the Spaniards, providing him with money, arms and military expertise with the condition that he free the enslaved in any territories that he liberated. Yet the states Bolívar created were recognised more quickly than was Haiti itself.

Clearly, whatever the British government's 'abolitionist' convictions, they did not extend to recognising the nationhood of the only state in human history founded by rebel slaves who'd won their freedom.[10] Furthermore, 'abolitionist' Britain stood by as France and then the US repeatedly punished Haiti for winning its freedom and its abolition of slavery. Under threat of re-invasion, the French extorted a debt from Haiti in 1825 of 91 million gold francs for the loss of their 'property' – i.e. the Haitians themselves. It took up until 1947 to pay this 'debt', and in fact Haiti had to borrow the money to pay the debt from French banks.

After independence, Haiti was afflicted by a series of fratricidal wars between the victorious revolutionaries that often had a racial overtone to them – blacks vs. mulattoes – and the legacy of that colour-based, slave-era privilege still afflicts every former slave colony to this day. The USA then invaded Haiti in 1915, removing the stipulation in the Haitian constitution that prevented foreign whites from owning land there, killing 15,000 Haitians and backing a brutal dictatorship for the best part of the twentieth century, and then, when Haiti finally went to the polls, the USA collaborated with the Haitian elite to have their democratically elected leader overthrown, twice.[11] To my knowledge, no senior British government official uttered even so much as a word in protest about any of this, though we can all be sure they would have found their moral indignation about 'human rights' if Russia or Iran had been the culprits.

But the duplicity of the British government as it relates to abolition did not end with attempts to crush the Haitian Revolution. Upon abolition in Britain's own colonies, it was the slave owners who were given compensation to the tune of £20 million, roughly £17 billion in today's money,[12] the largest public bailout until the aftermath of the 2008 banking crisis. The formerly enslaved were given nothing; in fact, they were expected to remain slaves for five more years under a system euphemistically entitled 'apprenticeship' and of course East Indian 'coolies' continued to be scattered across the Caribbean to labour as 'indentured servants' well after the abolition of slavery.[13]

We must remind ourselves that we are talking about a period of British history where it took almost a century of debate, reform and much consternation to abolish domestic child labour. Are we really to believe that a British parliament that had only just come to abolish the labour of its 'own' children felt such a loving affinity for faraway negroes? Furthermore, when the enslaved in the British Caribbean struck out for their freedom, sometimes in the mistaken belief that the British government had actually set them free, how did the local arms of the British state respond? After the 1807 act there were a series of major slave rebellions in the British Caribbean, first in Barbados in 1816, Demerara (British Guyana) in 1823 and then Jamaica's Baptist War in 1831. The Baptist War was the largest rebellion in the history of the British Caribbean, involving perhaps as many as 60,000 rebels.[14] The genuine fear that Jamaica and other territories might go the same way as Haiti cannot be overstated – indeed, had the Jamaican Maroons not helped British forces put down the rebellion it may well have developed into a full revolution. In response to that rebellion, Lord Howick, under-secretary for the colonies and the son of Prime Minister Lord Grey, wrote to the new governor of Jamaica that his information was that:

> The slaves were not being in the least intimidated or cowed by the dreadfully severe punishments which have been inflicted, but on the contrary as being quite careless of their lives, and as regarding death as infinitely preferable to slavery, while they are exasperated to the highest degree and burning for revenge for the fate of their friends and relations . . . it is quite clear that the present state of things cannot go on much longer, and that every hour that it does so is full of the most appalling danger . . . my own conviction is that emancipation alone will effectively avert the danger, and that the reformed parliament will very speedily come to that measure, but in the meantime it is but too possible that the simultaneous murder of the whites upon every estate which Mr. Knibb apprehends may take place.[15]

It is an odd way to express one's love for an oppressed class of people, to leave them in conditions so horrendous that they have no choice but to rebel and then, rather than ameliorate those conditions – remember £20 million was found for slave masters – to engage in mass executions of the very same people one had apparently set free out of sheer and undying love.

The British government's treatment of its own rebel slaves and its refusal to recognise abolitionist Haiti contrasts sharply with its relationship with the slave owning Confederacy, Brazil and Cuba. For decades after abolition, Britain imported countless tons of slave-made cotton from the American south, which stimulated all kinds of industries, and British banks and businessmen made a mint investing in slave-owned mines and slave-built infrastructure in Brazil. Brazil and Cuba did not abolish slavery until the 1880s but still received massive inward investment from British companies and merchants, with the government's knowledge of course. But in perhaps the most treacherous episode of the whole affair, the British anti-slavery squadron tasked with enforcing abolition on the seas received 'head money' for each African they 'liberated' – so no, it was not altruism – and they sometimes even sold the Africans they liberated back into slavery.[16] Finally, slavery was not abolished in British colonies like Hong Kong, Aden and Sierra Leone until well into the twentieth century.

So, despite Britain spending almost two centuries as the dominant transatlantic slave trader, with all the torture, rape and mass murder that entailed, despite Britain refusing to back abolition when other European powers had paved the way, despite Britain spending the 1790s warring to keep slavery intact all over the Caribbean, despite Britain trying to crush the only successful slave revolution in human history and then helping their French enemies attempt to do the same, despite Britain refusing to even recognise the first Caribbean state to abolish slavery, despite all of this, some 'historians', teachers and assorted nationalists are asking us all to believe the self-serving fairy tale that suddenly, in 1807 – just three years after Haitian independence – guided by William Wilberforce alone, Britain abolished slavery because it was 'the right thing to do'. What a pile of twaddle.

But the 'Wilberforce did it all' idea also springs from two other ideological founts, one the aforementioned classic white saviour trope and the other a seemingly human need for simple solutions to complex problems, for great men instead of the convoluted mess that is human history – in short, a need for heroes. Unfortunately, very little of human history is unsullied by the grit of reality and no humans are free from imperfections. Even if we take a far more prominent abolitionist than Wilberforce, a man who literally shed his blood for the cause of abolition – Toussaint L'Ouverture – we see these human imperfections and contradictions. Born into slavery but free by age thirty, the charismatic and militarily brilliant leader of what became the Haitian Revolution was at one time himself a slave owner. He instituted a draconian labour regime when he was governor of Haiti, had his own adopted 'nephew' executed for being too unkind to French 'planters' – slave owners – and even snitched to the British about a slave revolt brewing in Jamaica, of which the suspected instigators were hanged. L'Ouverture nonetheless did shed his blood and spent much of his adult life literally fighting for the abolition of slavery. Humans are complex. I suppose the difference between Wilberforce and L'Ouverture in this respect (other than the obvious fact that L'Ouverture's contribution was far greater) is that even the most hagiographic writings on L'Ouverture would not dare to suggest he did it 'all by himself'.

Any analysis of the ending of Caribbean slavery that fails to even mention the only successful slave revolution in history and the wider phenomenon of slave resistance, as well as multiple other factors, is not to be taken at all seriously. There is also the glaring contradiction of the creation of apartheid semi-slave states in southern Africa that stayed in existence until well into the twentieth century, and which took a combination of armed struggle, protest and worldwide boycott to formally topple. If the British government abolished the slave trade way back in 1807 because of an inherent love for justice and for African human beings, how do we explain the British government backing apartheid rule, which did not end until I was seven years old? Remember that a regime of forced labour based on white supremacy was the cornerstone of apartheid.

Let's be totally clear though, I am not disputing that Wilberforce played *a role* in the Abolition of the Slave Trade Act passing in 1807, nor am I disputing that for all its contours and complications that the abolition acts were steps forward, nor that some Britons did indeed have genuine anti-slavery principles back then, some much more demonstrably so than Wilberforce, such as Foxwell Buxton or Clarkson or the British workers that went on strike against slave-made cotton, and of course the black British abolitionists living and publishing in England at the time, such as Mary Prince Ottabah Cuagano and Olaudah Equiano. What I am saying is that power concedes nothing without demand or motive, and the abolitionist movement needs to be viewed much like the anti-war movements of today, if you will forgive the crude historical parallel. Think of it like this; there are today British citizens – perhaps millions of us – who, however fringe we may be considered in mainstream politics, are genuinely horrified at our government's foreign policy, its arms dealing and war-mongering, and there are also a few rogue MPs who constantly vote against the British war machine – but does any of that mean that the British ruling class generally take anti-war humanitarianism at all seriously?

Of course not. This is how they can support terrorists in Libya while claiming to save Libyans with humanitarian bombs, and then let people fleeing from Libya drown in the sea while the Foreign Secretary makes jokes about clearing away the dead bodies to a laughing audience; or how they can sell arms to the Saudis for them to kill Yemeni civilians at the exact same time that they are waging war in Syria under the rubric of humanitarianism.

The times have changed and the extremities of the crimes may be different and a little less direct, but the narrative and Machiavellian mentality have remained much the same. No one refers to the 'white man's burden' any more, as it's just too crude a phrase, so instead we speak of spreading democracy and human rights and of saving people from dictators, which funnily enough is almost exactly what the original nineteenth-century version of the white man's burden claimed to be motivated by. The Scramble for Africa was justified in largely humanitarian terms; Europeans needed to go in and save Africans from their slave-dealing elites, apparently. There is no doubt of course that these slave-dealing elites existed in Africa – they had been Britain's business partners after all – but the idea that the Scramble for Africa 'saved' the African masses is so ridiculous that even the most nationalistic of historians would find it hard to spin.

And here we come to the old adage, the third slavery fact we learned in school and offered to us again by Geldof and so many others: 'Africans sold their own people'. There are a number of obvious problems with the 'Africans sold their own people' cliché, but that still does not seem to have stopped people offering it as an 'argument'. First and foremost, does the fact that Britain had 'African' accomplices rid it of any and all wrongdoing? According to many, it does. Second, there was no continental 'African' identity before industrial technology, the Scramble for Africa, the redrawing of borders and the modern pan-Africanist movement created it in the twentieth century, and that African identity is still fraught with contradictions and conflicts. Between the sixteenth and nineteenth centuries, Africa was not a paradise where all humans sat together around the campfire in their loincloths singing 'Kumbaya' in one huge – but obviously primitive – black kingdom covering the entire continent and littered with quaint looking mud huts, any more than all of Europe or Asia was one big happy family. Africa had and has ethnic, cultural, class and imperial rivalries that every scholar of the period acknowledges are the very divisions that colonisers and slave traders played on. In fact, as the award-winning historian Sylviane A. Diouf notes, in none of the slave narratives that have survived do the formerly enslaved talk about being sold by other 'Africans', or by 'their own people' and only Sancho – who lived in England – even mentions the 'blackness' of those that sold him.[17] The victims of the transatlantic traffic did not think that they were being sold out by their 'black brothers and sisters' any more than the Irish thought that their 'white brothers and sisters' from England were deliberately starving them to death during the famine.

Oral traditions collected in eastern Nigeria in the 1960s speak of local groups that considered a particular family to be cursed because they had sold a daughter into slavery several generations ago; such treachery would hardly be considered grounds for a centuries-long curse if it were the norm. Even the major slave-trading states of western Africa – Oyo, Dahomey, Ashanti – all passed laws banning or limiting the sale of their own citizens, i.e. 'their own people', while they of course continued to raid for and sell other nations' people. The early kings of the Congo wrote letters to Portuguese monarchs pleading with them to stop sending traders because they were taking away people, and to only send teachers and priests instead, and Benin, one of the most impressive West African states of the period, seems to have been the only one that successfully protected its own citizens from the beginning of the trade.[18]

We need not romanticise pre-colonial Africa, we are not all descendants of 'kings and queens'; most of us whose ancestors were sold into slavery are probably descended from serfs, servants, existing slaves and soldiers from warring parties. With that said, it is interesting that Olaudah Equiano made such a huge distinction between the kind of slavery that existed in African kingdoms and the kind practised in the Americas. Countless European witnesses made this same observation – that African 'slavery' was nothing like the racialised chattel slavery practised on the sugar plantations of the New World, including English slave traders like John Newton:

> The state of slavery among these wild barbarous people, as we esteem them, is much milder than in our colonies. For as, on the one hand, they have no land in high cultivation like our West Indian plantations, and therefore no call for that excessive un-intermitted labour which exhausts our slaves; so, on the other hand, no man is permitted to draw blood even from a slave.[19]

Which brings us to Hugh Thomas's assertion that Africans were 'docile'. Reflecting the unscholarly value-judgment embedded in that statement, neither Hugh Thomas, nor any others who peddle it, offer any comparative data to try and prove the claim. They do not, for example, attempt to show that enslaved people in the Greco-Roman world, the European 'Dark Ages', eighteenth-century Russia or medieval Korea were any more likely to rebel than 'Africans'. In fact, specialists in studies of global slavery note just how relatively rare slave rebellions were across all slave societies – for what should be obvious reasons to a scholar.[20]

However, perhaps the most neglected area of study in the whole history of transatlantic slavery is the issue of resistance to enslavement in Africa itself. Most people are at least vaguely aware that there was some resistance from black people in the Caribbean but it's always fascinated me that people, even many in the black diaspora, seem willing to believe that 'Africans' – undifferentiated by class, region or ethnicity – just allowed their family members to be taken away, or worse, that they were all collaborators. Thanks to decades of painstaking research we know this is fundamentally untrue. There were literally hundreds of rebellions and attacks against slave ships up and down the West African coast carried out by organised guerrilla groups much like the Maroons of the Caribbean. As many as 483 of these rebellions are recorded in British, French and Dutch records alone. The average death toll in these skirmishes seems to have been about twenty-five and the historian David Richardson estimates that a million fewer people had to go through the middle passage because of this one form of resistance alone.[21] It is also estimated that one in every ten European slave ships to dock in West Africa experienced either a shipboard revolt or an attack from land.

It is notable that there were not any major rebellions against transportation to penal colonies, let alone a revolution in the UK, during all the years that Britons were being shipped against their will to Australia and elsewhere. But I will not suggest that this is because white Brits are uniquely docile, as there are several other more likely possible explanations: the British State was too well armed; class divisions were too strong; people were too divided. In two final examples of how complex the picture and experience of the transatlantic traffic were from a West African perspective, there is even evidence of wealthy African families sailing all the way to America to get their children back during the nineteenth century and there are copious records attesting to the practice of ransom, i.e the practice of people capturing and selling two or more people to get back a loved one that had been sold into slavery. Can such a person be called a slave trader with any degree of certainty? Can you be sure that you would not kidnap people you did not know to get back your child if faced with such a dilemma? I certainly can't.

To make the simple bald claim that Africans were docile or that they generally 'sold their own people', knowing that most West Africans of the time were not involved in slave trading at all, is like saying the English killed their own people when they invaded Ireland or fought the French, because today we see them all as white and European, and of course it's not as if the English ruling class were treating their own people wonderfully during the period in question. This colonial projection of Africa is useful to some as it avoids them having to use the usual tools to explain the behaviour of real human beings – economics, market demand, dynastic rivalries, ethnic enmity, class distinctions, pure profit-seeking, self-preservation, love and more. It allows one to offer a person's 'African-ness', a concept that did not yet exist in the period, as an explanation for their behaviour. 'Africans sold their own people' is the historical version of 'black on black violence'.

None of this is offered to excuse African elites then or now for their greed and caprice, nor black people generally for our human flaws, but rather to paint a full picture of a complex phenomenon, as we would with any other region, time period and the peoples living in it. Is an Irishman like Bob Geldof in a position to assert that Africans are eternally shamed? Is the story of Ireland so uniquely pure among the history of nations that it places Geldof in a position to cast this kind of aspersion on an entire continent? No, of course it is not. There was slavery in Celtic Ireland long before the English arrived – this justifies nothing the English did of course; Irish merchants collaborated in selling Irish people to traders as early as the Vikings. Anglophile Irish chiefs collaborated with the English in their conquest of Ireland, and Irish merchants and landowners forcefully stole land from 'their own people' in the midst of the worst famine in modern European history.[22]

As we've seen, the Irish in America became slave owners and ardent supporters of white supremacy, despite their own sufferings at the hands of the British. One of the staunchest Irish nationalists – John Mitchell – became a vocal supporter of black slavery despite the fact that one of the most prominent black churches in America managed to send aid to the Irish famine, even though much of its congregation was still enslaved. I don't say any of this to suggest that the Irish are 'eternally shamed' nor to suggest that Irish humans are uniquely flawed, or that these actions represent the morality of all Irish people. Indeed, some Irish nationalists themselves called out this hypocritical behaviour at the time. I say this simply to say that if 'Africans' are eternally cursed for the greed and caprice of some of their number then so is all humanity, including Geldof's Irish compatriots. It's also fascinating that Geldof did not assert that British people – much less all white people – were eternally shamed for their role in enslaving their fellow human beings, but whatever. The average Irishman would certainly resent being conflated with an Englishman, yet Geldof and others can gloss over centuries of diverse and complicated history with the 'Africans sold their own people' cliché. Oh, and by the way, I am aware that this chapter is about Britain and that Ireland is obviously not part of Britain, but Geldof is such a part of the British establishment and represents so well its colonial arrogance I doubt my Irish homies will object to me including him.

Which brings us on to the wider way in which the British Empire as a whole is remembered.

Back in 2005, future prime minister Gordon Brown let the world know that 'the days of Britain having to apologise for its colonial history are over' – leaving us all wondering when those days of apology were. In a 2014 YouGov survey, 59 per cent of Brits declared that they were proud of the empire. The historian Niall Ferguson gloated approvingly on his Twitter, 'I won'. I'd love to see a similar survey done with only British citizens whose families come from non-white former colonies, and of course the not-quite-whites of Ireland. Wouldn't the true measure of the British Empire's supposed benevolence surely be attained by asking the billions of humans that descend from the people it ruled if they remember it so favourably?

The fact remains; no one colonises another group of people out of love for them. Anyone familiar with the traditions of postcolonial scholarship will know that African, Asian, Irish and Caribbean intellectuals, and the peoples they represent, do not share Niall Ferguson's fond memories of the Empire, which is why he as a 'historian' must ignore the most prominent intellectuals of those regions. In the British Caribbean, the postcolonial tradition was pioneered by Walter Rodney, C. L. R. James and Eric Williams, who are still pretty much standard reading for any educated Caribbean adult.

In India, we could take Booker Prize-winning author Arundhati Roy, perhaps the most prominent global critic of modern India's corruption and its mistreatment of its vulnerable populations, and even an outspoken voice of dissent against Gandhi worship. Anyone familiar with Roy's work will know that she, unlike some Indian Hindu fascists, has no nationalist axe to grind, yet her assessment of Britain's empire in India and elsewhere is much like my own. We could also choose Pankaj Mishra, whose masterful book on the Asian intellectuals who challenged European hegemony to 'remake Asia' is a brilliant refutation of Eurocentric nonsense.[23] He also, incidentally, once gave Mr Ferguson quite an intellectual spanking in the *London Review of Books*.

If we go to Kenya, where Mr Ferguson grew up in the shadows of the gulag, we could talk to Ngũgĩ wa Thiong'o, unquestionably the most well-known Kenyan novelist and scholar and a man imprisoned by Jomo Kenyatta's repressive – UK-backed – 'independent' government. Despite his accurate and persistent criticisms of the corruption and brutality of African elites, has he resorted to forgetting that British rule was horrendous? Nope. In fact, you'd be hard pressed to find prominent intellectuals from any of Britain's non-white former colonies, or Ireland, who are both respected in their native lands and who share Britain's romantic and fond memories of its empire. Why is this so? To understand why people across the world have such a different understanding of British colonialism we must address a number of things.

First, Britons were submitted to generations of deliberate imperialist, militarist propaganda in all areas of culture, from education to the cinema, theatre and music halls and in the production of huge imperial exhibitions at Wembley and elsewhere.[24] The myopia this propaganda still produces was aptly captured when Secretary of State for International Trade Liam Fox said in 2016, in the run-up to the EU referendum, that 'the United Kingdom is one of the few countries in the European Union that does not need to bury its twentieth-century history.' Funny, because Britain is in fact one of the few countries in the world that literally did bury a good portion of its twentieth-century history.

During the period of decolonisation, the British state embarked upon a systematic process of destroying the evidence of its crimes. Codenamed 'Operation Legacy', the state intelligence agencies and the Foreign Office conspired to literally burn, bury at sea or hide vast amounts of documents containing potentially sensitive details of things done in the colonies under British rule.[25] Anything that might embarrass the government, that would show religious or racial intolerance or be used 'unethically' by a post-independence government was ordered destroyed or hidden. The Foreign Office were forced to admit in court about having hidden documents, then were unforthcoming about the scale of what was hidden, to the point that you'd be a fool to trust anything that is now said. But from what we know, hundreds of thousands of pages of documents were destroyed and over a million hidden, not just starting in the colonial period but dating all the way back to 1662. This operation was only exposed to the public in 2011 as part of a court case between the survivors of British concentration camps in Kenya and the government.

What this means is that it is completely impossible to write a truly accurate history of the British Empire, and anything written before Operation Legacy was revealed is certainly incomplete. It's revealing that some 'historians' – that is people whose profession is supposed to be guided by evidence – have not taken to reviewing their thoughts about the wonders of the British Empire even after such a revelation. The destruction of historical memory is not limited to documents – while Britain has preserved the HMS *Victory* as a tribute to Nelson, as well as other ships from key periods of British history, not a single slave ship survives.[26] You have to stand in awe of the intellectual obedience it takes to still cheer for empire after the revelation that the government hid or burned a good portion of the evidence of what that empire actually consisted of, but such is the use to which we put our free thinking. You see, imperial apologists would like to view themselves as the apogee of Western thinking, as great contributors to the impressive history of Western intellectual inquiry, when in fact they actually represent its ossification. They represent the very 'decline of the West' that they bemoan. Say what we might about the brutality of European colonial expansion but we cannot deny that European thinkers from Giordano Bruno to William Tyndale, Thomas Paine to Bertrand Russell, have faced persecution and even death to push the intellectual envelope in their respective societies and times. Liberal apologists for empire are nothing but glorified cheerleaders for the current powers and status quo, who on the one hand bemoan the moralism of critics of empire, yet simultaneously claim that what made the British Empire superior to all others in the world's history was its apparently enlightened morals.

Thus the propaganda continues. Most people are still not at all aware of what has been done in their name, such as the deliberate starving to death of millions of people in India, the imprisonment and mass torture of British-Kenyans in concentration camps in the 1950s, the removal of the population of Diego Garcia for a US army base, widespread use of torture and a swathe of secret wars that have seen the British military active for almost all of the last 100 years, including the supposed 'post-war' period. People are also unaware of the degree to which British rule was violently resisted everywhere it trod across the globe. This resistance was so widespread that the historian Richard Gott has been able to fill an entire mammoth tome with just these episodes of rebellion and tell the story of the empire in reverse, through the eyes of its resistors.[27] It's rather odd, then, that if what the British Empire was offering was so self-evidently a good deal for all, the restless natives so often picked up their guns to fight against it. Either the natives were too stupid to know what was good for them, or perhaps what was being offered was not such a sweet deal after all.

But the final reason we don't have a greater critical dialogue about the empire is plain old racism: many would not care even if they knew the history well. What we do is OK, what others do is bad. It is worth quoting the historian John Newsinger at length here:

> What they have to be asked is how they would respond if other states had done to Britain what the British state has done to other countries. How pro-imperialist would they feel for example if, instead of Britain forcing opium on the Chinese Empire, it had been the other way round? What would their response be if, when the British government had tried to ban the importation of opium, the Chinese had sent a powerful military expedition to ravage the British coastline, bombard British ports, and slaughter British soldiers and civilians? What if, instead of seizing Hong Kong, the Chinese had seized Liverpool and used Merseyside as a bridgehead from which to dominate Britain for nearly a hundred years? What if further British resistance provoked another attack that led to the Chinese occupying London, looting and burning down Buckingham Palace and dictating humiliating peace terms? What if today there was an Imperial Museum in Beijing that still put on display the fruits of the Chinese pillage of Britain? None of this is fanciful because it is exactly what the British state did to China in the nineteenth century.[28]

The primary difference between Britain and other empires was not that 'we were not as bad as the Belgians or the Third Reich' – which is true but is such a shit boast – but that Britain succeeded in dominating the globe and still kind of does, albeit as a second fiddle to the USA in the Anglo-American Empire. The question we should ask today is not 'were we as bad as the Germans?' But rather, is it possible to critically and honestly reflect on Britain's history in an attempt to build a more ethical future? Can Britain ever behave in the world like the democracy it claims to be, or is such a thing entirely impossible? Is it more important to cling on to power and prestige and outdated Victorian notions of dominance and superiority even if such a tendency may well help to accelerate another World War and helps cause unspeakable suffering globally? 59 per cent of Britons apparently think it is more important, and their prophets cannot even begin to imagine a world without empires and, you know what, it's entirely possible that they will be proved right. One could quite reasonably argue based on world history that brutality, corruption, duplicity and aggression are actually good politics and the public just need to 'grow up' and accept that, but that is an entirely different conversation than pretending that British imperialism was and is motivated by a higher morality.

However, as much as a tendency to dominate, divide and brutalise has been a seeming constant for the past few millennia at least, so too has the tendency of sharing and co-operation, of rebellion against dominant powers and attempts to create a more just order. The degree to which humans have secured a more just world has been born out of the struggles against empires as much as anything else.

While I'm sure Mr Ferguson and others would accuse me of 'working myself up into a state of high moral indignation' about the crimes of the British Empire, I'll bet that he and others like him will be wearing their poppy every 11 November; that is, they will be 'working themselves up into a state of high moral indignation' about dead people when those dead people are truly British – the Kenyans tortured in the 1950s were legally British citizens but naturally there will be no poppies or tears for them. The implications are clear – some ancestors deserve to be remembered and venerated and others do not. Those that kill for Britain are glorious, those killed by Britain are unpeople.

If we truly cared for peace, would we not remember the victims of British tyranny every 11 November too?

I speak about the British Empire so much not just because I live here and have been shaped by it – not that any historical interest needs explaining – but because its legacies are so clear and visible and because unlike the Spanish, Portuguese, German or Japanese Empires it still sort of exists, albeit in attenuated form as second fiddle to the American Empire, despite what our free press likes to pretend. Our ruling class and much of the citizenry seem to believe that it is still 'our' divine right to police the world and to hell with what the rest of the planet thinks. What is most fascinating about British intellectual discourse is that we can see brutality ever so clearly when it wears Japanese or German or Islamic clothes, but when it comes to looking in the mirror at the empire on which the sun never set – the eighteenth-century's premier slave trader, the mother country of the Commonwealth and one of the pioneer countries in developing and then putting into practice the Enlightenment philosophy of white supremacy – so many suddenly become blind, deaf and dumb, unable to see murder as murder.

It is often said that I am half-Scottish and half-Jamaican, I have even said so myself, but this is an oversimplification that probably originates in a subconscious choice. My father is indeed of Jamaican heritage through both parents, though he was born in the UK. My maternal grandmother is Scottish but my maternal grandfather is actually English. My mum's father was a very unpleasant man, and so deeply racist that he pretty much disowned his own daughter for falling in love with a black man. One of my few memories of visiting that granddad is of him telling me 'jokingly' to 'paint myself white because you're dirty'. I was maybe six years old. It's hard to overstate the impact adults' words have on a child, and even though I did not think much of my granddad because I barely knew the man, his 'joke' left such an impression that I remember the weather, the taste of the air, the quality of the light and the smell of freshly cut grass in his back garden at the exact moment he said it to me. Frozen like a photograph, it is my enduring memory of him. I do not recall being hurt though; oddly enough, I think what I felt was something more like embarrassment, disgust, maybe even pity for him.

My mum tried to maintain cordial relations with her parents but as it played out we saw them very little. My siblings and I got to know our maternal grandmother better once my granddad died, my older sister and I even went to visit her in Thailand, to where they had emigrated. Despite my granddad spending a lifetime complaining about the immigrants and darkies, he took his military pension and retired to Thailand and saw no contradiction. In typical expat style, he did not learn the language, did not integrate and did not particularly respect the culture; he lived in his enclave with other 'expats' from Australia and America and moaned about the Thais in their own country instead. After my granddad's death, my white gran went native and got re-married to a Thai man, much to the chagrin of some members of the family. My granddad would have turned in his grave, but given how horrible he was to his own children I can only imagine what he must have been like towards my gran.

By contrast, and perhaps surprisingly, even though my mum and dad split up before I was born and despite the fact that my dad was not very close with his own mother – families, eh? – my mum maintained a very close relationship with my paternal, Jamaican grandmother. So it was that I spent most of my Sundays as a child at the home of Millicent Roberts, eating typical Caribbean food, staring at her cliché Windrush generation pictures of white Jesus and Queen Elizabeth II and sweating half to death, because even in the height of British summer she refused to turn the central heating down, even a notch.

It was via my grandmother that my mum was introduced to the wider Caribbean community in Camden. As a result of all this, it was the Caribbean side of my heritage that I grew up surrounded by and so came to identify with most. I'm not sure if you've noticed? I say Caribbean rather than specifically Jamaican as the community was very much made up of people from all of the English-speaking Caribbean islands and Guyana; my 'step'-grandmother is from Grenada, for example. Weddings and funerals with the same soundtrack, the same rum cake with the white icing, Escovitch fish, hard food, carnival, sound-clashes, falling asleep at parents' 'blues dance' parties, Saturday school, sometimes church, Rastafarian fathers clashing with Christian grandparents, reggae music, lovers rock, jungle.

There are certain things that every British Caribbean of my age has seen and experienced. We, quite consciously I think, feel like the last generation with such a direct connection 'back home', as our Caribbean grandparents will mostly die as our children come of age, so our coming to adulthood very much feels like the end of an era. 'Who we will then become' is one of the great questions of diaspora. How will our children and their children after that navigate being born black in Britain and of Caribbean heritage without the wisdom and laughter, the cooking and the cussing, of Caribbean-born grandparents? Will we become black English, or is that still a contradiction in terms? Will these connections be severed or will we maintain those links in honour of the generation that came here and sacrificed so much in so many ways? Who knows?

However, in many interesting, anecdotal ways we have already tried to guard our sense of Caribbean-ness more fiercely than those on the islands, as is normal for a diaspora and especially one that has often felt under attack. For example, Celine Dion, Garth Brooks, Michael Bolton and a whole host of 'surprising' singers are practically musical royalty in Jamaica, yet their popularity on the island has not transferred to the diaspora at all, we have instead focused more acutely and narrowly on Jamaican music. Why? I am going to call it cultural defensiveness; a tendency to cling onto one's culture more fiercely when alienated from its source. I have seen a similar thing with heavy metal in India – it's massively popular in India itself but barely registers with the Indian diaspora in the UK. I would also partly attribute this phenomenon to the racialised way in which music has been marketed in the UK but regardless, whatever the reasons, people 'back home' seem to feel a greater freedom to like 'white stuff', if that's what appeals to them, without the same fears that they are trying to be something they are not.

In a similar culturally defensive vein, my uncle often tells me of his generation – he came here when he was four – becoming more Jamaican as they got older, re-learning and even faking Jamaican accents in response to the extreme social exclusion and racism of the 1970s. As Jamaican was the dominant black identity, people from other Caribbean islands and even from Africa itself would sometimes take on a Jamaican style, persona and accent. Despite the dominant depictions of the British state and media that focused almost exclusively on 'Yardie gangsters' – without any analysis of the Cold War geopolitics that brought those cocaine cowboys into being of course – my Jamaican heritage was a major source of pride and kudos among my peers growing up. Jamaican-influenced music was the dominant youth music and as black Brits we got a sort of 'racial credit' for the achievements of black America – it was assumed we were more in the know about RnB and hip hop and that we could relate to the black American ghetto experience in a way that others could not. Both these assumptions, it must be said, were pretty much true. Almost all Caribbeans have cousins in New York and hip hop did indeed come into British society via Caribbean interpreters, in that our cousins in NY would send us the latest mix tapes and they'd be in Brixton or Tottenham markets days after they'd hit the streets of the Bronx or Brooklyn.

Before hip hop was mainstream, if non-black people wanted a slice of black American culture they often had to come to 'the hood' in the UK and get it; which gave black Brits a certain cultural capital. On top of this, Jamaicans in particular and black boys in general were assumed to be both tough and good at sports – this can be a blessing and a curse of course. Sometimes stereotypes put fear in your enemies and as a teenager that can be useful! On the other hand, if you are not six foot and 'naturally' athletic, as I was, the expectations to be tough, to run fast and to be a good rapper can be very damaging.

My relationship with and experience of my Scottish/English identity was a little more ambiguous. Even though I rarely saw my white grandparents, my maternal grandmother's Scottish siblings did their best to keep in touch and I recall seeing some of them, particularly my aunt Mary, much more than my mother's actual parents. My Scottish great-uncle Kenny had caught wind that I was interested in science, so the first time I met him he wrote out a list of all the things Scottish people had invented and gave it to me so that I could feel proud of my heritage. I must say, in the small amount of time I spent with my Scottish family us being black never felt like an issue. In fact, there was a subtle feeling that they disliked the English – including my granddad – far more than anybody brown! I would not want to generalise this experience, of course, but looking back now it did affect me a lot. My mum was able to set up her Scottish identity, in addition to her German one, in opposition to the 'racist white English'.

While I am not suggesting that there is no racism in Scotland – or Germany for that matter – there is also no question that the culture and subsequent worldviews of the two countries, Scotland and England, are quite different, and the events of recent years have only served to amplify this. Despite Scotland's bouts of amnesia regarding its role in slavery and the empire, there can be no question that the imperial nostalgia, class hatreds and cultural arrogance that feed racism are far stronger south of the border. On the other hand, Scotland also has a tiny black population and a far smaller population of non-white people generally, so we must also say that Scotland's 'ethnic limit' has not really been tested in the same way England's has.

Despite being much closer to my Jamaican family and culture, I visited both Jamaica and Scotland just once each during my childhood: Jamaica for six weeks aged seven, Scotland for ten days aged ten. Both trips had a profound impact on my life and thinking and, as hard as this may be to believe, I was very conscious of this even at the time.

In the summer of 1991, my gran took me, my older sister and our cousin Dwayne back to her village of Dunsville in Saint Ann's, the same parish as Marcus Garvey and Bob Marley, no less. A few things stand out in my memory from the trip. During the first two weeks, I was exposed to my own staunch English nationalism. My seven-year-old self berated Jamaica to my sister for its being backwards and not having – in our gran's village at least – indoor toilets, too many bloody mosquitoes, bus drivers that took mountain bends without regard for human life and let people bring chickens and goats on the bus and, to top it all off, they had no trains at all. I found a litany of things not to like about Jamaica; I cursed the island for being small, underdeveloped and visibly poor. My sister, by contrast, loved Jamaica from the moment we landed and she could do such an authentic Jamaican accent even at that age that nobody would believe she was really English. I was thoroughly jealous.

Yes, despite all the benefits of pan-African Saturday school and seven years of my grandmother's and great-grandmother's stew chickens and coconut creamed rice and peas, I was a thoroughly Westernised snob who, though poor by UK standards, looked down upon Jamaica's 'third world' poverty with much disdain. Who knows, had I never taken that trip I might still feel that way today. However, as the first two weeks passed I slowly warmed to JA. I got used to the cold showers, the death-defying bus rides and to shitting outside and I actually started to enjoy myself. I hunted lizards with my cousins, I swam in the river, climbed the gullies and hills, and went on countless adventures through the dense forests. I even wiped my bum with a stinging nettle by mistake after being instructed to 'jus use a leaf na man'. It was several days before I could sit comfortably again! My sister, cousin and I learned folk songs and games that we still remember to this day, we learned a secret language where the syllables are distorted – the children called it 'Jamaican Gypsy' language – and of course we perfected our 'Jamaican' speech, the ultimate passport to authentic blackness back then. I was carried up Dunn's River Falls by my super-hero-looking uncle Bob. I visited my great-grandfather's grave and got a real sense of my family heritage. By the middle of the trip I had come to love Jamaica and even to think of myself as Jamaican; how impressionable young minds are, and how quickly and often they change. By the end of the six weeks I had had such a transformative time that I begged my mum to move to JA so we could continue life there.

It's not that the trip was perfect. I saw domestic abuse and homelessness, there was a severe hurricane and Jamaica was much more dangerous back then than it is today, but the beauty of the landscape, the friendliness of the people and the immaculate pride of the children in their school uniforms or on their way to church combined with the physical and cultural freedom that I felt more than made up for the shortcomings. I've had a love for Jamaica and its/our culture ever since, which has been solidified by decades of reggae music and yard food, by knowledge of its history and the influence of its intellectuals, J. A. Rogers, Orlando Patterson and Marcus Garvey to name but a few.

This diaspora identity solidified in opposition to the Britishness that black people were denied, much like my uncles before me, if one generation further removed. While very few of my age group went as far as to create fake Jamaican accents for ourselves, we identified with an idealised version of the island over and above the country that we had been born into – in fact, we identified with blackness over and above being British. If England played any black team at football or cricket we would cheer for the black team; I vividly remember cheering for Cameroon at Italia 90, for example, though I'm sure this has changed for the generation younger than myself. This may seem 'ungrateful' to some, but given that we grew up watching black English players suffer the indignity of monkey chants and having banana skins thrown at them it's hardly a surprising reaction.

Without being blind to its enormous challenges, one cannot deny that Jamaica is unique; one of the most brutal slave colonies in human history just over a century ago, the tiny island has exerted an unparalleled influence on popular culture relative to its size – much like Britain, though minus the imperialism – it has given us some of the greatest academics of the black diaspora, dominated athletics during the past decade, produced the founder of the largest black organisation ever, the Godfather of hip hop and the 'Third World's' first superstar, this guy called Bob Marley who you may have heard of. In other perhaps surprising areas of achievement, despite still having serious problems with violence against women Jamaica is also one of only three countries on Earth where your boss is more likely to be a woman than a man, and as mentioned earlier in 2017 the country ranked eighth in the world for press freedom, thirty-two places above the UK. Whatever challenges the country still faces, it is infinitely more democratic than it was at any point during the 300 years it was ruled directly by Britain. Yet much of Britain has come to see a people whose not-too-distant ancestors British people owned as inherently violent; perhaps there is a subconscious subtext of the many slave rebellions still haunting British–Jamaican relations.

That Jamaica is one of the most violent countries in the world is of course not disputed, but what is disputed is that this violence requires no explanation beyond simple stereotypes. The simplistic representation of Caribbean men as inherently bad fathers for example is pretty ironic given that for centuries Caribbean history was shaped by men from Europe sexually exploiting indigenous and African women and leaving their 'half breed' children to be raised by black people or to be enslaved. The 'yardified' image of Jamaicans in the UK is all the more fascinating because the Jamaican middle and upper classes look upon ghetto people with a similar snobbery and because the UK is the only place in the world I have been where Jamaicans are seen so negatively. Even in the US, where the CIA-backed Jamaican drug gang known as the Shower Posse wreaked much havoc,[1] the enduring stereotypes of Jamaicans are still that we are hardworking, skilled, over-educated and business savvy; you only have to ask anyone in Brooklyn or Fort Lauderdale to confirm this. It is actually a cliché to say someone 'has as many jobs as a Jamaican', as seen in the 2016 film *Moonlight*, though of course neither of these stereotypes tell the whole story. Elsewhere in the world, when people ask me 'where are you really from?' (many people still refuse to believe that there are black people in England), when I respond with 'Jamaica', the immediate response is usually one of warmth, often accompanied by shouts of 'Bob Marley, Bob Marley'. Since I have grown my dreads this reaction has only become more common. I have seen the mention of Jamaica evoke smiles from Zimbabwe to Thailand, India to Germany, Brazil to Sweden. Reggae music has become a globally popular culture and though some engagement with it is rather gimmicky reggae is generally seen quite rightly as an anti-establishment, pro-people cultural force.

It's a shame that successive Jamaican governments and the Jamaican elite have not yet found an effective strategy to convert this global goodwill and cultural capital into a programme to uplift the nation. It pains me to see a country with so many brilliant and talented people still suffer from problems that are well within its capacity to solve, but JA – like elsewhere – is riddled by class divisions, local corruption and, most devastatingly, insurmountable neocolonial pressures – IMF debt, structural adjustment, capital flight, foreign interference and other post–Cold War geopolitical legacies.[2]

There is one other issue that I remember as a vague presence back in 1991 that has relevance to this book, namely colourism. Jamaica may well be a black-majority country, but of the twenty or so 'big families' that are said to control virtually all of the wealth of the island, or at least that portion not owned by foreigners, none are black. They are mostly white, with a few families of Syrian and Chinese origin thrown in for good measure. What does it mean to have the old plantocracy and later migrants into the country control all the wealth and power? Of course, there is no guarantee whatsoever that a black elite would be any more just per se, but it is nonetheless an interesting thing when the power and wealth in a country are controlled by people who do not share the heritage of Africanness and the extreme experience of chattel slavery of the vast majority of the population. Unlike in, say, most countries in Africa – where the black elite have their own distinct history and identity and may even have connections to traditional precolonial nobility – slavery did away with all that in the African populations of the Caribbean, and while that would not negate the existence of class, it has produced a 'black' identity and solidarity that can't quite exist in the same simplified way among the Yoruba and the Igbo, the Wolof and the Fulani.

Class in Jamaica and indeed the world is racialised. To this day you cannot fail to notice as you drive from the well-off neighbourhoods of uptown Kingston to the ghettoes of downtown that the living conditions get progressively worse and the skin colour gets progressively darker. Part of this legacy of colour-coded class distinctions is that being 'light skinned' carries with it the assumption of wealth and privilege. There are no specific incidents that I recall from that trip in 1991 but just a vague, aching suspicion that people treated me and my sister better than our 'fully black' cousin. I remember phrases like 'high colour' and 'redskin' and the general sense that because we came from 'foreign' and were mixed we must have money, a perception that continues when I visit today. The reality that my white family is actually 'poor' – again by UK not Jamaican standards – and that my siblings and I are now the most educated and affluent genera-tion in the family on either side, does not matter. The other real-ity, that middle- and upper-class black Jamaicans, few as they may be, almost undoubtedly enjoy a better quality of life and are certainly better educated than the average poor person in Britain doesn't matter either; the racialised ideas are still there.

This colourism has even been a bone of contention within the family itself, and my grandmother, for all her Jamaican pride, will still not accept that her roots lie in Africa – her perception of the continent is overwhelmingly negative, despite my decades of banging on about African history. When I told her I was going to Zimbabwe for the first time back in 2011, she told me to be careful because Africa – the country – is danger-ous. Jamaica is far more dangerous than almost every country in Africa of course – including Zimbabwe – but actual facts and details about Africa matter little even to my loving, African origin, colonially educated black grandmother.

'High colour' as status and privilege has deep roots in the colour codes of law that governed all slave colonies, and thus the reality of light-skinned privilege still plagues Caribbean and Latin American societies to this day. The reproduction of anti-black sentiment in majority-black countries may well seem paradoxical to many, but as we have seen race is a very pliable idea and societies change for the better only very, very slowly. Centuries of blackness acting as a signifier of non-human chattel slave status and as a badge of dishonor are still being wrestled with every day. That's not by any means to say that all Jamaicans hate being black, on the contrary, Jamaicans are some of the proudest people on the earth – the rest of the Caribbean may even argue, with some justification, that we are too proud – but it is to say that history will not die easily. It is also to say that skin bleaching has some real-world logic to it in that people who are not dark-skinned black still all too often have more real-world privileges, even in Jamaica.

Even with the colourism, poverty, violence and other challenges, I came back from the 1991 trip of a lifetime a changed person, and I knew it. I now visit Jamaica regularly, have presented two documentaries on Jamaican music and bigots will be happy to hear that I may well choose to relocate back 'where I came from' – but who knows how I would have come to view that side of my heritage had I not had those six weeks there back in 1991. Thanks, Nanny Milly.

Three years after my tip to Jamaica, I visited Scotland. The journey to Benbecula was long and arduous. A train from London to Glasgow, a coach from Glasgow to the coast and then a three-hour stormy boat ride to the island. I don't travel well at the best of times, let alone in a storm, and I vomited on that boat trip until there was nothing left but bile. The ship tipped and swayed; one moment I was looking up at the stars, the next I was staring into the blackness of the night sea, but eventually we arrived. Over the next ten days I went for walks around Stinky Bay – filled with rotten seaweed, it really did stink – ate Scotch broth and got a good old lungful of highland air. My Uncle Kenny and Aunty Peggy were much more welcoming than my mum's dad had ever been.

One day, I collected a bag full of heavy stones from the bay to keep as mementoes. When we got back to London we realised we had run out of money and didn't have enough cash for the whole family to get on the bus. My mum put us children on the bus with my heavy stones and the rest of the luggage and she walked all the way back to our house from Euston Station, a three- or four-mile journey. Bus fare was actually relatively cheap back then, but that's how close to the bread line many families live; literally every penny counts. I remember carrying those stones from the bus stop home and regretting ever collecting them. My mum had told me it was over-zealous, but I was a ten-year-old city boy let loose on the great outdoors. I chose not to listen and suffered with a sore shoulder for the rest of the week as a consequence. The stones are still at my mum's house, though, so it seems a small price to have paid for the memory.

By the time I went to Scotland, as far as I was concerned racism was pretty normal and certainly something to be expected whenever one ventured out of the relatively 'safe space' of our inner-London environment. I was on edge and very conscious that I was in totally white spaces. I became conscious of my body; paranoid about looking like a thief, I would stand far from the shelves in shops and only pick up what I knew I was buying, something I still sometimes find myself doing as an adult, just to avoid having to cuss someone. Day by day, I waited for the racial abuse that I was sure was coming. I think I was even slightly annoyed; I wanted to get it out of the way. The trip went on and the abuse never came. In fact, people, even old people, were generally just quite nice. It was odd – I didn't know how to process these white people. Looking back now, it was the first time I had spent a protracted period in such an overwhelmingly white environment and not encountered the discomfort of obvious racism.

When 'race' finally did surface, it was actually quite funny and sort of sweet. One of my cousins around the same age as me asked, in total innocence and fascination, 'why are you brown?' (You have to say it to yourself in a Scottish accent to really feel it.)

Notice that she didn't say 'black' or 'coloured' – the latter phrase was all the rage back then – but brown, an accurate(ish) description of my skin colour, not a pejorative preconditioned social category designated black. 'My daddy says it's because of the sun,' she added. It was clear that my cousin had no idea that brown people were supposed to be muggers or immigrants or criminals and certainly not 'Chinese black nigger bastards', and perhaps her father never knew these things either – after all, this was a tiny island with just one school way out in the Outer Hebrides, where people barely had televisions to teach them that darkies were to be feared. Because my upbringing had given me an unusual political vocabulary for a ten-year-old, I remember thinking quite consciously in that moment that this proved that racism was learned behaviour. I never went on to become that close to my Scottish family, they're in the Outer Hebrides after all, but I left with a respect and fondness for my Uncle Kenny and Aunty Peggy, and even for Stinky Bay. From that day forward, I went into a kind of subconscious romanticised denial of my 'Englishness', and that's why you might have heard me say I'm half Scottish.

It is often said that travel is the best education. These two trips, both undertaken before I was eleven, had managed to teach me much about the stupidity and fluidity of race, about how my own racial identity changed from place to place and how the people in the hills and gullies of St Ann's or the islands of the Outer Hebrides can be more enlightened and welcoming than some of us from the educated bright lights of the big cities.

We have looked at blackness and whiteness, we have even looked at race and slavery, but we have not yet actually asked what 'race' itself is. Today, race most often connotes very distinct groups of people usually defined by skin colour, and especially the black–white binary and images of Jim Crow America and apartheid South Africa. 'Race is a social construct' has become such a cliché phrase that we perhaps never stop to think about how little it actually tells us. Race may well be socially constructed, but how, why and when did this happen?

The idea of race, i.e. the idea that human phenotypes or ethnic/religious origins tell us something significant about the genetic, moral and intellectual capacity of human beings, and that this something is permanent, unalterable and hierarchical, was only properly codified in the eighteenth century. Ethnocentrism, bigotry and even a type of 'proto-racism' have existed for millennia, but race and racism as we think of them are very new.[3] Race and ethnicity are often conflated, as race used to mean what we now think of as ethnic or national groups. Today ethnicity, as distinct from race, is a grouping of human beings based on culture, religion, geography or language. The demarcation line for what separates one ethnicity from another can be and in fact almost always is vague and imprecise. People can share the same language, religion and nation yet perceive themselves to be ethnically different.

Race is much more crude and can unite two peoples that share none of these things in common or divide two peoples that share all of these things in common. Ethnicity, much like race, can be and has been a lethal division used to justify subhuman treatment by dominant ethnic groups, but just because ethnic tensions share many of the characteristics of 'race' does not mean we should conflate the two. Joseph Ziegler,

Benjamin Isaac and Miriam Eliav-Feldon outline the clear difference between race and ethnicity in the book *The Origins of Racism in the West*:

> The Spartans kept their neighbors, the Messenians, in perpetual collective submission and categorized them as 'between free men and (chattel) *douloi*'. The helots were treated with notorious brutality and their hatred for the Spartans was commensurate. Yet there is no suggestion they were ever seen as anything but Greek, nor is there evidence that they were seen as inferior by nature.[4]

So the Spartans considered the Messenians to be ethnically different but not racially different; that is, not permanently and unalterably inferior. Racism proper claims to be based on scientific truth. Thus while anti-black prejudice had existed to a certain degree in the Middle East among Jewish people and Muslims, and even in ancient Rome, it never developed into racism in the way we have come to understand it. Similarly, anti-Jewish pogroms, ghettoisation and hatred of Jewish people had existed in Europe for centuries, but it was only when the Nazis picked up the current of pan-European race science and applied this to a long and deep seated anti-Jewish prejudice that we got biological racism toward the Jews. As alluded to earlier, the Nazi Nuremberg Laws were directly inspired by American race laws in the Jim Crow south, and thus the scientific racism that had been used to justify colonising, and even where 'necessary' exterminating, Africans, Asians and the indigenous people of America and Australasia was returned to Europe and visited on Jewish people and others.[5] If we go further back in history, it seems that European hatred of Jews in the medieval era informed the development of racial ideas about the 'other' in Africa and Asia,[6] much as anti-Irish racial thinking informed British attitudes towards other 'savage' groups.

Yet the origins of race as a concept also has roots in a dialogue that was actually nothing to do with 'race' at all. Ziegler, Isaac and Eliav-Feldon continue:

> The word 'race' first emerged in France, not in Spain or Portugal. It was not coined to denigrate a despised minority or an alien people with strange skin colour or to justify colonisation or enslavement. The word emerged in the context of the discourse on nobility in the fourteenth and fifteenth centuries and was hence not initially racist. It was linked to the transformed and growing importance of blood in defining and describing nobility in general and royal nobility in particular.[7]

Racism as a word only really came into popular usage during the 1930s, and specifically in relation to the anti-Jewish rhetoric of the Nazis and American hatred of other European immigrants.[8]

We will almost certainly always have a degree of ethnocentrism in human societies but to conflate this with racism proper is lazy and dangerous. Ethnocentrism can be overcome, but overt racism or the idea of permanent hierarchical racial difference is a chasm much deeper and more difficult to surmount. Thus German prisoners of war were able to dine with white Americans during the Second World War, but their African-American 'comrades' and 'countrymen' were not. Thus the post-war British government preferred to pay to settle German and Italian prisoners of war in Britain than allow 'too many' non-white British citizens from the Commonwealth to come here, even though the Commonwealth citizens were paying their own way. The Germans and Italians were seen as ethnically but not racially different thus they could be – and have been – made into white people and thus truly British or American. Despite the Nazis' genocidal rampage and their attempts to take over the world and the war with Germany, a German was still preferable to a black person in British and American post-war racial 'logic'.[9]

The idea of racial hierarchy only lost much of its credibility because its three most unapologetic twentieth-century proponents were all defeated, to a greater or lesser extent. They were, of course, the Jim Crow South, apartheid South Africa and Nazi Germany. But there is absolutely no reason to assume that what the scholar George M. Frederickson calls 'overtly racist regimes' could not return, though today an obsessive focus on essentialised cultural, ethnic and religious differences often serves many of the same functions as overt racism.[10] While the overtly racist regimes have fallen, one only has to spend a little time on the Internet, looking at comments on videos or following social media threads about migrants, police brutality, terrorism or any other potentially racialised issue to see that the idea of race and racial hierarchy is perhaps as strong as it ever was for many millions of people today.

7 – POLICE, PEERS AND TEENAGE YEARS

The first time I was searched by the police I was twelve, maybe thirteen years old. There was no adult present and I was not read my rights; this is both completely illegal and entirely normal. Apparently, someone 'fitting my description' had robbed someone. During that same year, I saw one of my older friends get chopped in the back of his head several times with a meat cleaver by another boy of his age. That these two trends – illegal and racialised treatment by the state and the attempted murder of one working-class black boy by another – would enter my life for the first time in the same year is more coming of age than coincidence. The violence of the state, the violence of my peers – both integral and inescapable parts of black male adolescence in London.

In fact, violent working-class youth gangs have been part of life in British inner cities – as has the over-inflated moral panic about them – for well over a century, as this *London Echo* report from 1898 makes clear:

No one can have read the London, Liverpool, Birmingham, Manchester and Leeds papers and not know that the young street ruffian and prowler with his heavy belt, treacherous knife and dangerous pistol is amongst us. He is in full evidence in London – east, north and south. The question for everyman who cares for streets that are safe after dark, decent when dark, not disgraced by filthy shouts and brutal deeds, is what is to be done with this development of the city boy and the slum denizen? Not one tenth of the doings of these young rascals gets into the press, not one half is known to police.[1]

From the panic over 'garroting' – a form of street robbery often involving a choke hold – of the 1860s onwards,[2] the history of these gangs in Britain is a very well documented historical issue, dramatised in the BBC TV show *Peaky Blinders* and written about in scores of books. They remain a national problem to this day; in 2015 a national study found the north-east of England to have the highest rate of knife crime in England and Wales, and in 2017 many of the most horrendous knife crimes, such as the stabbing to death of a two-year-old and a seven-year-old and the murder and dumping in the woods of a sixteen-year-old girl, did not happen in London and were not committed by black teenagers. Glasgow was dubbed the Chicago of Britain as long ago as the 1920s because of its notoriously violent gangs,[3] and while teenage stabbings seem to have been drastically reduced in the city, the violence of organised crime is still a very serious issue facing Glaswegians.[4]

So while violence of the organised-crime and teenage-gang varieties has been with us for some time and continues to affect regions of the country where very few black people live at all, if you live in London and read the London press, you'd be forgiven for thinking that a) black boys are the only demographic that have ever been affected by this issue and b) London is one of the most violent cities in the world. In reality, class is a far bigger factor than race in this issue and, as noted above, London is not even the most dangerous area of Britain, let alone Europe, let alone the world. So while my narrative in this chapter will focus on working-class black boys in London, that is much more a result of proximity and familiarity than because I'm adopting the silly and obviously racist 'black-on-black violence' narrative so loved by US and UK media and law enforcement. We will deal with the 'black-on-black violence' trope later, but for now it's enough to note that even in London, when you adjust for class, the 'ethnic model' of explaining street crime falls away entirely.[5] It's also important to note that while London feels incredibly dangerous for teenagers it remains, in reality, a far safer city than media hysteria would have you believe, and the vast majority of murders in the city are committed by adults, not teenagers. All of this must be kept in mind as I tell you some genuinely horrific instances of violence that I experienced growing up.

In some cultures, they mark your entrance into adulthood with a spiritual quest, a physical challenge, a camping trip, a commune with the elders or with an exchange of long-held ancestral wisdom. In the inner cities of the UK, teenage boys racialised as black are instead introduced to the fact that the protection of the law does not apply to our bodies. There is no equality before the law. The whole of society knows this to be true, yet they pretend otherwise. When you meet your own powerlessness before the institution that claims to be protecting you, you feel both stupid and cheated. Stupid because how could you possibly have been so naïve as to believe any of the fancy rhetoric about equality when the signs were clear all along? Cheated because you nonetheless know you have been wronged.

During your coming of age, you will also come to know that boys just a few years older than you are now killers. Boys that helped you build sandcastles and pushed you on the swings, boys you looked up to as great footballers and fast runners, boys that you saw spill ice cream on their T-shirts and cry when they fell on the tarmac and split their knees open. Some of these very same souls now kill each other and while you don't yet quite understand how or why, you will have to learn, fast.

Some of your older friends and cousins will inevitably go to prison, some will be killed and a very small number will succeed in attaining the trappings of British middle-class life via the roads or by legal means. As you look at your 'olders', your realistic life options – if you can't play football or rap – will smash you in the face. You will shit yourself.

While London is not a dangerous city by global standards it is hard to overstate just what a scary place London is to be a working-class black male teenager. You are in one of the wealthiest cities ever built, yet the vast majority of your friends and family live in some of the worst poverty in Europe;[6] the opportunities seem to be everywhere yet very few people you know manage to grab them. You know West African 'uncles' with PhDs from back home who have ended up working as cleaners and security guards and while you don't judge those jobs – everyone has to earn a coin – it's not what you want for your future.

The first time I was searched, or at least the first occasion I remember – there were so many it has become kind of jumbled – went roughly as follows. I was on my way home from the youth club at my school, it was a warm summer evening and still light outside though it must have been at least 7 p.m. As I turned the corner just one street from home, I saw a police car in front of me and I knew they'd seen me too. I did my best trying-not-to-look-guilty walk, even though I had not done anything wrong. They pulled over and told me to wait there. As one officer made his way over to me he asked 'Where are you from, Tottenham? What are you doing round here?' Tottenham is a much rougher and distinctly blacker area than Camden or Archway, even though it's just a short bus ride away; we both knew what he was trying to say. The officer's question already let me know that in his eyes I was dirt; that is, matter out of place.[7] As the three officers got close, two of them held my arms and told me they were going to search me because someone fitting my description had robbed somebody round here earlier that day. I tried to read them my rights. Mr Muhammad, one of our teachers – you'll meet him more in the next chapter – had given us black boys a sheet with information about our rights when stopped by police printed on it, as he knew from experience that such encounters were absolutely inevitable for us.

The officers didn't care. Two of them held my arms, another rummaged through my pockets and then a fourth officer emerged from nowhere holding a camera and filmed the whole thing, pointing the camera in my face. I knew this was odd even then; in all the times I have been searched since, never has an officer pushed a camera in my face. They found nothing on me, of course; I was still a full good boy at this point, I didn't even smoke. I'd tried weed just once, way too young, because my older sister gave it to me! As quickly as they had come they left, no apology, no words of consolation, and no explanation. Gone. I walked the rest of the way home and thought about what had just happened. I concluded that I was officially becoming a man now, so I didn't bother to tell my mum about the encounter when I got in.

Over the next few years being searched by the police became virtually a bi-monthly experience. The most explicitly racialised time was in Elephant and Castle, when a group of us happened to be with our white friend. The police searched the four black boys only, and said 'keep it real' to our white mate while doing their best 'gang sign' poses as they drove off, obviously making fun of the fact that he hung around with niggers. The most embarrassing time was perhaps when I was on my way to the Royal Institution maths masterclasses mentioned earlier. As I stood there having my pockets rummaged through, the absurdity of racialised policing really hit me. I could literally be one of a handful of children on free school meals – of any ethnicity – that was also in the top 1 or 2 per cent of mathematicians of my age and be on my way to an elite maths class during the summer holidays, but I'd ultimately still be viewed as little more than a potential criminal by those with the power. I was late for class that day and did not bother to explain why to the teachers because I simply assumed – or feared – that my rich white professors would refuse to believe that the police just stopped people for no reason, and would end up looking at me with suspicion.

Once I was older and could afford a car, my main contact with police has been getting pulled over and having my car searched. One time, not far from my mum's, they rummaged through all the receipts I was keeping in the glove box for my company tax return and threw them all over the car. I complained; one officer told me to fuck off. I remember wondering how many young entrepreneurs who were not black experienced this kind of thing. By the logic of British capitalism, I had done everything right; a working-class boy that had used his talents to start a company and could now even afford a brand-new car. By the professed logic of the system, I should be rewarded and praised for my entrepreneurial spirit rather than harassed, presumed to be a criminal and spoken to by 'public servants' as if I was not a taxpayer.

Another time, when I was driving my girlfriend's car, we were pulled over on Sloane Square. The officers rummaged through her laundry bag on the side of the street. They posed the same questions I'd been asked years before, only slightly updated: 'What are you doing here? This car is registered to Croydon.' Matter out of place again. Apparently, some officers don't understand that the literal purpose of a vehicle is to travel. My trauma surgeon friend had the humiliation of the police calling the hospital where he works when they pulled him over, because they just could not get their head round the idea that a young, athletic-looking black man driving a Mercedes could be a doctor and not a drug dealer. He literally saves lives for a living and gets paid well for it, but can still be assumed a criminal and treated accordingly. Class and race have a funny relationship, eh? A young black man can change his class location by learning to save lives, but it still will not free him from the stereotypes associated with blackness.

When I started writing this book, I had not been pulled over in about five years – a personal record. The last time I had been pulled over was about 5 p.m. on a weekday. I had just picked up my nephew from school and noticed that a police car was tailing me. As we pulled up outside our house, the police flashed me and I stopped, as is the usual procedure. The officer got out and came to my window to speak to me. 'Is this your car?' 'What are you doing here?' 'What do you do for a living?' 'There have been an unusual amount of car thefts in this area'; the usual slew of questions and statements. I replied that it was five in the evening, that I clearly had a child sitting in the back, and that the child was visibly in full school uniform, thus it was not at all difficult to deduce where I might be coming from and what I might be doing. I informed him that it was indeed my car and that he could have easily called the DVLA to check if the car had been reported stolen before bothering to waste my time. I also told him that I taught theoretical physics at Cambridge University for a living. This lie had become a standard joke of mine when I got pulled over; I figured if the police wanted to mess with me then I'd mess with them. I kept an entirely straight face and I know the officer fought the urge to question me further on it, perplexed by the complexity of the title, with all the implications of education, class and access that would come with such a profession. Had I said that I was a rapper, that too would have come with its own set of assumptions. I could just as easily have said that I teach Shakespeare for a living, which would have actually been partly true, but for some odd reason I did not think of that.

When I informed the questioning officer that we were about to enter our home and pointed to the house in front of us, he could not hide his shock. 'You live here?' he asked in disbelief and resentment. What fascinates me is that it's not as if I was living on The Bishops Avenue; granted, I was living in a relatively nice part of W10, but I promise you it was nothing so plush as to warrant shock that a black family could be living there. It may have even been an ex-council place, just done up well, but in all fairness a regular policeman certainly could not have afforded to live there. It was clear that I now had the upper hand, so I put some questions to the officer myself; I asked him what he thought he was showing my nephew about this society by questioning me about car thefts on our run back from school.

The officer got shirty and said something like 'no need to have an attitude, mate' before walking off sheepishly. I talked to my nephew about the experience but he already seemed to understand quite well the relationship between black people and the state; his father is from a pretty rough estate in south London and he regularly visited his grandmother, who still lived there.

That would have been my last example, but then a couple of weeks after the chief of the Met had announced her new strategy to get tough on 'teenage thugs', called for more 'stop and search' and emphasised the problems with gangs and black boys in London, and just a week before I was due to hand my final draft into the publisher, I got to have another rather comical encounter with the police. I was driving on the A40 near Baker Street on my way to a meeting and I saw a police van flashing its lights, I moved to the side to let them pass but they stayed behind me, so I moved again to let them pass and they moved behind me again. I realised what was happening, and as I looked into my rear-view mirror I could see the officer motioning for me to pull over, so I did.

The officers jumped out quite hyped up, or at least that's the way it seemed to me, and I wondered why they would flag me down on such a busy road unless they thought they'd discovered something serious. The officers came to my window and to the passenger side, and started asking questions about the car. Apparently 'cars like this are used by gang members'. I laughed at this assertion; I'm sure it was the car that made him think of gangs, rather than who was in it. Then a female officer who had been trailing behind her colleagues came to the window, looked in and clearly recognised me. She pulled one of the questioning officers aside and immediately his whole demeanour started to change. While his colleague ran my licence, he asked me what I thought they should do, and if I had a better suggestion of how to police gangs in London. The change in attitude of the officers, once they realised I was 'someone important' rather than just another potential gang member, was stark. Perhaps if police just approached the public in general with that level of respect things would be different. My class privileges had come to the fore and momentarily trumped their racial assumptions. I informed the officer that I did actually have a proposal on this very subject, which I was writing to the mayor and the leader of the opposition with, which is true.

I could give a hundred more absurd examples from family and friends. I could even offer the case of the brothers who were brutalised on camera outside of Brixton station for selling books.[8] No, you did not misread that; they were manhandled on camera by the police for having a community bookstall, something any sensible agent of a state genuinely dedicated to education would praise. This was in 2016, and few incidents show more plainly and stupidly the relation between race, capitalism and gentrification than young black men being violently arrested on camera in front of a huge crowd in a historically poor black neighbourhood that is currently in the midst of a very visible middle-class white takeover, all for displaying books and taking charity donations. This was not about the books or trading licences at all – it was about the allocation of space, about belonging, about who is deserving of access and of rights. It was about matter that finds itself out of place. Dirt.

You see, racialised stop and search is not really about fighting crime, and the effectiveness of random stop and search as a policing tactic in general is ambiguous at best. Also to believe that a fourteen-year-old who has left his house with the intention of killing another human being, or who thinks so little of his own life that he will kill over nonsense, is going to be deterred by the potential threat of stop and search reveals a worryingly shallow understanding of human psychology. What racialised stop and search is about, in London at least, is letting young black boys and men know their place in British society, letting them know who holds the power and showing them that their day can be held up even in a nice 'liberal' area like Camden in a way that will never happen to their white friends, if they still have any left by the time they have their first encounter with the police. It is about social engineering and about the conditioning of expectations, about getting black people used to the fact that they are not real and full citizens, so they should learn to not expect the privileges that would usually accrue from such a status. Racialised stop and search is also a legacy of more direct and brutal forms of policing the black body in the UK, from back in the days before political correctness. The era of sus and the notorious Special Patrol Group or SPG – the unit responsible for the beatings discussed in Chapter One.

Looking back today, many people, even some police themselves, admit that the policing tactics of earlier decades were racist, though they will often admit this only to claim that things are almost perfect now and that they have sifted out all but a few bad apples. For them, the problem with policing now is simply the community's attitude to it, or rap music or single-parent families.

But let's return to the case of Glasgow, the city once dubbed the most dangerous in Europe which has seen a massive reduction in youth gang crime in recent years and where, if official stats can be trusted, the frequency with which young people are carrying knives is at a thirty-one-year low. The confrontation of the issue in Glasgow has revolved not just around stop and search, but around treating this kind of violence – i.e. teenage violence that is largely unconnected to proper organised crime – as a public health issue, and acting accordingly. A blitz of stop and search was used to give the public health policies time to kick in after which stop and search was scaled back, but it was ultimately understood that stop and search alone could not possibly be a serious long term solution. This approach has been led by the violence reduction unit, or VRU, and contrasts sharply with the approach towards 'teenage thugs' advocated by the Met Commissioner Cressida Dick as recently as 2017.[9]

Dick also emphasised the racial demographic of the teenage thugs in London as being 'black' and 'Asian'. Again, this is in marked contrast to the rest of the country, where knife crime persists but the 'whiteness' of the perpetrators or victims is never mentioned. It's also noteworthy that fourth generation English kids are referred to by their skin colour and the continent of their great-grandparents' origin. It is also worth noting that more than 80 per cent of the murders in London committed up until November 2017 were not committed by teenagers, so I'm a little surprised that there has not been a call to lock up more 'adult thugs'. Despite the fact that Britain already has by far the highest number of prisoners per head of population in Western Europe[10] – 50 per cent more than Germany, 30–40 per cent more than France – and by far the highest number of child lifers, with no comparable crime rates to match, here we have the chief of the Met calling for 'tougher sentences'. A slew of PhDs have long since shown that this approach simply does not work, if common sense hadn't told us so already.[11]

Our 'closest ally', the United States of America, has almost 1 per cent of its population in prison, by far the highest ratio in the world. The 'three-strikes' rule in some states there sent people to prison for decades for such petty crimes as stealing biscuits and video tapes. That is not an exaggeration. Yet with millions of people in prison, retention of the death penalty and other draconian punishment laws, the USA remains by far the most violent of the 'developed' countries in the world. So if the Met are proposing 'tough on teenage thugs' stop-and-search tactics in 2017, we can all safely conclude that this approach will obviously not solve a problem that has affected Britain's inner cities for over a century and a half and will likely help to actually make it worse by deepening and expanding an excluded criminalised underclass.

The day I first saw someone stabbed was rather unremarkable in other respects. I had gone for a kick about with a friend at the park, and then went to my local barber's in Archway with that same friend to get fresh. I was waiting for my turn; I think it was a weekend and black barber shops had not yet decided to do appointments back then, so the waiting time was often hours. It was a summer day and quite hot, and I was practically falling asleep when I noticed a commotion outside. One of my 'olders' – literally the older boys in your area that sometimes serve as your mentors/friends – was shouting expletives at someone. As far as I was aware he had recently got out of prison, and one of his conditions of release was that he was not allowed to be in London, so I was surprised to see him. I looked closer and saw blood on the sleeves of his torn jacket. I saw two other boys of the same age, one who I did not recognise and one who I had grown up with very closely, close enough to call 'cousin', waving plastic bags with knives inside them. The bags were there for the double purpose of preventing the assailant's DNA or prints getting onto the murder weapon, and of obscuring from the victim what kind of knife was coming for them.

My older friend was already a very naughty boy by this time, so this was not a random attack over nothing, like so many other stabbings in London, but part of an ongoing feud between young men already on their way into a life of organised crime. The 'black-on-black violence' cliché obscures this huge distinction between random attacks and those that are actually part of gang feuds or crime, but I can tell you first hand that many of the boys that get killed genuinely have nothing to do with street or gang stuff at all and are simply caught in the wrong place at the wrong time. My older friend was different; after being expelled from school at thirteen he was following that path to its inevitable conclusion.

He had also been to youth prison already, had been sent back to Nigeria as punishment and had now come back to the UK. The punishment trip 'back home' is a cliché among the black diaspora. Sometimes these trips back to Nigeria or Jamaica genuinely did work in terms of fixing a child's behaviour; school 'back home' is much tougher, life is generally harder, but there is also a communal discipline and a cultural sense of accountability that is hard to recreate in London. It's interesting that many black parents have felt sending their children back to far poorer societies would cure their bad behaviour in

England, suggesting that the parents see England as part of the problem. In my older friend's case, however, the trip had the opposite effect, he came back feeling that boys in England were soft compared to the reality encountered in Nigeria. It saved him in one sense, I suppose – in the year he was away there was a very gruesome murder in our area of a young boy who had a very big name in the streets. Some of my older friend's crew went to prison for that murder so if he had been in the country he might have been involved. That murder led to a spiral of street rivalries that resulted in many deaths. Anyway, back to the day in question.

My 'older' also had his knife on him, which he had now taken out, and was calling his attackers 'pussyholes'. I had not noticed that one of the attackers had disappeared. My friend retreated from the street into the doorway of the barber shop, just a yard or two from where I was sat. I noticed the other attacker reappear inside the shop; he had used the other entrance through the women's salon to sneak up behind my friend. It happened so quickly I couldn't even warn him before the meat cleaver came down on the back of his skull – twice? Three times maybe? What seemed like endless amounts of blood spewed everywhere. I remember being struck by the stains running down the fridge, the fridge that we used to buy our ginger beer and grape soda from. It was also the sound that was most unsettling, the sound of blade cracking bone, puncturing veins and tearing into flesh. Maybe it's because I love music so much, maybe I am just strange, but every time I have seen someone get stabbed it's been the sound more than the visual of the violence that's really struck me. I got used to that sound.

My friend was already fifteen stone at that age and a seasoned 'road man', but even I was shocked at the toughness of his reaction to being literally chopped in the head several times; he did not drop to the floor, he did not even scream. He chased his stabber out of the shop promising to kill him and calling him a pussyhole a few more times. The attackers ran off, satisfied they had done enough. Someone passed my guy a towel to wrap his head while he waited for the ambulance and he finally showed some signs of pain, while continuing to promise death upon his attackers. What is most remarkable to me, looking back now, is that nobody even stopped cutting hair. An attempted murder among what were in reality mere boys was thought to be so mundane as not to warrant any panic. Even I only made a brief trip to the phone box – remember those things? – to call my other friend and tell him that his older brother had been chopped in the head and that he should go to the hospital and check in on him. My friend, knowing his big brother's lifestyle, did not seem that taken aback, and it's only now I realise the horror of having to make that call as a mere child – I thought I was a man already at the time. I knew their mum well, I stayed at their house frequently, and I also knew I could not tell their mum what had happened as it was against the rules. She would obviously find out soon enough but it was not my place to say.

I returned to the barber's and waited for my Saturday trim. I remember a girl crying at the scene, the girl that my friend had come to the barber's to meet – it was pretty obvious to all she had set him up on behalf of the other boys, a very common tactic in 'the hood'. I don't remember the police turning up and though they must have it would not have made a difference; nobody, including me, would say they saw anything. So there is no confusion, despite our dislike of police the code as to what constitutes 'snitching' is much more complex than outsiders want to imagine. For example, had the attackers been stabbing a grandmother people certainly would have tried to intervene and would have had no problem handing over the granny attacker to the police, had we not killed him in the process first. But three young men stabbing each other, when all were known locally as rude boys, was never going to generate a swathe of willing witnesses, even though at least ten of us saw what had happened. What's more, even the victim would not have wanted anyone to talk; it would be street justice or none at all.

What's striking about my own reaction is that I was not traumatised. Despite never having before seen an act of comparable violence before that day, it was as if I was expecting such an incident and had mentally prepared for the encounter. My friend went to the hospital and recovered pretty quickly. He was then sent back to prison straight from the hospital for violation of his bail conditions.

Many more of my peers were stabbed before my eyes, a few boys I knew personally got killed, others went to prison for murder and there were many more police searches too. I went to clubs and parties where people got shot, extreme violence became a normal and accepted daily possibility. There were other dangers too, I recall seeing crackheads openly smoking up in a pre-gentrified Dalston Kingsland station, I saw a heroin addict overdose in Finsbury Park, I recall Broadwater Farm and Stratford Rex and under-eighteens raves and CS gas and beatings and bats and blades and the constant stench of danger.

Just a few short years after that first stabbing in the barber shop and that first search by the police, I was a completely different person. At thirteen I was still a rather soft boy to be honest; while very tall for my age, my physical stature masked an insecure, naturally geeky little boy. But by sixteen, despite all the benefits of pan-African Saturday school, a loving mother, the distraction of a potential career in professional football, many male role models and even straight As at school, I'd still become the stereotype in many ways. I carried my own knife inside the pocket of my silver Avirex jacket. It was a flick knife given to me by another local boy who I was not that close with but who happened to be on hand when I was attacked over some foolishness by two grown men, one of whom was armed with a long blade. I kept it. I liked it, it made me feel safer, less vulnerable and also gave me a magnetic sense of doom, danger and power – a sense that I was tough. However, my knife sat uneasily with my reality and my prospects. I started to smoke weed the night before football matches and I committed petty crimes. One of my friends sometimes took his dad's gun from under the bed; they lived opposite a crack den and so his dad kept the gun for protection. We took it to the streets, and the gun was brandished more than once. I got into fights, bottles and weapons came out, yet I somehow remained relatively unharmed – a bruised lip here and battered ego there, but all in all I emerged relatively unscathed physically. I had become a very volatile young man, quite capable of articulating my thoughts and quite willing to smash someone's face in given the right circumstances.

How did such a transformation occur in such a short space of time? How did the sweet, smiley eleven-year-old that wanted to be a scientist become the scowling, knife-carrying man-boy of sixteen? How did the knife-carrying sixteen-year-old then turn into the adult that teaches Shakespeare and lectures at Oxford? At eleven I was a 'mummy's boy'; I cried far more than my older sister and she made fun of me for it. By eighteen my sister knew that I was capable of grotesque violence – she had had to talk me and my friends out of trying to kill one of a group of boys we had got into a fracas with earlier that day. In an odd twist of fate, my friend who had been chopped in the head also talked us out of this action and thought we were being stupid. To him, a man that was now knee-deep in organised crime – don't worry mandem I am not dry snitching, my friend did his time! – killing someone over something so small as a glorified punch-up and a bruised ego was stupid – he had graduated beyond his teenage self, and now only major street beef would be worth contemplating murder for. Strangely, he was also the first one of my peers to ever give me a book. It was a novel called *The Fourth K* by Mario Puzo, and incidentally he'd found his love for espionage novels while in prison, not in school. He also had the most eclectic music tastes out of any of the man dem; he played me Nirvana and Radiohead before anyone else.

Oh, and to be fair to me and my other friends, the boys we were contemplating killing had pulled a gun on us in front of children, so we felt initially justified. Retrospectively I can see that I was not mentally well, and neither were most of my friends and peers, but how is that so obvious now despite none of us realising it properly back then?

I make these confessions not to appear tough or to add some ghetto drama to my narrative but simply because they are true and because they're important. When I look at the countless young black boys – and others – in jail in the UK and throughout the world and say, 'that could have been me', I don't mean it in the figurative 'we are all black' or 'I was poor too once' sense, I mean it literally could have been me. I made many of the same mistakes, I just never got caught, and that is complete luck and nothing else. When we look at the prison system we cannot fail to notice the backgrounds of the prisoners and the guards, overwhelmingly from poorer families, in contrast to the judges and lawyers; generally from much better off families. It all seems like one big racket.

For people who have never gone hungry, never been deliberately abused by the state or lived in 'the ends', the prospect of prison seems so distant that many may believe that only certain kinds of boys go there, only certain types of young men are prone to making these types of mistakes. Do yourself a favour

– visit any primary school in any 'hood' in the UK, black or otherwise, watch the children's playfulness, their sensitivity, their willingness to learn and then ask yourself in all serious-ness how any of these little spirits will become killers within the next decade. In fact, you could equally visit any of the top private schools and ask how some of those children go on to become the political psychopaths who justify wars with all sorts of profound rhetoric, knowing full well the killing is for profit and for strategic advantage. Rich people crime good, poor people crime bad.

I am not saying that teenagers have no agency, are incapable of making good choices or that all young working-class boys choose to carry knives like I did – clearly the overwhelming majority do not. But I am saying that teenagers, including myself back then, can see clearly that the professed values of the system do not tally with its actions and outcomes. We recognise that willingness to do violence is an almost univer-sally admired male trait from Wall Street to West Hollywood to Whitehall. Crime does pay and young people can see that as clearly in their ends as they can out there in the big wide world. The problem with our crime is just that the scale is too small.

Thus I had become both everything I was 'supposed' to be considering the odds – council house, single-parent family, drug-dealing uncles, Caribbean 'immigrant' – and everything I was not. I went to mathematics masterclasses and two years later I battered other boys with weapons. I spent time in the black book store and outside of Dalston station debating poli-tics with the Nation of Islam and other black sects that could be found there, I hung out with the middle-class white girls from my school, and on the block in Tottenham and Harlesden where white people did not exist and certainly no one was middle class. I likely had my knife on me in all these locations. My Tottenham friend also played for West Ham with me; my

Harlesden friend was a barely reformed roadman whose former street partners had either been killed or were now doing life in prison, and his dad was a genuine gangster. His gangster dad – one of my 'uncles' – was a breed of roadman Britain has never admitted to the existence of – the politicised, well-read, suit-wearing, organised black gangster. He could recite dissertations on the Russian Revolution, the troubles in Northern Ireland or Castro's Cuba, yet he was also as hard as they come. A natural leader with charisma and charm by the bucket load, he is the kind of man that other men follow into war. His crew robbed banks, banned the sale of class A drugs from the estate they controlled, ran a security firm and built a boxing gym for the local children. They also had ties to the guerrilla struggles being waged in Angola, Mozambique and Zimbabwe in the 1970s. In another life, born into another society, he may well have become a history professor or a military general. How do such supposed contradictions occur?

In the case of my own personal contradictions, I think there are a number of reasons. My own fragile ego played a role; I wanted to be tough, I did not want to be a victim. It was expected – I was six foot by thirteen after all, I could rap and play football, so being a 'pussy' was never going to cut it. I was also shit-scared and the fear of getting killed or even being known as a 'pussy' was far greater than the fear of doing a little time for carrying a knife. My family was poorer than my friends that lived in the 'real' hood and I'd been through a much tougher childhood than some of them in many ways, but I did not live on 'the block' so to speak, so I felt a need to prove myself as an outsider in their world. I succeeded, to a degree at least.

Yet the failures and stupid decisions of my own ego do not explain why such conditions exist in the first place in one of the richest cities in the history of the species and in the centre of an empire that considers itself the very birthplace of modern democracy. Do all nations produce teenagers willing to kill each other over virtually nothing? Because I promise you that the vast majority of the stabbings in London are over almost nothing; a wrong look, a perceived disrespect, a silly comment, getting caught in a rival postcode. Describing these young boys as gangs is quite an exaggeration – even the previous Met commissioner observed that most of London's knife crime has nothing to do with gangs.[12] It is no justification of their – nor my – potentially murderous behaviours to say that these young men, young men like I was for a period of time, are desperately crying for help, despite the tough façade.

Gangsters, i.e. persons involved in actual organised crime, tend to be too busy making money to kill someone for looking at them the wrong way. When they kill, it tends to be via the gun or even at a certain level kidnap and . . . well, you can imagine. The point is that male children in our society are willing to kill each other over very little. We can blame the families alone; claim the cause is single parents and fail to ask why middle-class kids whose parents get divorced rarely end up stabbing people. We can repeat the cliché of 'your environment does not define you', but none of us who are lucky enough to have attained a very decent living would choose to go and raise our children in Easterhouse in Glasgow or Croxteth in Liverpool so clearly we do not believe that bullshit cliché. The life expectancy difference between Britain's poorest areas and its richest is almost a decade – your environment literally does define you, despite the few who may transcend it.

Which brings us on to the two most obvious things that connect the teenage killers of London and Glasgow to those of Liverpool and Durham. They are almost always poor and they are almost always men. What is it about masculinity in our society that makes young men from entirely different ethnic backgrounds and geographic regions often react to the challenges of being poor with such territorial displays of violence?

Accra in Ghana is obviously much poorer than London and the city faces many issues, yet teenagers stabbing each other over iPhones and postcodes is not one of them. I know for much of Britain it is easier to believe that there is a certain kind of boy that gets involved in all that sort of stuff, that someone like me, an open exponent of education, could not possibly fall prey to such a mentality – if only things were so simple. The sense of hopelessness and fear felt during those formative years is so intense it is hard to even remember the sensation properly. The pressure to accumulate, the understanding that poverty is shameful, the double shame of being black and poor, the constant refrain of materialism coming from every facet of popular culture, the empty fridge, the disconnected electricity, the insecurity of being a tenant with eviction always just a few missed paycheques away, the stress and anger of your parents that trickles down far better than any capital accumulation, the naked injustices that you now know to be reality and the growing belief that one is indeed all of the negative stereotypes that the people with the power say you are.

These are the factors that aided my own ego in turning me from a wannabe Max Planck to a wannabe gangster. I ultimately take responsibility for my own actions, but there is still a story there and being treated like and presumed to be a criminal for years before I ever contemplated actually carrying a knife is part of that story. If I had listened to my mum and gone to private school at seven it's unlikely that I would have made the same friend groups, been exposed to the same things and have gone through any of the above, yet at my core I would have been exactly the same person, just shaped by a different set of experiences and conditions. Some on the right would like to lambast a person like me as the much-maligned 'social justice warrior' or 'virtue signaller', but I am actually quite the opposite. It's precisely because I have been exposed to my own potential for murder, because I know that I am not inherently a good person and that we all change to one degree or another according to our circumstances, that I have such an interest in trying to help create conditions that encourage the best in people. I have been, or at least felt, desperate, and desperate people do desperate things. I'd rather live in a city and a society and a world where less desperation exists: this is as much common-sense self-preservation to me as it is 'altruism'.

Yet even with all of these pressures I can tell you that the vast majority of my peers did not succumb to the pressures like I did. The other boys I played football with, often from very similar backgrounds, did not understand why me and my friend wanted to be rude boys when we were potentially on the way to becoming Premier League players. I can tell you that if most youts in the hood could genuinely see a legal path to just a decent middle-class living without having to be spoken to and treated like a total idiot for thirty years, 95 per cent would take it. I have no survey to back this up other than hundreds of conversations, years of educational workshops in prisons and just plain common sense. Just recently a friend of mine, himself a former drug dealer turned fully legitimate businessman, went on to one of the most notorious council estates in London and offered a young rapper that lived there a record deal. This young boy is knee deep in street life, yet he took the deal, which came with the express condition that he leaves the street life, in a heartbeat. This is a rapper who in his songs boasts about selling drugs and murder 'because that's what sells' – young black boys understand what the market demands of them quite well – yet even he, like other 'gangster rappers' before him, would much prefer to tell stories over music than kill anybody or sell drugs.

The plain reality is that even in a developed, wealthy country like Britain very few people want to spend their lives working for someone else with very little prospect of a serious improvement in their lives or those of their children, so people have to be conditioned to accept this reality. Many of the young kids that get expelled from school and hit the streets refuse to accept this conditioning. There is intelligence in rebellion, they are just channelling it in the wrong direction. My friend and I – the other footballer turned rude boy – were both natural rebels, I just found my path to a more productive rebellion earlier than he did. After he stopped playing football it took him ten more years of the harsh lessons of street life to realise and accept that he was probably better off just getting a job after all.

Though I am individually much better off than my parents ever were, that extreme violence remains only a few wrong turns, misunderstandings or family feuds away. For example, my little brother is essentially middle class, he has never missed a meal and he has been all over the world at sixteen, yet the first victim of a stabbing he knew was his other older brother. So even in his middle class-ness he is not too far removed from the reality of the hood. His brother (my stepbrother) was stabbed in the neck on his way home from school one day. That side of the family lives in Tottenham where the riots of 1985 and 2011 occurred.

In reaction to these various formative experiences, a noticeable demographic shift can often be seen in boys' friend groups around the age of thirteen in areas like Camden. Throughout primary school, children seem to pick friends across the economic and racial spectrum and friend groups tend to broadly reflect the diversity of the area. This was my own experience, despite some very strange things occurring as a result of this 'racial mixing'. One example will suffice; one of my white friends moved away from the area and thus left our school. I kept in touch with him and went to stay at his new house in the sticks. We played football in the mud, rode our bikes, roller-skated and all of that good stuff. When we sat down to have dinner that evening his older brother asked his parents for permission to tell 'Paki jokes' at the dinner table, saying, 'Kingslee doesn't mind.' I was about nine, he was fourteen, his parents were at the table and I assumed they would stop him so I smiled uncomfortably. His parents did not stop him, they in fact encouraged him and he sat at dinner glee-fully making fun of smelly Pakis and starving Ethiopians – the famine there was still in recent memory – while his parents and my friend laughed along. Needless to say, it was the last time I ever went to stay with him.

So I don't want to give you a romantic picture, it's not that children are not conscious of race during their primary school years, far from it – it just seems they are more willing to look past the conditioning and the difficulties when making friends than they will be as teenagers. I have observed this process of ethnic socialisation many times with my younger brother, my nephew and in countless schools that I have visited.

For me personally, because I was among the top academic performers my chosen friends in primary school – as opposed to extended family 'cousins' – tended to be the rich white kids. The other children who received free school meals were not generally in the top working groups of course – class differen-tiation in academia starts early. So by virtue of usually being in the working groups with the 'rich white kids' – apart from when I was placed into special needs – they became my friends. They were probably not millionaires, but with two professional parents, two cars, skiing trips during the holidays and a house-hold fizzy-drinks-making machine, they seemed incredibly rich to me at the time. I went to France with one of my rich white friends and his family one summer and I stayed at some of their houses, though I don't ever remember them staying at mine – looking back now I think I was probably embarrassed that we were poor, because I did invite my poorer mates to stay.

The racially mixed friend group tends to stay intact throughout primary school, but then a mystical process occurs during the first two years of secondary. No one says anything openly but you all know what is happening: your lives are becoming too different and unlike before you are no longer willing to look past these differences. You can no longer relate to one another across lines of race. We are destined for different things and we all know it, so by year nine your friend group becomes exclusively black, with one white boy that loves hip hop and probably has a black girlfriend. I have seen this occur as surely with my sixteen-year-old brother as it did with me. I have also been to enough schools in the area and spoken to enough parents and peers to know this is a common pattern. We all learn our race and our place. Thus I gravitated first to Hackney, where my earliest teenage best friend lived, then to Tottenham for the latter years of secondary and then finally in my later teens to Harlesden. I became a kind of ghetto nomad and because I was from Camden, an area that everyone knew had poor pockets but was not considered a rival hood in the way that any of the above mentioned areas would be, I could get away with it. A Tottenham boy rolling in Hackney or vice versa was in serious danger, as the two areas were in direct beef, and a boy from either of those areas would probably have been greeted with much more suspicion than I was in NW10. My Tottenham friend remained mildly suspicious of my Harlesden friend and his Brixton-based brother even after years of rolling together, and it was certainly at least partly because of that 'rival hoods' suspicion.

How much of this self-segregation is caused by the seemingly natural human appetite for tribalism, and how much is due to the social processes that shape a shared identity? I would argue that through school and the different treatment and assumptions of teachers, encounters with police, and portrayals of ethnic groups in print and TV, by thirteen we have learned the meanings and implications of our racial identities quite well and have bonded over common experiences and perceptions. For black children, encounters with the state and its agents, outright interpersonal racism and much else teach you a sense of shared blackness and by thirteen this black identity is usually solidified. Ironically, this sense of shared blackness creates two completely contradictory behaviours. First it creates a fierce loyalty to your 'man dem', a sense that you are taking on the world together, and so you become willing to die to defend your friends – your 'niggas' – as if you were at war. In fact, if your friend was not willing to risk his life for you you'd very much doubt his friendship. Yet this very shared blackening also begets fear and thus aggressiveness towards other young black boys who are not familiar. You internalise both a sense of black unity and common struggle and at the same time a sense of self-hatred, a belief that other young black boys are a danger to you, and both possibilities wrestle one another constantly. When you see another group of unfamiliar young black men, everybody is tense, you don't know yet whether you will give them the black nod or the 'screw face' – literally where you screw up your face to try and look scary – whether you'll holla 'wa gwan blood' or 'where you from cuz?'. The difference could be life changing for all of you.

Class has to be kept in mind too, as these segregated friend groups emerge even for black children who are essentially middle class, whose parents are professionals, who go to church on Sundays and never miss a meal. Even those black children, who will never carry a knife and profess their loyalty to their niggas, make social choices about friends very early. I have visited enough African-Caribbean societies at universities to observe the outcome of this pattern, even in the most educated section of the black population. Similarly, I'm sure the gang mentality that forms in poorer non-black communities bears much emotional resemblance to what I am describing here.

By thirteen I was no longer that close to any of my white friends. I had the occasional one who I played football with but none of them could possibly ever be my 'brothers' in the way that my black friends were.

As you already know, the 'rich' children lived walking distance from me, as did the kid who was selling drugs for his dad at age eleven and the boy whose mum burned his head with an iron when he was a baby because he was crying too loudly – or at least that's what we were all told about the massive hand-sized burn scar on his head, and knowing his family it seemed entirely plausible, sadly. That boy got expelled on the first day of secondary school, went to prison and was killed by another boy we grew up with before the age of twenty-one. The boy who sold drugs for his own father is now in prison for many years, and not for the first time.

The 'rich' kids from my area, my top-group primary school friends, are all doing fine, of course. I barely need to check in with them to know that, but on the odd occasion that I do bump into one of them and ask what they are up to I usually find out that they are now barristers or film directors or working for the UN or something like that. None of them are in prison and none to my knowledge have yet been murdered. There have been a few working-class success stories of course, I am one of them after all, but these are very much the exception to the rule, even in liberal multicultural Camden.

Then everything changes again.

Between the ages of thirteen and twenty-five I was constantly aware that my fragile masculinity could be challenged at any moment, that a failure to respond correctly could result in my

death, or irredeemable embarrassment. I was aware that my A*
school grades would not save me from PC Plod digging through
my pockets, aware that the school system and the larger society
did not really want to see me prosper despite all their liberal
claims to the contrary, and I shit myself. I shit myself and I
learned to screw up my face instead of smiling, I learned to
shout instead of crying and I learned to fight my peers even
when I really wanted to hug them.

Then an immense sense of relief descended on me sometime
around the age of twenty-five. I know this was not just my experience, I have spoken to so many others who have confirmed that
this epiphany is common and murder stats peaking between
eighteen and twenty-two would also seem to bear it out as a real
thing. There is no ceremony, nobody congratulates you, you just
wake up one day and it's over. You take a deep breath and you
just know you have made it through and things will never quite
go back to the way they were before. In a similar way to your self-
segregating friend group years earlier, nobody ever says anything,
though it is understood by all. The youngers can somehow sense
that you are an older now and thus there is no real need to feel
threatened by you; no one asks you what you are looking at or
what ends you are from any more.

Internally something changes too. You no longer care
anyway, there is a shift and things that would have enraged you
a year before no longer even register. I was on a train about five
years ago and a young boy of maybe eighteen was 'screw-
facing' me. Perhaps because I was wearing a tracksuit he
thought I was his age, maybe he recognised me and was trying
to prove a point, who knows? It had been so long since I had
experienced this kind of thing that it took me a moment to
realise why the young man was so upset and why he was holding his face in such an uncomfortable position. Once it registered that he was trying to screw-face me I couldn't help it, I

just burst out laughing. I saw it dawn on the lad that I was obviously ten years his senior and in no way willing to entertain this foolishness any more, and he looked away, quite visibly embarrassed. Had this been a decade earlier one of us could easily have ended up in hospital.

But this science does not work for everyone, some 'olders' never grow out of the hype, some are never lucky enough to be exposed to new and life-changing experiences as I was and some are still so unhappy with themselves that murdering someone over trivialities remains an everyday possibility. Yet for the most part, unless you are involved with actual organised crime, the 'gang' bullshit and ends beef will subside past the age of twenty-five; wisdom and the hard lessons of life combine to grow you up. You realise the injustice of it all, you see that class and race conditioned your whole generation and that social mobility is largely a myth. You can see how life panned out for everyone who was expelled or dropped out of school at thirteen and it was never ever well.

Yes, you have survived, but it is bittersweet; some of the best minds of your generation have been wasted, the children that grew up with the safety blankets of money and whiteness have gotten twice as far working half as hard, they are still having the same cocaine parties that they were having twenty years ago and they still have not ever been searched by the police once, let alone had their parties raided or been choke-slammed to death. They have just bought a flat in Brixton; they go to one of the new white bars there. They pop up to the new reggae club in Ladbroke Grove, the one that serves Caribbean food but also gets nervous when more than two black guys turn up. They have no idea that the building used to be a multi-storey crack house. By twenty-five, even if you don't read Stuart Hall, if you grew up both black and poor in the UK you will have come to know more about the inner workings of British society, about the dynamics of race, class and empire than a slew of PhDs ever will. In fact, PhDs and scriptwriters will come to the hood to drain your wisdom for their ethnographic research, as will journalists next time there is a riot. They will have careers, you will get a job. Wash, rinse, repeat.

Once this awakening comes you will even find yourself repeating the same lectures to teenagers that old men used on you, hoping they will not make your mistakes. You will give them all of your worst horror stories; the dead peers, the friends and cousins that will not get out of prison until they are in their fifties and sixties, the football and music careers cut short, my man's little sister that got killed over her brother's beef. You insist that things are much better for this generation than they were back in your day, then you remember the polite smile that you used to do when someone you respected gave you this same lecture. You know it's little use. You continue anyway but you know that the youngers will make their own mistakes by the rules of their own world, just as you did. You tell yourself that if you can just turn one head, get one person to think differently, that all the hot air will be worth it and maybe that's true. You repeat the lecture again tomorrow.

Then there is me, my doctor friend and my composer and lawyer mates; the exceptions that prove the rule. Trapped between two worlds, we can afford to still live in Brixton or Ladbroke Grove while we watch our communities be removed from under us, but it's not as if we have enough money to buy the block. We try to not be gentrifiers by fighting for the community in our various ways, yet we can afford to buy extortionate coffee and we quite like a nice wine and, well, quinoa is good for you. We've even tried hot yoga a couple of times – oh no, we are officially internationally middle class.

We are too smart and now too successful to be ignored entirely, but we are still outsiders in essence. My friends that work in the city or in hospitals refrain from having political discussions with their white colleagues or bosses, especially about race. When newspapers claimed Mark Duggan shot at the police my now-middle-class black friends knew this was nonsense immediately; they left their workmates to talk, as it's the only way to stay sane. The riots happen, they understand why, but they grit their teeth and listen to the simple analysis or outright dehumanisation. Rashan Charles gets choked by the police on camera and dies, and someone in the office says, 'Well, he should have just obeyed, he shouldn't sell drugs.' My friends refrain from reminding their colleagues that they saw them snorting coke on their lunch break. My friends visit their cousins in prison, they don't talk about it to their colleagues; my barrister mate volunteers in his old hood every Sunday teaching English, but at work every week he hears how the police and the judges talk about the poor, about people of colour and about the immigrants. He bites his tongue and does his job.

A terrorist attack happens – meaning the perpetrator is assumed to be Muslim, of course – and my friends of course deplore the attackers and feel total sympathy for the victims, yet hailing from Kenya, Zimbabwe, India, Ghana, Nigeria, Iraq and Jamaica they know, unlike their colleagues, that Britain is not some innocent virgin nation quietly minding her own business that has been placed under siege. They refrain from giving any context out of fear of being seen as terrorist sympathisers, which of course they are not – their grandmothers or children could just as easily be in the wrong place at the wrong time and get killed by these brainwashed murderers. I know so many people that lost friends after the riots in 2011 and during Brexit; everyone's real opinions come out in a crisis. I once made good friends with a very successful businessman of my age, we bonded over a mutual love for literature and Jodorowsky's graphic novels, then one day he made a passing comment to me about his workers who had had the gall to ask for better pay: 'What would they be doing if I didn't employ them anyway? Drinking, gambling, committing crimes?' I could not be bothered to argue that day, and he probably has no idea to this day that this comment is why we are not friends any more – he was born into money, I made what little I have 'myself'. We may both have been eating at the same restaurant in Venice, but we are not the same.

Which brings us to the elephant in the room; the history of the British class system. Despite all the rhetoric about meritocracy and equality of opportunity, Britain is still – like every nation on earth to some degree – a society where the social class and area you are born into will determine much of your life experiences, chances and outcomes. The quality and type of education you receive, and your likelihood of interaction with police, social workers, prison or other state institutions, will all be influenced by class. If you visit any prison in this – or any – country, the vast majority of its prisoners from any ethnicity you choose will be people from poorer backgrounds, obviously.

We live in a country with a particularly vicious class system when compared with other similarly developed Western European countries, and the results of this can be seen when we look at our huge prison population, terrible child poverty rates, the thousands of old people who freeze to death every year because they cannot afford to heat their homes, the millions of people living off food banks, the crisis of homelessness and the return of such Victorian diseases as rickets in the poorest parts of the country. These things are all the results of political decisions taken, decisions informed by the perceived class interests and worldviews of our rulers and their rulers. You will never as long as you live hear British politicians saying that we cannot bomb some far off, probably oil-rich country because we don't have the money, and of course the history of British class conflict is inseparable from British imperialism as Britain was literally able to expel its class tensions onto the people of Australia, America and Southern Africa. Had Britain's elites not had transportation as a safety valve, who knows, some of the genocidal violence inflicted on the Australian Aboriginal population may have been aimed at them. As the most accomplished British imperialist Cecil Rhodes aptly put it 'if you wish to avoid civil war you must become an imperialist'. In marked contrast to the wars we can always afford you will frequently hear the same people talk about not having the money for any number of things that affect the lives of poor people, such as adequate fire safety, decent pay for nurses and teachers and winter fuel for the elderly: this is classism. The state makes choices about the interests in which collective resources will be spent. Poor people have no real voice in British politics, but we do have an unelected second chamber of 'lords' influencing policy. None of this is conducive to having a truly democratic society and we may not be able to substantially change it, but it is important that we at least understand what's going on. Class affects everything – culture, confidence and worldview – and the class system is so entrenched in Britain that even a person's accent carries with it implications about their social background.

Whether or not teenagers always have the language to articulate these things, I think an understanding of class starts to dawn on young people sometime around thirteen. In children from poorer backgrounds, there is a change in confidence, an unwillingness to speak, a fear of being embarrassed and, for the boys especially, a turn towards aggression that often begins to manifest around this age. Having lived it myself and having visited well over a hundred secondary schools across the UK, I can say that this immense change for the worse is near universal. There is something about that age – about the combination of puberty and all its sexual confusion and competition, about being old enough to start noticing how fucked up the world is and how many holes there are in your shoes, with the dawning of the reality that your dreams will not come true, that you will most likely be just as unhappy as your parents and that fifty years of dead-end work awaits you – that kills most working-class kids' confidence.

'Why should I learn Pythagoras, sir? I'm never gonna use it, am I?' 'Why should I care about Shakespeare? He's for posh people.' I tell teenagers they are wrong when they tell me these things, but in reality I am telling them a lie in the hope that one or two of them will be foolish enough to believe me and that those foolish ones might become the poor kid that 'makes it'. But, in general, they are actually correct. It's not that life in post-industrial Britain is materially awful by global standards, clearly it is not and clearly things are quite substantially better than they were a century ago, but it seems to me that the drudgery of it all encourages many teenagers to just give up on their dreams and accept 'their place'. This remaking of humans to fit social norms is of course what education is about, from 'tribal' initiation systems to state schools.

With regards to policing, Sir John Woodcock, then HM Chief Inspector of Constabulary, said back in 1992:

> What is happening to the police is that a nineteenth-century institution is being dragged into the twenty-first century. Despite all the later mythology of Dixon, the police never were the police of the whole people but a mechanism set up to protect the affluent from what the Victorians described as the dangerous classes.[13]

So despite all the lovely comforting stuff we are told, senior police understand very well that the primary function of policing is to protect property. Despite all the pretence about serving the people, and some of the genuinely good and difficult work police have to do, such as dealing with rape victims and missing children, the police are primarily enforcers for the state and for the state of things as they are. When this is understood you can make sense of 'illogical' police activities like spying on justice campaigners or environmental activists as if they were the Mafia, to the extent of going undercover and marrying members of activist groups. If you delude yourself into thinking the police's primary function is to serve the people none of this makes any sense.[14] When masses of the public protest government injustice, such as millions protesting against an unjust war, it's obvious that the police are there to protect the state, not 'the people'.

When viewed in the historical context that governments themselves evolved as governments for the wealthy, explicitly excluding the poor, and that it took literally centuries of struggle for people who were not 'propertied' to have the right to vote and therefore any say in political affairs, all of this makes perfect and simple sense. Marx and his intellectual descendants may well prove to have been wrong about socialism and how society will evolve – we'll see – but much of their analysis of the way capitalism works is so clearly and plainly accurate that if it was given to any working-class child at school they would immediately be able to make total sense of much of the 'Marxist nonsense', as it's so often called. (Interesting that despite being two of the fathers of racism the works of Voltaire and Kant for example do not evoke such odium as Marx among mainstream intelligentsia; naturally African and Asian scholars can be all but ignored.)

As such, in a racialised society it's only natural that working-class people in general and black people in particular would come to dislike the police. This is both politically logical and an obvious recognition of reality, even for more successful black people that 'make it'. Who are the only members of British society who have openly and repeatedly gotten away with unlawfully killing our family and friends? Who, after having grossly failed them, decided to spy on the Lawrence family instead of bringing them the justice they deserved? Who expect us to believe that Smiley Culture really stabbed himself while making a cup of tea during a drugs raid? Surely, even if that was true, someone should be in prison for negligence? Who attacked the miners at Orgreave? Who lied after Hillsborough? The job of the police is to protect the state and working-class people obviously do not control the state in any meaningful sense.

To be black, poor and politicised in Britain is to see the ugliest side of the police and indeed of Britain itself; it is to see behind the curtain and not be fooled by the circus, and to feel crazy because so many others cannot see what is so clear to you. When my safety was threatened when I was growing up the last thing I would have done would be to call the police, it would not even have crossed my mind. The police brutalised pretty much every black Caribbean man of my father's age that I know, with impunity. Cynthia Jarret died when they raided her home, they shot Cherry Groce and despite all of the suspicious deaths in custody and even in cases where inquest juries have returned a verdict of unlawful killing, the police are never punished.[15] I know some people reading this will find it very hard to believe that police used to just grab black men off the street and beat them for no reason, but I suggest that if you are one of those people you just talk to some black people over the age of fifty about their experiences, or if you need white confirmation, talk to some Irish people of that age, as they were often treated relatively similarly back then.[16]

It made no difference whether someone was a criminal – ignoring the politics of that term – or not; my father, stepfather and working uncles all got their beatings, as did my 'road' uncles too, of course. I grew up hearing these stories. Even now, with all of my academic work and fully legitimate business interests, I still get nervous when a police car is behind me and I still wouldn't call them if my personal safety was under threat. Given this history, I was hardly surprised that day back when I was thirteen that I had my first encounter with the police. I was black and I was working class – of course they were looking for me. And I'd been expecting them.

8 – WHY DO WHITE PEOPLE LOVE MANDELA? WHY DO CONSERVATIVES HATE CASTRO?

'The crushing defeat of the racist army at Cuito
Cuanavale was a victory for the whole of Africa! . . .
The decisive defeat of the apartheid aggressors broke the
myth of the invincibility of the white oppressors. The
defeat of the apartheid army was an inspiration to the
struggling people inside South Africa. Without the defeat
of Cuito Cuanavale our organisations would not have
been unbanned. The defeat of the racist army at Cuito
Cuanavale made it possible for me to be here today.'

Nelson Mandela, 26 July 1991,
speaking in Matanzas, Cuba[1]

The boy pulled at his dead mother's sleeve. Her white shirt
caked with dust and blood, she lay on the ground, frozen.
Mangled limbs fixed in the patterns of a falling runner. The
boy cried and pulled and even nestled himself affectionately
under his mother's armpit, but she was still dead. Around them,
stretched over the grass and dirt, lay mothers, fathers and children, scattered, bleeding, dead or dying. Just moments earlier,
the sound of song could be heard, but the brutal crack of bullets
had left in its wake only silence punctured by screams.

This scene from the 1987 film *Mandela*, starring Danny
Glover, was my first introduction to the brutal reality of apartheid. I'm pretty sure I watched the film not long after it came

out, which would have made me just four or five years old. In all the years since then I have not watched it again, yet that scene, which depicted the notorious Sharpeville massacre of 1960 in which sixty-nine people were shot dead, scores injured and many paralysed by bullets in their backs as they fled, has stayed with me as if I watched it yesterday. Thousands of black South Africans had gathered at the police station in Sharpeville to protest the racist pass laws of the South African government. They were unarmed, but this did not stop the police from deciding to massacre them. The film recreated these events in fairly brutal and graphic detail. This was the first time I'd ever had to think about how cheap human life, and particularly black human life, could be.

I watched this film with my mother, stepfather and older sister; as you may have noticed by now my family home was very politicised. The anti-apartheid struggle was the first political issue I recall entering my life; the African National Congress (ANC) freedom charter was on the wall in our house, along with the Malcolm X 'By Any Means Necessary' poster. Even though South Africa was thousands of miles away, the black British community was heavily involved in anti-apartheid campaigning and organising. Anti-apartheid activists saw clearly the relationship between the British state's support for a foreign, racist settler colony and its domestic racism.[2]

After all, can it really be a complete coincidence that the most tumultuous decade of Britain's domestic 'race relations' history was also the decade of the apex of the struggle against apartheid? As I have mentioned, my pan-African Saturday school was named after Winnie Mandela, in honour of her contribution to that very struggle and in recognition of an internationalist understanding of white supremacy and colonialism. I grew up watching 'Mama Winnie' appear on television in the years approaching Nelson's release from prison and my family went on many anti-apartheid demonstrations. I saw a brilliant production of the South African play *Sarafina* at the Hackney Empire several times during 1991. The play depicted the Soweto uprisings of 1976 and featured the legendary South African jazz musician Hugh Masakela, who I got to meet. As you can imagine, within this cultural and political environment I had already got a sense of the incredible brutality of imperialism and white supremacy long before my tenth birthday.

You could question the wisdom of allowing a five-year-old to watch a film clearly designed for an adult audience, and I certainly remember feeling disturbed and upset, but even now I remember watching that scene as a turning point in my life, the moment at which I first realised adults could be so horrible and that the world was well and truly messed up. You could criticise my parents for playing me something so brutal at such an age but I think that would be a mistake. The reality is most children in the world do not have the luxury of hiding from the brutalities of systemic injustice and as tough as my upbringing may have been by British standards, there are certainly more children on the planet even now whose lives more closely resemble the lives of a child born in Soweto or Sharpeville than one born in Camden. I think my parents did the right thing, even though it was painful and confusing and it left me with so many questions that I could not properly formulate.

'Mummy, if the police are supposed to protect people why are they shooting them?' 'Why are all the police white and all the people protesting black?' 'But they were only singing; why did they kill them?' 'What is going to happen to that little boy now that his mother is dead, Mummy?'

If the overriding white nationalism of Anglo-American governments is to be fully understood then we need look no farther than the issue of apartheid South Africa. Decades after the supposed war against fascism, the British and American governments and the capital they served could be found supporting a regime whose ideas were rooted in the same kind of genocidal racial 'logic' as the Nazis. The governments of Britain and the US, who had styled themselves as the world's policemen and who had invaded numerous countries on apparently 'humanitarian' grounds, would obviously not be invading South Africa, perhaps the most universally unpopular regime of the late twentieth century. No, they would in fact support it. While Margaret Thatcher claimed to be against apartheid 'on principle' she consistently opposed sanctions against the regime. Westminster, Cecil Rhodes and Winston Churchill had played crucial roles in constructing apartheid in the first place, despite the number of black South Africans that had fought on the British side in the Boer War and would fight for them again during the Second World War – the war to end fascism, remember. It is inconceivable that if the race roles in South Africa had been reversed Britain and the US would have supported a black government committing such outrages on its white population.

Britain, France and the USA had consistently blocked calls from the international community to impose an arms embargo on South Africa, even after the murder of schoolchildren and the banning of opposition political parties and groups; this is usually what the great powers call 'supporting democracy abroad'. To think this kind of naked support of a government who believed black people to be subhuman would not have an effect on the domestic black population is obviously totally ludicrous, but successive British governments either did not care or were willing to manage the contradiction. As you've already seen, we were very much still second class citizens in the 1980s.

Black Britons, for reasons that should be abundantly obvious, were overwhelmingly against apartheid, though the situation in southern Africa was much more complex than one struggle – the divisions of ethnicity, traditional nobility and actually potentially having to run a country all complicated matters and divided loyalties. I also appreciate that it is easy to be radical from thousands of miles away, when the boot is not on your neck and the bayonet is not in your back. Nonetheless, anti-apartheid was an issue around which the vast majority of black Brits were united (which is what made Frank Bruno's tacit support all the more galling). It's also worth remembering that Jamaica and Barbados were the first countries to impose sanctions on the apartheid regime, and naturally that stand filtered down to Caribbean descendants in the UK.

Across Britain more widely, hundreds of thousands of people participated in marches and demonstrations against apartheid, high-profile artists recorded tribute songs and lent voices of support to enforce a cultural boycott of South Africa, and the concert at Wembley Stadium in honour of Nelson Mandela's seventieth birthday that called for his release from prison was graced by some of the biggest music stars from across the globe. From 1986 to 1990, activists in the UK organised a non-stop picket outside the South African embassy in London. The response of the state was to arrest activists and try to ban the protest. Think about that; the British government having its own citizens arrested for protesting a foreign racist settler regime. It seems that large sections of the British public have long been more forward thinking than those in power.

When Nelson Mandela was released from prison in 1990 it was a momentous occasion for us. The iconic photo of Nelson and Winnie with their Black Power fists in the air graced the covers of newspapers the world over. The *Voice*, Britain's most popular black newspaper at the time, ran the photo with the headline 'Free At Last', in obvious reference to Martin Luther King Jnr. The *Daily Telegraph*, on the other hand, ran the headline 'Armed struggle will go on, says Mandela', a very misleading headline given that the internationally backed apartheid regime and their black collaborators were still massacring ANC members and supporters and that apartheid itself had been rooted in grotesque violence.[3] Now that Mandela's ANC has become the ruling party in South Africa, it's easy to forget just how precarious things were back then, even after Mandela's release. Soon after his release, a second concert was held at Wembley Stadium and Mandela graced the stage to address the world.

In my family home, at the Hackney Empire and across the black British community and anti-racist activist circles, the mood was one of celebration and victory. While the more cynical (and astute) among the adults knew even then that justice would not really be served, that those who had committed decades of atrocities under the apartheid regime would not be punished, nobody questioned that this was a significant moment, that the powers that be had been forced to compromise and that the last white settler regime in Africa had been formally defeated.

In later years, my connection to the struggle became more personal; one of my schoolfriends was living in the UK in exile after his father had been killed by the apartheid regime. In our secondary-school hip hop group, he rapped:

To me the Truth and Reconciliation Commission
　　seems insane
Since lies and suffering is all we seem to obtain.

Even a teenager could see that truth and reconciliation were not justice.

From his release from prison until his death, Mandela became a virtual saint in the mainstream media, an elder uncle to our broken world, praised by everyone from Bill Clinton to the Pope. When Mandela died, the *Daily Mail* ran with the headline 'Death of a Colossus', Downing Street flew the flag at half-mast and then Prime Minster David Cameron called Mandela 'a true global hero'. Statues of Mandela now stand outside of the Southbank Centre and even in Parliament Square – along with two of the architects of apartheid, Winston Churchill and Jan Smuts. How is this possible, you might legitimately ask. How can people that love the makers of apartheid also love the breakers of it? Surely something must be amiss here?

Why did the opinion of the white conservative mainstream and respectable liberals suddenly come to view Nelson Mandela as a hero at some unknown point in 1989? Remember, sections of the British press had accused the ANC of wanting to establish a 'Communist-style black dictatorship' in South Africa, Margaret Thatcher had labelled the ANC a 'typical terrorist organisation' (it was recognised as such in the USA until 2008[4]), and opposed sanctions, and the federation of Conservative students ran a 'hang Mandela' campaign. While there is no evidence that a young David Cameron participated in the hang Mandela campaign, he certainly did travel to South Africa in 1989 on a fact-finding mission paid for by a lobbying group that sought to lift sanctions. So why all the Mandela love post-1990 from people that were at best ambivalent to black South African life at any point before then, and at worst openly hostile to it?

I know why I love and respect Madiba, and I know why my community and people that were anti-apartheid before it was fashionable do. We love Madiba because he risked his life and lost his freedom for twenty-seven years for opposing one of the most unjust regimes in history. We love him because even when he was offered his freedom in 1985 in return for a capitulation to apartheid, Madiba refused, telling the South African people that his freedom was inseparable from their freedom. And yes, we love Madiba because he had the courage to take up arms against a morally indefensible racist settler colony. We also love Mandela because, even once he was released, he never forgot those countries that had supported his struggle, no matter how unpopular their leaders became in the mainstream press. But what about all the new-found Mandela worshippers? Why did they suddenly love Madiba?

Was it that the white mainstream had suddenly come alive to the evils of white supremacy and in a moment of moral epiphany – much like the manner in which 'they' ended slavery – had discovered that Mandela's struggle was a just one? Were they suddenly committed to the freedom charter? Did they wish to see the wealth of South Africa even mildly redistributed? Are those that belatedly learned to love Mandela committed to trying to eradicate the things for which Mandela lost twenty-seven years of his brilliant life or are their motivations rather more sinister?

We can glean some insight by contrasting how these same organs of the press and political institutions have chosen to remember or depict another man and country of whom Mandela was a great admirer; Castro and Cuba. Somehow these belated anti-apartheid types have either forgotten or do not know that the only non-African nation to send its troops to actually fight the apartheid regime was Cuba. Not only that, but Cuba provided medical aid and military training to the ANC in exile. Cuba's role in helping to bring an end to formal apartheid in Africa was decisive and Mandela, until the end of his long life, never forgot it. He once wrote that 'the Cuban internationalists have made a contribution to African independence, freedom and justice unparalleled for its principled and selfless character.'[5]

The first foreign country Mandela visited upon release from

prison was Cuba, where he met and shared a podium with Fidel Castro, a man he referred to as 'my brother' and 'my president'. So how is it possible that Mandela's new-found white conservative fan club came to such different conclusions about Castro and Cuba than Mandela himself did? To understand, we must visit the history of how apartheid actually ended, because like all achievements of black freedom before it, the fall of apartheid seems to be remembered as a gift from newly enlightened white rulers and liberal campaigners putting pressure on odious regimes. This could not be further from the actual truth.[6]

In 1974, the dictatorship that had governed Portugal collapsed under pressure from the Carnation Revolution, and the new leftist government stopped the military actions of the previous regime in Portugal's African colonies of Guinea-Bissau, Angola and Mozambique. These three territories were the last vestiges of direct European colonial rule in Africa and all three countries had already been undergoing military struggles against Portuguese rule, supported by Cuba and, to a much lesser and more ambiguous extent, the Soviet Union. With the change in government in Portugal and independence declared in Angola, a new set of problems arose that would play a key role in ending apartheid. Angola had declared itself independent under the leadership of Agostinho Neto's leftist MPLA, a movement that was openly hostile to South African apartheid and had links with the ANC. In response, the apartheid regime invaded Angola; they had already been occupying neighbouring Namibia for almost a decade, imprisoning and torturing children as they had in South Africa itself. In response to requests from the Angolan government, 36,000 Cuban troops deployed into Angola between 1975–76 to assist in the struggle against the racist regime in Pretoria. For all the bravery of MPLA and SWAPO (the Namibian liberation movement), it is entirely inconceivable that they would have won without this

Cuban contingent, a contingent in which Afro-Cubans had a significant presence. Or at least that's what the African revolutionaries themselves maintain.

Up until 1987, the apartheid regime made repeated encroachments into Angola and armed a brutal and unscrupulous proxy leader named Jonas Savimbi of UNITA, to try to overthrow the Angolan government. However, at the crucial battle of Cuito Cuanavale, referred to by Mandela in the epigraph of this chapter, the Cubans, Angolans and SWAPO defeated the apartheid forces. The negotiations after this defeat led directly to the independence of Namibia, the unbanning of the ANC and the fall of (political) apartheid. Perhaps as many as 400,000 Cuban personnel would serve in Angola over these years and Cuban troops would stay in Angola to help protect the country and train the Angolan army until 1991, by which time South Africa had granted Namibia independence and agreed to set Nelson Mandela free from prison, directly as a result of the defeat at Cuito Cuanavale.

This is the military background that popular Hollywood history likes to forget when discussing the fall of formal apartheid. The role of Cuba was both unique and decisive. This one fact alone, a major contribution to the fall of white supremacist apartheid, should enable most people to have at least a nuanced view of Cuba and/or even arguably rank the country as a major contributor to extending human rights struggles, but popular propaganda – in the West at least – ensures that that is not the case. Africans, Asians and Caribbeans have certainly not generally forgotten the Cuban contribution to fighting settler-colonial racism. For a long time, it was thought that Cuba was acting in Africa simply as a proxy of Moscow, but US intelligence documents told a different story and even Henry Kissinger came to admit this was not the case, saying Castro 'was probably the most genuinely revolutionary leader then in power.'[7]

So if the ending of apartheid is now universally agreed to be a good thing, and Cuba played such a central role, how is it still possible to have such differing views of Castro and Mandela and of Cuba and South Africa?

The short answer is that the mainstream media has been so successful in distorting basic historical facts that many people are so blinded by Cold War hangovers that they are entirely incapable of critical thought, but the other answer is rather more Machiavellian. The reality is that apartheid did not die, and thus the reason so many white conservatives now love Mandela is essentially that he let their cronies 'get away with it'.[8] The hypocritical worship of black freedom fighters once they are no longer seen to pose a danger or are safely dead – Martin Luther King might be the best example of this – is one of the keys ways of maintaining a liberal veneer over what in reality is brutal intent.

Apartheid used racism to justify stealing enormous tracts of land by force and treating a huge black workforce like they were subhuman, with no real rights, no freedoms to travel in their own country and no real recourse to the law with respect to the abuses of their oppressors. Needless to say, this exploited black labour force, along with the fantastic mineral wealth of southern Africa, produced uncountable fortunes for transnational corporations, and some of the highest living standards in the world for most white South Africans. Given a basic understanding of apartheid's economic underpinnings, it would not be unreasonable to ask whether that economic relationship between black and white, between large transnational corporations and black labour, has changed since 1994. If apartheid was primarily an economic system, surely to claim as we do that apartheid has ended there must then, by inference, be something resembling economic justice occurring over there in southern Africa?

Sadly, this is not the case. Yes, formal, legalised,

unapologetic, political white supremacy has been defeated in South Africa, and that is a cause for celebration for any human that believes even vaguely in justice. Nonetheless, the afore-mentioned economic relationships have not seriously been altered in all the years since Mandela was released from prison, and this is a direct legacy of compromises that were made in those initial handover negotiations.

After the apartheid handover, the South African central bank was to be run by the same man it was run by under apartheid. The apartheid-era finance minister also kept his position. The debts incurred by the apartheid regime had to be paid off by the newly elected ANC and the ANC essentially accepted the IMF/World Bank neocolonial model that has been such a disaster for other poor countries. A newly elected black government paying back loans taken out with international creditors by a white supremacist regime; it would be laughable if its effects were not so sickening. I'm not sure there has ever been a clearer case of odious debt in history. No corporation was forced to pay repar-ations to the victims of murders and other abuses carried out under apartheid to benefit them. Killers and torturers were not imprisoned, as would be usual after a regime 'fell', but rather were invited to confess their crimes and walk free. To this day, South African whites, who are still a small minority, control a hugely disproportionate amount of all forms of capital in South Africa.

This was not justice or the end of apartheid, but rather its morphing from a system that was unapologetically racial to one that is now unapologetically economic and by inference, given South Africa's history, still racial. This legacy leads us to the Marikana massacre of 2012, the single largest massacre in South Africa since the infamous Sharpeville massacre of 1960 – thirty-four striking miners were shot dead by police and to this day no one has been prosecuted. Lonmin, the company that the mine belonged to, is based in London. In 'post-apartheid' South Africa, the message is still clear – black life is expendable in pursuit of profit. A few black shareholders, CEOs and politicians do very little to alter that reality, as those in power clearly feel very little solidarity with the dead and their families. Again, I must re-state, because I don't want what I am saying deliberately misunderstood, that the ending of political apartheid is to be celebrated. Majority rule, however flawed, is always preferable to racist minority rule, and the ANC have made some very interesting geopolitical moves that we know a settler government would not have made, such as refusing Britain's overtures to help invade Zimbabwe (according to Thabo Mbeki at least) and sending arms to the democratically elected Lavalas in Haiti while their democracy was being destroyed by Haitian elites and their US backers.[9]

But when black South Africans claim the ANC and the post-apartheid order has failed them, they more than have a point. The average black South African still lives in conditions of extreme poverty, often with a lack of access to basic amenities and with little hope of real change in sight, and the country remains one of the most violent and unequal in the world. In the past few years there have been repeated waves of xenophobic anti-African attacks against African migrants from other countries, resulting in scores of deaths. These attacks have been justified in the language of bigots everywhere – 'they are coming over here, stealing our jobs' – and have even been encouraged by a Zulu king who described migrants as 'head lice'. Though he insists his words were taken out of context, his repeated xenophobic remarks make this quite unlikely. That this mass mob violence is mostly directed at poor African migrants is very revealing; it seems some black South Africans have internalised the very anti-African, anti-black ideas in opposition to which their parents shed so much blood. With that said, African

ethnic differences and conflict obviously pre-date settler colonialism by hundreds of years. Almost everywhere in the world, it
seems people love to pick on the most vulnerable. Though it
must also be pointed out that South Africans have mobilised
against this xenophobia with repeated marches calling on the
government to do more to protect foreigners, attracting as
many as 30,000 people.

Obviously this cannot all be laid at Mandela's door, any
more than Cuba's achievements – outlined below – can be cred-
ited to one man alone, but Nelson Mandela was more than
smart enough to know the ANC's compromises would mean
continued misery, poverty and a virtual police state for most
black South Africans, though perhaps he a had a longer-term
vision. I would not presume to judge a man who spent almost
as much time behind bars for his principles as I have spent alive,
or claim that I could or would have done any better. Only time
and the future of South Africa will reveal the full political
consequences of Mandela and the ANC's decisions. However,
it's worrying that the British Conservative government –
formerly such a good friend to the apartheid regime – was in
2016 willing to secretly use the British Army to prop up the
ANC in the case of unrest.[10]

In almost complete divergence from the hero worship of
Mandela, Fidel Castro has become an almost pantomime
villain in the Western popular imagination, particularly in the
USA, and Cuba has been under sanctions for decades, in
marked contrast to apartheid South Africa. When Castro died,
even a journalist at the *Guardian* ran with the headline 'Forget
Fidel Castro's policies, what matters is that he was a dictator'.
But that very same journalist told us that we should 'stop calling Tony Blair a war criminal' and informed us that 'the Left

should be proud of his record'. In all fairness, I was pleasantly surprised that the coverage of Castro's death generally seemed to be far more thoughtful and balanced than I had expected – outside of the usual gutter rags. I imagine that was not so much the case in America.

With Castro frequently labelled a 'human rights abuser' (in marked contrast to Mandela), we have to ask where post-Castro Cuba stands in human-rights terms in comparison with post-Mandela South Africa. Seeing as both struggles were so inter-twined and the popular treatment of Mandela and Castro stands so obviously juxtaposed, it would be reasonable to expect the living conditions of the average Cuban to be far worse than those of a South African – especially considering the enormous wealth and industry South Africa has and the lack of sanctions imposed on the country. That is if 'human rights' are really what motivates the Mandela good, Castro evil brigade.

That is not what we find, which is why Cuba's most ardent critics avoid directly comparing Cuba to countries with similar histories and simply resort to adjectives. Once Cuba is directly compared to other former slave states of the Caribbean and South America, or to a country like South Africa, it starts to look like quite a different proposition.

In addition to playing such a significant role in the ending of apartheid, Cuba has managed to avoid the ravages that drug trafficking wrought on the rest of the region. The murder rate in Cuba is four times lower than the average for Latin America, or to put it another way, the murder rate in many US cities is ten times worse than the murder rate in Cuba. The same is true in relation to nearby Jamaica, and South Africa frequently ranks in the top ten for murder rate in the world. The kinds of massacres of workers that occurred at Sharpeville and Marikana simply have not occurred in post-1959 Cuba, and even the most ardent anti-Cuba ideologues could not try and pretend that the kind of police brutality that is so common in South Africa, Jamaica, Brazil and even the USA exists on anything like that scale in Cuba. The extreme inequality and particular history that makes Latin America the most violent region of the world is due in no small part to a long history of the United States supporting dictators in the region, and this is part of why so many of the people there look to Cuba as a source of hope and pride – it is the one nation that stood up to Uncle Sam and won out.

There is one area of achievement which even Cuba's critics have not been able to dismiss: healthcare. While you will often hear people grudgingly admit that Cuba 'has good healthcare', the scale of their programme and how many other countries they support is rarely properly appreciated, so it's worth looking at them here in length.

In 2015, Cuba became the first country in the world to eliminate the mother-to-child transmission of HIV and syphilis. More recently, even Richard Branson felt compelled to pen an article about Cuba's extraordinary medical achievements and how the idiotic embargo prevents ordinary Americans from benefiting from Cuba's medical innovations.[11]

Cuba currently has more healthcare workers in foreign countries than all G8 countries combined.[12] In 2014, Cuba had 50,000 healthcare workers in sixty-five countries; that is more than the Red Cross, Médecins sans Frontières and UNICEF combined. Since 1960, over 101,000 Cuban health workers have provided care in 110 countries. There is even a history of Cuban medical outreach to countries openly hostile to Cuba, such as Nicaragua during the Somoza dictatorship, and even the USA.

To show just how far Cuba has come in this area, in 1965 Cuba had one physician for every 1,200 people, but by 2005,

Cuba boasted one physician for every 167 people – a number unequalled anywhere in the world. In 2014, the island had 83,000 doctors, some 5,000 more than Canada, a wealthy country that has a population that is over three times larger. Recent World Health Organization data put Cuba's health indicators, such as life expectancy and infant mortality, in line with the US and Canada.

In addition, Cuba has offered free – that is, the cost is borne by the Cuban people – medical scholarships to thousands of students from across the world on the condition that they return and serve the poor in their own countries. As of 2014, over 23,000 students from eighty-three countries had graduated from the ELAM campus (Cuba's international medical school) since 2005. Cuban healthcare workers are often among the first responders in major global crises such as the Ebola outbreak in 2014 or the earthquake in Pakistan in 2005.[13]

These facts are recognised by such 'Communist propaganda outlets' as the World Health Organization and all of the national governments that Cuba helps. To anybody that actually cares about global justice, human life and human rights, Cuban medical internationalism is without a doubt one of the greatest humanitarian enterprises of the twenty-first century. Cuba does not demand that Jamaica or Haiti or Liberia sell off their water systems, or incur crippling debt or elect Communist leaders that Cuba approves of in exchange for this help, the Cuban people elect to do this work out of genuine revolutionary solidarity with other, overwhelmingly poor black and brown people in the global south. Britain offers nothing like this scale of condition-free support as far as I am aware, even to its former colonies, and 'we' are currently in the process of dismantling our own domestic NHS.

So if the average Cuban is several times less likely to be murdered than the average South African – either by another

Cuban or by the state – has access to healthcare, housing and education to a far greater degree and can expect to live more than ten years longer, it would be quite fair to say post-Castro Cuba is faring better than post-Mandela South Africa on many important human indices.

But let's even suppose for a moment that everything that has ever been said about Cuba was totally true, let's even also say that Castro barbecued dissidents alive while drinking cold beer and sodomised people with knives, or banned women from driving, that still would not explain why conservatives or mainstream politicians more generally have such disdain for him, seeing as they are fine with such deeds in other contexts. When we do look at some of the regimes that our government(s) have armed and/or otherwise done business with, we see some of the greatest human rights abusers of the post -1945 world – Pol Pot in Cambodia, General Pinochet in Chile, Suharto in Indonesia, Nigeria during Biafra, Israel and the horrendous Saudi war being waged in Yemen right now. The list is long and responsible for millions of deaths and unimaginable misery.[14] It takes an extremely gullible person to truly believe that 'human rights' is what motivates our government. Conservative and even 'respectable' liberal opinion has chosen to adopt Mandela as a hero and Castro as a villain because of, in my opinion, a number of factors, plain old intellectual obedience being one of them. Yet anyone that is willing to have a nuanced, even favourable view of the likes of Tony Blair and Barack Obama but unwilling to extend that nuance to Castro and Cuba is obviously not motivated by the behaviours of the men in question and how they wielded political power, but rather by ideology, nationalism, bigotry or ignorance.

To be clear, I am not one of these religious leftists who thinks St Castro can do no wrong; I'm well aware that there were mistakes, shortcomings and abuses of power in Cuba and that Cuba has many challenges still to overcome – including its own internal racism. There are many valid reasons to critique the Cuban Revolution and Castro himself. However, what I am saying is that it takes quite substantial delusions of grandeur to believe that you or I could have done a better job of running that country while under blockade from the wealthiest nation ever, having to deal with state-sponsored terrorism and being under constant threat of assassination and the coups that the US/UK have exported to so many other places.[15] I have had a hard enough time writing this book, let alone trying to run a country, but if the success or failures of the Cuban Revolution are to be honestly assessed, surely they have to be looked at in comparison to other similar societies? It's much easier to focus on the demonisation or demagoguery of an individual than actually discuss the outcomes of a political process. By focusing on the person of Fidel Castro, or of Mandela for completely opposite reasons, we can avoid any real analysis of the legacies of the apartheid struggle and the Cuban Revolution. Of course, such a comparison would make the Cuban Revolution's achievements – and shortcomings – vis-à-vis South Africa and other similar nations quite plain to anyone who can count.

Why is any of this important to race and class in the UK, you may ask? First, because these global anti-racist struggles were connected. Many of the same people that faced down British fascists at the 'Battle Of Lewisham' in 1977 were active in anti-apartheid throughout the 1980s. Second because, as a global power, Britain's domestic politics and public opinions affect the whole world, as domestic British politics are in turn affected by global events. My childhood was shaped by the presence of the anti-apartheid struggle in the same way that my young adulthood was shaped by the invasion of Iraq – these things have informed how millions of us view our own society and its place in the world. But it's also important because the Castro–Mandela dichotomy exposes the way the mainstream loves to worship a supposedly non-racist country as long as it leaves the accepted class hierarchies in place, but hates a society that has revolutionised some of its class relationships despite its actual material contribution to global anti-racist struggle. Either way, genuine anti-racism cannot be what motivates such favouritism.

While Cuba's achievements might look meagre to the average middle-class liberal or conservative Briton, to the average Jamaican, Haitian, Brazilian or Indian what Cuba has been able to do for the masses of its people is impressive indeed. The average middle-class liberal Brit might be able to brush off a society not falling prey to American imperialism, attaining universal healthcare and education and even assisting many Commonwealth countries in that regard, but for those of us whose parents or grandparents came from places like Jamaica, Nigeria and India, who go 'back home' regularly and thus have some realistic yardstick by which to measure Cuba, the legacies of the Cuban Revolution look quite different. I have seen Cuban doctors in Jamaica training people and saving lives with my own eyes, and while it's easy to idealise the achievements of a socialist state while living in comfort in Britain, it's equally easy for others to ignore the fact that Cuba has made advances in some key areas that almost no other 'third world' country has, nor even the richest nation on Earth.

When I was child, black and brown voices in British politics were generally quite fringe to say the least. That situation has changed quite a bit, and though we should not overstate things, it really shows no signs of being reversible. As the percentage of the British population that hails from Africa, Asia and the Caribbean grows

– it's projected to be 30 per cent by 2050 – how will this affect dialogue, debate and the subsequent direction of British politics? Those of us who are directly connected to the 'third world' have very different renderings and rememberings of political events than mainstream opinion, and our traditions cannot help but continue to shape and be shaped by the future of Britain.

Part of this ideological battle is fought over popular memories of historical figures like Mandela and Castro, and can be seen playing out in real time in the 'Rhodes must fall' campaign – a campaign in Britain directly inspired by students in South Africa demanding that the worship of white-supremacist colonial figures like Cecil Rhodes be stopped, that statues of them be torn down out of respect for the victims of atrocities they promoted and in recognition of the hope for a different world order from one defined by empire, racial hierarchy and cold war geopolitics.

At the outbreak of the First World War, the vast majority of the world was colonised by European powers – and the Ottomans – and race was a fully accepted way of accounting for human difference in international affairs among the great powers. Despite some doubts about overt displays of white supremacy, even after the carnage of the First World War British, American and French elites felt confident enough to reject out of hand Japan's suggestion that a clause recognising racial equality be inserted into the treaty of Versaille.[16] It would take another world war and the genocides perpetuated by the Nazis for the 'enlightened' governments of the democratic Western world to entertain the idea that white supremacy might not be a given.

Even when the Second World War ended, the colonised world still had an entirely different project confronting it than the European societies under whose flags they had fought. While European states focused on rebuilding themselves with massive amounts of help from the United States, their colonies now had

the space, capacity and experience to fight for their own freedom against the very people with whom they had fought shoulder to shoulder against fascism. Make no mistake about it; in
1945, even after using their colonial troops to defeat the Nazis,
both Britain and France had every intention of holding onto
their white-supremacist empires.

It is one of history's great ironies that the most extreme
incarnation of white supremacy, the Nazis, did more to undermine white dominance, damage Western prestige and make
space for 'third world' freedom struggles than any other force
in the previous three centuries. For reasons of self-preservation
only, you would have thought that western liberals would have
learned this lesson, yet we live in a world where literal card-
carrying Nazis getting punched in the face or being refused
platforms to speak garners more liberal outrage than twelve-
year-old Tamir Rice being executed on camera by the police
while playing alone in the park. Only when I see the free-speech
purists campaigning for the right of a Salafist who thinks 9/11
was wonderful to speak at America or Britain's top universities
will I perhaps believe in their sincerity. The way these people
speak of free speech you would think that McCarthyism was a
thousand years ago.

In the years since 1945, mass movements among the black,
brown and yellow world majority have fundamentally remade
the world; decolonisation may well turn out to have been the
most significant historical process of the second half of the
twentieth century, but you would never know this from mainstream historiography.[17] Through this process, which included
some radical critics from within the colonising societies themselves, the accepted racial hierarchy of the world has been so
comprehensively redrawn that today even most bigots find it
embarrassing to be called racist. Both Mandela's ANC and
Castro's Cuba played complicated roles in this racial remaking

of the world and both men had tremendous respect for the contributions of the other, but we do history a serious disservice when we allow it to be reduced to simple dichotomies.

My childhood was indelibly shaped by the struggle against apartheid in South Africa, even though I lived thousands of miles away and the momentum of that struggle had swung decisively against the apartheid regime by the time my earliest memories were formed. Nelson Mandela was already a name synonymous with freedom and wisdom, justice and principle, by the time I took my first steps. However, it was not until over a decade later, when in my late teens I started to do a little reading and research of my own, that I even heard mention of Cuba's contribution to anti-apartheid. This obvious omission, along with the simplistic narratives that surrounded Mandela and Castro, was a valuable lesson to me about how the powerful craft history and news media to their own ends. This realisation that major parts of recent political events could quickly be forgotten or indeed totally ignored if they did not fit the script helped encourage me to always seek multiple sources for a given story or situation, and compelled me to always distrust or at least question what I was being told and why I was being told it. A trait that frequently brought me into conflict with my teachers.

9 – THE KU KLUX KLAN STOPPED CRIME BY KILLING BLACK PEOPLE

I was visiting my soon-to-be secondary school. These visits are a ritual; they are designed to give students a sense of the scale and scope of big school, to make sure the new terrain is somewhat familiar come September. During the visit, I got to meet the rest of my future year group and we toured around the school; I remember being impressed by the science labs with their Bunsen burners, but most impressed with the size of the football pitch, of course.

I'd like to note that my secondary was actually a pretty good school; it has produced a notable number of creatives and certainly played a key role in my development. I had some great teachers there and even better friends. Nonetheless, like everything else in life it was full of contradictions.

Back to the visit; we also got to meet some of our future teachers. One look was enough. It may sound dramatic or presumptuous but that's often all it takes. Eyes tell so much when they are left to wander unguarded. I could tell from that first simple glance that it was going to be a long five years and that my relationship with this particular teacher was going to be a major source of stress throughout secondary school. Adults think they can fool children but children are often able to judge a character so accurately and so quickly it's almost like a sixth sense. So it was when I first met that teacher. Her eyes could not hide her disdain for this mouthy, overconfident, articulate, obviously working-class boy. I could feel a sense of racial discomfort coming from her as well; I'd started to be able to sense this type of feeling.

I officially joined the school that September and my initial impression was proved right in quite spectacular fashion. My clashes with this teacher began almost immediately. Our world-views were so radically different – my political heroes were Muhammad Ali and Malcolm X, hers were Margaret Thatcher and Winston Churchill – it was never going to work out. She believed in Britain's inherent moral superiority and that the British Empire was essentially a civilising mission, while I had an unusual amount of information for a teenager – courtesy of pan-African school – that contradicted, or at least challenged, much of what she believed. When we argued about the Scramble for Africa she reproduced the old railways argument, the one that goes something like, 'colonialism gave the natives railways, so it was good, the end'.

Another time she went as far as saying that 'Europeans did not actually know Africans were human so you can't *really* blame them for enslaving Africans, whereas when they got to China the humanity [of the Chinese] smacked them in the face.' I was not aware of the Opium Wars at the time, nor did I have much information about the treatment of Chinese indentured labour, so I'm not sure how exactly I countered this. I wish I had known back then that British-ruled Hong Kong was governed by some of the same kind of racist apartheid laws as South Africa and other colonies. In short, the Chinese were treated just like other subject races, albeit for a shorter time period – so clearly British imperialists were not 'smacked in the face' by the humanity of the Chinese, despite the historical achievements of Chinese civilisation. In the end, I think I asked something like 'Why did colonisers and enslavers rape their human property so frequently if they didn't know that they were human?' Anyway . . .

This teacher used to refer to certain boys in our class as 'sandpit boys', meaning to infer that they had the mental aptitudes of five-year-olds playing in a sandpit. These were generally boys who were not fortunate enough to have had the radical community education and, perhaps, the family encouragement that I had benefited from. One of these boys in particular I knew from primary school – he had a mother that was a severe alcoholic and often suffered clear and obvious parental neglect. Rather than investigate what the reasons might be for their lack of confidence and participation in the classroom, the teacher labelled them sandpit boys. By contrast, Anne Taylor – my favourite primary school teacher – went well beyond the call of duty and used to feed this same boy. She even bought him some shoes once. How big a difference a teacher's personal attitudes can make.

I don't think 'chavs' existed as a term back then, but no doubt it was that type of stereotyping of people from less fortunate family circumstances that the form tutor was aiming at when she called them 'sandpit boys'. By association of class, I should have been one of the sandpit boys. After all, was I not on free school meals just like them? Did my clothes and shoes not speak of my family's dire finances? Could you not hear the poverty in my accent and see it in my skin, my walk and my eyes? But I was among the top of the class for all subjects (except art of course!), something which strangely bothered some teachers, this one included, but seemed to spare me the nickname. Nevertheless, I felt a class affinity for the 'sandpit boys'; I felt like I could see what was happening to them and wished I could give them what I'd been given.

During another debate, this teacher compared the exclusion of girls from our lunchtime football games to Jim Crow-era US racism. While I totally accept the severity of gender oppression, this seemed to me a rather odd comparison given that there were no signs excluding girls from the football pitch – let alone lunchtime lynchings – and that the state did not enforce this 'no girls on the pitches' policy, and I said as much to her. What her comment did show was that she was able to recognise how gender conditioning could subtly shape the expectations and behaviours of girls and prevent them from going somewhere that they were not 'really' being prevented from going, for there is no doubt that the boys controlled the football pitch every lunchtime, and would have probably viewed girls trying to play football as an incursion.

My teacher could not, however, understand how young boys from poorer, less educated families came to be intimidated by an education that no one was 'really' preventing them from attaining. She told me confidently that all women had harder lives than any men on the planet (she meant brown and black men, of course), not out of feminist solidarity with the brown and black women of the global south – as you will understand more fully in a moment – but rather to tell me that I was essentially complaining about nothing when I spoke about historic racial injustice.

My relationship with her and a few other teachers meant that school felt like a battleground instead of a joy, a constant war of attrition with people who did not want the best for me but nonetheless were supposed to be educating me. The teachers that were in my corner told me I could not let 'them' win, I could not drop out of school or allow myself to be expelled like so many of my friends. It was almost as if I was representing not just myself but rather that my academic success – and that of one or two others – was a vindication of young black boys as a group. The school, for all its Camden liberalism, knew very well that black students were being expelled at much higher rates than other students, but did not really attempt to investigate the issue. In just one example of how far this ambivalence spread, my sister's sociology teacher told her that when a new group of students joined the school certain teachers would bet, based solely on a child's name before even having met that child, about the likelihood of said child actually finishing school. If the child were named Leon Smith or Wayne Johnson – typical black names – then they would bet against him. More often than not, they were proved right.

All of this is just the background to the final showdown.

During one particular debate in Year Ten, the shit really hit the fan. Some context: there was another teacher in our school who was a member of the Nation of Islam and he ran an extra-curricular history class for black students. It's worth remembering that Spike Lee's Malcolm X film was still in public consciousness and the NOI had also been very visible during the Stephen Lawrence trial, so people tended to be more aware of who the NOI are than they would be today. These extracurricular classes became a source of tension for some teachers and the school temporarily suspended the classes, though they never explained why. I started a petition in response to this suspension and for whatever reason the classes were reinstated. I was never sure if my petition had any effect or not, but I was caught in the act of collecting signatures by the deputy head, who looked rather embarrassed. That same teacher from the NOI had designed a history module called 'Black Peoples of the Americas' that he managed to get onto the school history syllabus. The other teacher declared quite openly that this was her least favourite module and that she hated teaching it. It is in the context of that module that many of our most heated debates about race took place.

One day during the module, we somehow got onto debating the NOI, and she asserted that the 'Nation of Islam was essentially the same as the KKK, but black.' This has become a rather clichéd argument among some white conservatives, and it essentially equates black people who are living under apartheid saying not nice things about white people with a tradition of actual violent terrorism. The message is clear: white people's hurt feelings are conceptually equivalent to black humans' actual lives. No matter that mainstream white anthropology had argued for generations that black people were not human and many societies set up literal human zoos to demonstrate that; no matter that during the era in which the NOI's racial ideology was formed all of Africa was colonised and racial slavery was still in living memory for some; no matter that black people's supposed sub-humanity was enshrined in the founding of the USA and that lynchings were still common when the NOI was founded in the 1930s. None of that context was needed in terms of explaining the appeal of the NOI's ideas. If whiteness is used to legitimise slavery, genocide and colonialism, is it really a surprise that at least a minority of people victimised in this way would turn around and argue that white people were inherently evil?

Anyway, I argued back that no matter what their opinions were on racial evolution – or other flaws for that matter – the NOI had no history of lynching white people, of collecting their body parts as souvenirs, of bombing white churches and of killing children and pregnant women. What's more, the NOI did much good, like cleaning up drug addicts and policing some of America's worst black ghettoes, helping to stop crime (the NOI had indeed sent some its members, unarmed, to challenge the drug dealers in some of the toughest US inner cities). The debate had been raging for pretty much the whole lesson, ranging over various subjects, and I knew the class were siding with the logic of the fifteen-year-old boy rather than the middle-aged university-educated teacher with greying hair. Losing the argument was clearly too much for her to bear and her response was so profoundly racist, even by her standards, that it still shocks me to this day. She blurted out:

'The Ku Klux Klan also stopped crime by killing black people.'

Now I know you are probably reading this in disbelief, but I'll repeat it for clarity and so you can be sure it's not an extended typo.

'The Ku Klux Klan also stopped crime by killing black people.'

Now imagine standing in front of students whom you are supposed to teach, in one of the most multicultural areas in the world, and saying that killing black people, including children, with all the spectacle and pomp of a summer fete, is somehow crime fighting. The genocidal implications of this statement are obvious. I'm sure that she and the many others that think like her would indeed be totally happy to see black humans wiped from the face of the earth. I'm equally sure that for such radicalised extremists having to teach self-assured little black boys who have actually read a few books must be like torture. How many more people like her have to teach children they actually hate, but just happen to never have had their hatred brought to the surface?

I told her to fuck off about ten times in response. My composure was completely gone and the slight arrogance that I had been feeling at outsmarting my teacher had been ripped away from me. Now I felt only rage and hurt. I knew she did not like black people but I had not fully grasped the extent and depth of her hatred before that day. I felt dirty and ashamed, and something that was like confusion but wasn't quite that. Black people have never really been able to understand the revulsion and compulsion to violence that our skin generates in these kinds of people, a hatred so profoundly illogical I doubt even those that feel it can really explain it.

I had the distinct urge to throw my chair at her and I am pretty sure that, had she been a man, I would have done just that and certainly got expelled as a result. The class collectively gasped, a few other students made statements of protest and shook their heads; they knew a line had been crossed. She looked at me, resigned. She had said it now, it was out in the open and there was no use in apologising, so she did not even bother trying. I can't remember how the rest of the lesson panned out and whether I stormed out of the class, I just remember swearing repeatedly, shouting and really wanting to punch her in her bright-red face but knowing that hitting a woman, even a woman that wished death on me, was not something I could bring myself to do. I also feel like there was something approaching relief in both her and me; I had always wanted her to expose herself fully and she had trodden carefully, sort of, but clearly she found restraining her real opinion quite challenging. Now I had the full truth, though it did indeed taste bitter.

Her comments became a mini scandal, students that were not even in the class seemed to know before the end of the day. I went home that night and when I told my mum what had happened I realised that I obviously had to act; something about repeating her words made their full absurdity clearer and gave the situation an urgency. My mum was in total agreement and support. I decided to write to the school governors to complain. Surely someone with beliefs like this, expressed so publicly and openly, could not be permitted to go on teaching? How could she possibly teach people she believed to be half-human, innately criminal savages? I had already learned to distrust the levers of power and so doubted that she would actually lose her job or face any severe disciplinary action, but I at least hoped that the governors would do *something*.

What actually transpired was a profound lesson in institutionalised racism and the protection of abusers by power. The headmaster somehow ended up with my letter and he called me into his office for a meeting. I explained the events to him roughly as I have retold them here and he sheepishly promised to talk to the teacher in question and clear it up. It was instantly obvious to me that he would have preferred me not to have put him in this 'uncomfortable' position, of, you know, actually having to do part of his job and administer justice. Then, in a moment of almost unwriteable irony, he gave me – or should I say tried to bribe me with – a book about Martin Luther King. I still have the book somewhere, it's called *The Children*.

The incident became, for me, the perfect embodiment of Dr King's statement to the effect that the greatest impediment to racial justice in America was not the open bigot but the indifferent and cowardly white liberal, more concerned with a quiet life than justice. There is no question that my Martin Luther King-reading headmaster would have thought of himself as a liberal, as open-minded and certainly non-racist, and maybe he was all of those things, yet he chose to do nothing when confronted by such profound abuse.

A few weeks passed and I had not heard back from the headteacher, so I went to see him. He told me that the teacher had denied saying what I was accusing her of saying, but had admitted to playing 'devil's advocate', and essentially that he was not going to take any action, not even by asking the other thirty or so children in the class that day what had happened. She would keep her job, there would not even be so much as a hearing and from what I was told – though it may be an urban myth – she was promoted after I left the school. I am not suggesting that the school thought so much of me that it waited till I left before promoting her, but rather that they did not care enough about her white-supremacist views to not promote her. Perhaps if I had been a 'rich' kid with a hotshot lawyer for a parent and the ability to go to the press and generate a story – kind of like I am now! – the school may have felt compelled to do something, who knows? But not only was I black, I was also poor and had no such connections. I'm also pretty sure that had the teacher from the Nation of Islam said that 'Nazis stopped greed by killing Jews' he would – quite rightly – have been seen as a psychopath and lost his job immediately.

I left the whole affair wondering how many other teachers thought like this one and what impact does their racism have on their ability to effectively teach students from Britain's former colonies?

My mum and I demanded that I be removed from her classes. The school reluctantly, but perhaps also a little relieved, agreed. I never forgot the larger lesson, though; many self-proclaimed, selectively reading, MLK-quoting liberals will choose to support or at least ignore injustice rather than rock the boat when in positions of power. The following year, when I took my GCSEs, I was still extremely angry about the whole affair and so I chose to write a protest on the exam paper of the subject she taught me about the 'cultural and ethical bias of my teaching' rather than to do the actual exam. I still remember the exam board observer seeing me sat, arms folded, trying to encourage me to 'have a go'. It was understandable that she assumed I was a struggling student rather than a wannabe revolutionary and I really wanted to let her know why I was not writing but of course I could not, so I wrote the same protest passage out over and over again so it would look like I was at least trying. I got a U as a result and, despite all my other A stars, it is probably the exam grade I am still most proud of.

Was my experience in secondary school unique, isolated, the result of one bad apple, or is there a general pattern of conflict between teachers and black students? Is there any evidence that the systemic discrimination against black students that we saw in action in primary school continues into secondary school? Unfortunately, the answer to the second question is a resounding yes.

In academic circles concerned with race and education there are two 'buzz' phrases, 'the exclusion gap' and 'the attainment gap'. The exclusion gap refers to the fact that black students have historically been always at least three times as likely to be excluded as their white counterparts, some years six times as likely. However, there is a significant difference between the rates of expulsion for black students of Caribbean origin and those hailing from Africa, with 'British-African' students being far less likely, especially in recent years, to be expelled than those whose great-grandparents came from the Caribbean. At first glance, this difference in outcomes between two different types of black students, which is also replicated in academic attainment, might seem to confirm certain stereotypes of 'Caribbean' communities; however, at three or more generations removed many of these 'Caribbean' children have never even been to the Caribbean so what we are really comparing is fourth generation black English children with children mostly born in the UK to African parents. Also a close inspection of the relevant research shows that a more sophisticated explanation will be needed. For example, a 2006 DfES report into the exclusion gap found that:

- Black Caribbean pupils are three times more likely to be excluded from school than white pupils.
- When FSM and SEN were taken into account, black Caribbean pupils were still 2.6 times more likely to be excluded from school than white pupils.
- Excluded black pupils were less likely to fit the typical profile of excluded white pupils (such as having SEN, FSM, longer and more numerous previous exclusions, poor attendance records, criminal records or being looked-after children).[1]

In translation, this means that even black English students of Caribbean origin from less 'challenging' family circumstances, even those with decent grades and good previous attendance, who have displayed better previous behaviour, are still far more likely to be permanently expelled than other ethnic groups. Why is this such a huge problem? Because permanent exclusion from school virtually dictates the future of a person's life. In the words of Martin Narey, former Director General of HM Prison Service, 'The 13,000 young people excluded from school each year might as well be given a date by which to join the prison service some time later down the line.'

The 2006 DfES report concluded

> The clear message of the literature is that, to a significant extent, the exclusion gap is caused by largely unwitting, but systematic, racial discrimination in the application of disciplinary and exclusions policies. Many cite this as evidence of Institutional Racism. The Department has a legal duty to eliminate such discrimination under the Race Relations (Amendment) Act 2000.

So the empirical data and government studies pretty much echo what black people have been saying ever since the 1960s; that black students in particular have been treated unfairly within the British education system for decades, beyond just the usual challenges of being poor, and that little to nothing has been done about it, beyond lip service. Of course, many will still claim, even when presented with the hard data and thorough investigations, that it is all in black pupils' and parents' imaginations or that, yep, you guessed it, we just have 'a chip on our shoulder'.

The 'attainment gap' refers to differentials in performance between ethnic groups in schools and what could cause them. Before we look at the evidence I would like to point out the obvious fact that I am not suggesting that all differential achievement between human groups in a given area of activity is the result of discrimination, what I am arguing is that where clear evidence of discrimination exists it should be removed, and then if individuals and/or groups do not take advantage of the opportunities afforded, we can talk more clearly about personal responsibility. As you already saw in Chapter Three, under the old empirical baseline assessments black students actually outperformed their white counterparts, but now that the mode of assessment has been left entirely to teachers' whims that is no longer the case. You also saw how much teachers under-assess black students' intelligence throughout primary school to age eleven. This pattern unsurprisingly continues throughout secondary school.

Warwick University investigated teacher bias by observing the proportion of black Caribbean pupils who are entered for higher-tier maths and science tests at age 14.[2] Being entered for higher tier allows a student to be awarded as high as an A*, whereas being entered for foundation means the highest possible mark is a C. They found that, at the same level of previous academic attainment, for every three white British pupils entered for higher tier only two black 'Caribbean' pupils were entered. These figures hold even when we account for gender, free school meals, maternal education, home ownership and single-parent households, in addition to their prior academic attainment. Once again, teachers' assessments underestimate the academic potential of black students.

Both the Warwick study and the Bristol one examined in Chapter Three looked at every state school in the UK, painting a bleak picture for black students. This means that under the current system of setting and tiering it is literally mathematically impossible for above a certain percentage of black students to get top-grade GSCEs, as they are significantly less likely to be entered for higher-tier GCSE papers even when they have the same previous academic attainment and family circumstances as white students.

To recap the odds stacked against black children in British schools, black students are:

- Under-assessed at five
- Dramatically under-assessed at eleven
- Significantly less likely to be entered for higher-tier exams when they have the same previous academic attainment
- 2.6 times more likely to be expelled even when control factors are taken into account

Despite all of this, in recent years, in particular since 2013, black children of African origin have surpassed the national average in GCSE attainment, with some 'national' groups such as children of Nigerian and Ghanaian origin faring particularly well. This is extraordinarily impressive given that children of African origin are concentrated in Hackney, Peckham and Croydon/Thornton Heath, which are some of the poorest and toughest regions of the capital. If we were not so addicted to social Darwinism, black African students might well serve as an example for other working-class students to imitate.

Yet despite all of the actual evidence of obvious neglect and/ or stereotyping of black students regardless of class, over the past few years a trend can be observed in the British media of positing Working-Class White Boys as the victims of the education system:

THE LOST BOYS: HOW THE WHITE WORKING CLASS GOT
    LEFT BEHIND – *New Statesmen*[3]
IT'S NO SURPRISE THAT WHITE WORKING CLASS BOYS DO
    BADLY AT SCHOOL: THEIR MORALE IS LIKELY TO BE LOWER
    THAN MORE SUPERFICIALLY 'OPPRESSED' GROUPS –Tim Lott,
    Guardian[4]
WHITE BOYS LET DOWN BY THE EDUCATION SYSTEM – *Daily
    Telegraph*[5]
WHITE BOYS 'ARE BEING LEFT' BEHIND BY THE EDUCATION
    SYSTEM – *Daily Mail*[6]

After noting the obviously sympathetic tone of the articles
across the print media spectrum, from the *Guardian* to the
Mail, in marked contrast to the manner in which some of the
publications report about so called ethnic minorities, we are
left to examine the actual data and ask if these headlines are
accurate. It's interesting that all of the articles in question
choose to focus on race rather than the British class system as a
whole, as it's a matter of fact that the gap between white working-class boys and other ethnic groups in the same social class
is far smaller than the gap between poor white boys and the
white middle class. The message from these journalists and
those that pedalled this narrative is clear: it's fine for working
class white kids to fail relative to the white middle-classes – but
they should never fall behind the darkies. Furthermore 'working class' here is being defined only as those on free school
meals, which does not include 86 per cent of the white population.[7] Students from poorer backgrounds who receive free
school meals do much less well in exams than students who do
not; this holds true for every ethnic group in Britain. Girls also
do better than boys; again, this holds true for every ethnic
group.

I'd like to be clear at this point that I agree working-class white boys have been neglected at every stage of British society – that is what classism is and does – so it's not support and sympathy for working-class white boys that I have an issue with, it's the notable lack of support for similar issues when they affect other demographics within the 'working class' more clearly, and also the ludicrous assertion that the white working class are being neglected because they are white. Of course, within British society the working class is taken to mean the white working class more often than not anyway.

It won't matter how many empirical studies you can provide, including the DfES's own report, or studies that have looked at every school in the UK or decades of academics and leading experts in the field showing empirically and measurably that anti-black racism is still a serious systemic issue adversely affecting outcomes for black students; many will do intellectual backflips to conclude something else is the cause, even when the black person talking to them is already successful and educated and therefore has nothing to 'make excuses' about. Naturally, it's far easier to believe that there is just something wrong with black people than really accept the scale of the mundane injustice of everyday black life in Britain; decades of unfair expulsions, potential wasted and dreams derailed.

In this national context and against this backdrop of history my experiences in school start to make complete sense, not as isolated incidents with a few bad apples but rather as systemic problems. There is an inability among some white teachers to be able to cope with the 'wrong' student being top of the class, and said teachers deploy a range of actions to mitigate it, from open bullying – my magic button – to sly attempts to hold me back – special needs group – hitting me, sending me out, telling me I am unable to read things well within my capacity, even advocating genocide at the extreme. Because I went to a very mixed school with lots of middle-class white children, unlike my cousins in Harlesden and Brixton, I was able to see even more clearly that my treatment by these teachers stood in marked difference to the manner in which similarly 'smart' white and even other non-black children were treated.

I was one of the lucky few who had the right family and community support to make it through the tumult, but what about all those other black children represented in this data? All those unfairly marked down, the gifts and talents they have overlooked, shoved into lower tiers where they really have no place being, but where they are now locked into a limited range of possible achievement that will affect their entire life. For some this will all sound a little conspiratorial, but the scholarship is pretty clear if you bother to read it. My individual experience is just one number among all those graphs and lines.

Black American culture was an ever-present force in my upbringing. In our house James Brown got as much play as Dennis Brown, and Billie Holiday, Ella Fitzgerald, Aretha (she needs no second name), Nina Simone and all the icons of black American music were names that I knew as well as any reggae artist. This influence was so strong that the first time I performed publicly it was to dance to Ray Charles's song 'Shake a Tail Feather' with my siblings and cousins on stage at the Hackney Empire, in front of a packed house. Black British identity more broadly was and is fashioned out of the material left from our home countries – Ghana, Jamaica, Nigeria – our concrete experiences and reality here in Britain, and from the inspiration of other black populations, mostly America. We grew up with Malcolm and Martin posters on the wall at the barber's and in our food shops, our parents used the language of black power for their own ends and even set up their own Black Panther parties, we watched the *Cosby Show* and *A Different World* and both delighted in and envied HBCUs, the Historically Black Colleges and Universities, wishing we had our own.

For those of us that are Caribbean, we grew up with cousins in New York sending us the latest DJ Clue or Red Alert mix tape, or VCRs (remember those?) of the latest stage shows where US rappers and Jamaican dancehall artists had performed on the same bills, usually somewhere in Brooklyn. We experienced black American culture not as a foreign presence but as an extension of ourselves; our overseas family who were articulating to the world what we felt we were going through too.

While there are huge differences in the experiences of black Britain and black America, we focused on the similarities and solidarities. We watched LA react to the Rodney King verdict and we remembered Brixton or Handsworth in 1985; we transposed Cliff Huxtable into an old West Indian granddad and we knew that Kool Herc, Biggie's mother, Pete Rock and KRS-One were from 'yard' too. We know Colin Powell is also of Jamaican origin, but we don't claim him.

The black bookstores that could once be found in every major area of African-Caribbean settlement in Britain were filled with volumes of scholarship from as many black Americans as Caribbeans or West Africans, just as our record stores gave prominence to Jamaican music but you could certainly find any soul, RnB or hip hop you would need at Red Records in Brixton, Body Groove in Tottenham or Honest John's in Ladbroke Grove. Thanks to gentrification and changing technology, two of these three iconic stores are now gone. The legendary Blacker Dread record shop in Brixton, that for so long serviced the UK's premier sound systems and the public alike with their 7s and 12s of the latest music from Jamaica, has similarly vanished.

The next time I remember stepping on stage I was ten and I rapped 'Slam' by the Queens hip hop group Onyx and 'Sound Boy Killing' by Jamaican dancehall artist Mega Banton to my, definitely confused, classmates and teachers at an end of year talent contest. This performance symbolised the syncretism of my generation; British-born to British-born parents, we started to identify with the US as much as the Caribbean. As a result of this decline in exclusively Caribbean, predominantly Jamaican influence, we produced new worldviews, attitudes and art, or at least a new negotiation between the 'roots, reggae and rasta' of our parents and the new dancehall, hip hop and RnB coming from the ghettoes of Jamaica and the states.

During my teenage years, local UK variants of MC-based cultures also rose to prominence via an extensive network of 'pirate' (illegal) radio stations and club nights. UK garage brought a Jamaican sound system aesthetic and set up to an originally American genre, mirroring the fusion that gave birth to hip hop. There was also the uniquely UK-based hybrid 'jungle', which fused Jamaican reggae and dancehall with the Amen break – the same drum break that is the basis of much legendary hip hop – and UK rave music. I loved jungle for the rawness of the baselines, the speed and intensity of the drums and the incredible use of samples that gave it a totally unique sound, a sound laced with the grit of Bristol and London's council estates echoing the indelible, irreversible influence of Caribbean ex-pats on British music. Jungle was a stamp on the face of safe and respectable British music and it was that grit that attracted the rude boys and gangsters from every hood to come to jungle raves. Guys did not dress up, they came to a jungle dance as if they'd come straight off the block; guns were brandished and shots were fired, but as jungle started to cross over it morphed into a safer, softer variant of itself that seemed to me quite consciously designed to appeal to a whiter, more middle-class audience and to keep the rude boys away. I think it worked on both counts. Naturally the British media and law enforcement took ample opportunity to racialise the gangster minority as a general black problem in a way they never did with the drug overdoses and sexual assaults that remain a common issue throughout the UK rave and festival culture.

Garage raves had some of the same problems with violence as jungle did despite the fact that the atmosphere was totally different. Garage blended soulful and smooth samples with a much slower, much more danceable beat than jungle and consequently garage raves were far better dressed and had a significantly greater female presence. I went to more garage raves than I could possibly count, long before I was supposed to; at fifteen years old I was at the now-legendary Pure Silk New Year's Eve 1999 rave at Wembley conference centre, with 10,000 other revellers. It was £50 a ticket, back then! Garage was big money, street dudes cleaned a lot of cash, and young black entrepreneurs, DJs and MCs became hood rich long before the mainstream had taken any notice. Me and my homies made unforgettable memories.

I MC'd over jungle and garage on my father's sound system between the ages of thirteen and sixteen. I still love dancehall, and Bounty Killer remains one of my top ten lyricists in any genre, but none of these genres or scenes would influence me quite like hip hop did. My dad and stepdad had acquainted me with NWA, Public Enemy and Big Daddy Kane but I was too young when they were at their peak to really experience them in all their glory. Being born in 1983 meant I was just seven when Public Enemy's legendary album *Fear of a Black Planet* was released, but my parents played it so much I memorised almost all of the words.

In the mid 1990s, when I started to get hairs on my chest and I got my first job, I struck out and found my 'own' hip hop. I was thirteen years old, working for £20 per day on Saturdays at a local DIY store, and any week that my family did not need the money I'd be off to the West End to the nerdy record stores that stocked hard-to-get US imports, or up to our bootlegger in Tottenham, and I'd spend my entire £20 on CDs. I had two 'bootleggers' (a person that copies and sells black market CDs), both of them black Americans, one from Roxbury in Boston and the other from Brownsville in New York, two of America's most notorious ghettoes. The stories they told us of 'the hood' back home only added authenticity to the purchases. It's probably hard for people under twenty to remember now what a precious commodity a CD was, but I felt absolutely no qualms about forgoing a few meals so that I could get the latest US rap release. I had no other access to the music; these records were not played on the radio, not even by the hip hop specialists, and there was no Internet, there was only the import CD shop and the bootlegger.

As my age group searched for new meanings and identities, American rap provided a soundtrack for what seemed like a reality we shared with our black American cousins: we lived in public housing, some of our uncles and fathers went to prison, we were relatively poor, we knew people who had been shot and stabbed – and likely those doing the shooting and stabbing too – just as we knew members of our community who had been killed and brutalised by the police and never gotten a hint of justice. At its best, our identification with black American culture helped give us the political strength and insights around which to organise, in the same way that my gangster uncles had come of age politically by reading Huey Newton and watching Muhammad Ali interviews. It instilled in us a new vocabulary and new ways of understanding race and class and inculcated a sense of shared blackness, a sense that we were not alone in facing the challenges coming our way. But our over-identification with black American culture was also not without its challenges and problems. We struggled to find our own voice based on our own realities and many of us MCs even rapped in fake American accents, as I did until I was thirteen. One day, as I showed my older sister my new bars, tinged with Staten Island slang and drawl, she told me off for being fake and made me try rapping in my own voice. I had become so enthralled with US hip hop that I found it difficult to even conceive of spitting in my own accent, despite the fact that the London Posse and others had been doing so on a national scale for years already. I felt that a British accent was not authentic enough, perhaps even not 'black' enough to be real hip hop. Luckily, I got over this crisis within a week and have never rapped as if I were American since.

Many of us have also chosen to adopt some of the destructive consequences of the black American experience; the best two examples I can think of are the attempt to create 'Bloods and Crips' style gangs in London and the uncritical adoption of the word 'nigga'. Gangs have a number of sociological, economic, cultural and interpersonal sources, they do not arise in a vacuum, and the Bloods and the Crips emerged directly in the wake of and fall out from black American attempts at mass political self-organisation during the 1960s. While there are certainly some economic and political similarities between Compton and Brixton, and there was certainly fall out from black British attempts to self-organise in the 1980s, the adoption of 'colours' in South London in the mid-2000s was as much an imitation of US corporate rap culture as it was the result of any directly collapsing political movements and deindustrialisation. Of course, London's gangs, despite all media exaggerations, have come nowhere near the levels of violence of those in USA – or of those in Northern Ireland for that matter – but the fact that we chose to identify with west coast American gangs rather than London's own centuries-long gang history or even the infamous Shower Posse of Kingston and New York that had a presence in London during the 1990s speaks volumes about how influential black American culture had become.

I make no secret of the fact I used to use the word 'nigger' in my music every other sentence, and indeed the only song of mine to get played on mainstream radio had the tagline 'Shakespeare with a nigger twist'. However, by my second album I had all but given up using the word for a number of reasons. First, it made me extremely uncomfortable to have crowds of young white people scream 'nigger' back at me, so that just was not going to work. Second, one of my elders gave me a bloody good talking to about its use – shout out to Uncle Toyin – but lastly, I just decided it was fake and destructive for us to call each other 'nigger' and pretend it was a term of endearment. While they are our extended family, we are not black Americans, we are Caribbean and African ex-pats living in UK and I concluded, based on my studies of history, that while racism was everywhere, nowhere was the attempt to create this nigger – a figment of the white imagination – more intense, brutal and long lasting than in the USA.

I came to feel that even in the American context the use of the 'n word' had become rather gimmicky, shorn of all original meaning and divorced from the context of its birth. The nigger; a fictional subhuman creation of the white racist imagination; a fiction that could justify actual humans being worked like beasts of burden, redlined,[1] segregated, executed by law enforcement, experimented on by medical science,[2] exhibited in zoos, bombed by their own government,[3] having their towns torched by terrorists and having to fight for almost a century to earn the right to shit in the same toilets as white people. All of that vanishes from view with the way nigger is now used in hip hop.

Now the nigger is presented as an autonomous black creation, a self-styled ghetto godfather rather than as the echo of white-supremacist perversion and relative black powerlessness that it is.[4] Young black boys and men know this to be true despite what we may tell ourselves; no truly self-loving people celebrate their own death, especially not for the entertainment of the primary beneficiaries of that death. I often work in prisons where, as you can imagine, a large section of those I work with are young black men. Some of the work we do is around creative writing and the young men write raps invariably filled with boasts about how many niggers they will shank and shoot. I don't judge them, how could I? I used to carry knives and I even used to rap quite like that even though I knew better, I simply ask them what they would think if I rapped about killing honkies. I remind them that my white family are poor, that we come from Scotland, that Glasgow is often more violent than London and that twenty million plus Russians alone died in the 'white on white violence' of the Second World War.

Despite all of this and without exception, all of the young black boys I have put this question to have one of two reactions; they either laugh out loud at the absurdity of rapping about killing honkies or they tell me that it would be racist for me – a man of mixed heritage that used to rap about niggers – to rap about killing honkies. They can never explain a logical reason as to why that is the case but the inference is clear; these young black men, like the world at large, value white life over black life. Though I do recognise the argument is slightly flawed in that even though I am technically 'mixed race' I am racialised as black and thus it would still be perceived as a black man rapping about killing white people, it has nonetheless been a revealing experiment.

I must confess, though, that I am quite the hypocrite on this issue – and much else of course. I still love so-called gangsta rap though I recognise the oddity of a black icon boasting about killing other 'niggers' for the entertainment of little Hank in Milwaukee; niggerish-ness can be a multi-billion-dollar commodity as long as it makes no mention of its relationship to whiteness. It's not that I wish the word to be deleted nor even that I wish people would stop saying it; as I mentioned, much of my favourite music ever is 'gangsta rap' and I accept that for a whole host of reasons violence is a fundamental part of human entertainment, from Shakespearean tragedies to Korean revenge cinema to mixed martial arts – all of which I also enjoy.

It's rather that I wish there was a greater range of voices making their way into mainstream popular culture – as has started to happen again a little with the likes of J. Cole and Kendrick Lamar – and that I hope out of respect for the ancestors and the struggles they fought that the context and pain attached to that word is not drowned in a sea of pool parties and post-racial fantasy.

It is also compelling that African and Caribbean music – that is music made in a black context primarily for black consumption – does not use the word nigger, and even the most 'gangsta' of Jamaican dancehall artists can be found offering profound political analysis of Jamaica's class dynamics and the corruption of its elites, something that has been almost entirely absent from 'mainstream' hip hop over the past twenty years. It's equally interesting to ask why reggae music has made such obvious inroads right across Africa over and above US hip hop, despite not having anywhere near the same level of corporate backing. What would the effect be on black musical production if black Africans had the same disposable incomes as white Americans? How does the self-perception of black people in majority black societies affect their worldviews and cultural tastes, if at all?

We may want to remember that after returning from his first trip to Africa, Richard Pryor announced that he would never call another black man a nigger again so long as he lived. Travelling around the continent, he marvelled at the fact that there were 'no niggers there' and added that in his time there, 'I have not said it [the word], I have not even thought it.' While uttered in the guise of comedy, this might be one of the most profound reflections on the black condition ever offered. Pryor understood instantly that the metaphysical category of the nigger could not possibly have the same meaning in Africa as it did in America.

While the physical legacies of white supremacy in Africa are clear enough, from the skin bleaching to the colonial borders to the languages of government, or from the segregation that is still so apparent in the former settler colonies, the state of spiritual and cultural crisis that Pryor denotes with the appellation 'nigger' simply does not seem to exist in the same way for Africans. Perhaps it's just diaspora romanticism, but I felt that same feeling when I first set foot on the continent. It's a quality that cannot be explained unless you have experienced both states. People who have experienced niggerisation or lifelong racism often walk as if they are apologising for their existence; it was only when I saw black people that did not walk that way that this became clear to me.

To a degree, I also feel this same unquantifiable phenomenon in the Caribbean; there is a cultural and spiritual freedom that people have growing up in a place that they feel belongs to them and they belong to, however severe the material challenges in that place may be. It's worth mentioning that Pryor was among the pioneers of the artistic use of the word, which he used in his comedy to shock at a time when everyone was aware of the dehumanisation implied by the word 'nigger'. Yet here he was realising what racism had done to the black American soul, how it had made nigger an acceptable denotation of actual human beings and just how destructive that was.

A friend of mine once told me a story that exemplified the importance of the way we use words and the images and ideas we attach to them. He comes from Brixton though he is of Nigerian, specifically Yoruba, heritage, he has been to prison and all that jazz, and one day he was on the block with the youngers when the following ensued.

He was lecturing the youngsters about traditional Yoruba values, values he admitted to having violated by being on 'the roads' and going to prison. He asked the group of young men he was talking to – also of Yoruba origin – to imagine themselves as 'black youts' and tell him what associations went with being a 'black yout'. He then asked them to see themselves as 'Yoruba men' and asked them what associations went with that identity. The images they associated with each identity were diametrically opposed. When he asked them if they could see 'Yoruba men' going to prison for selling crack or stabbing each other they said no; when he asked if they could see a black yout doing those things they all answered yes. Obviously Yoruba men are perfectly capable of any number of behaviours in reality, but the automatic associations are nonetheless interesting. If 'black yout' can carry such connotations for black youth themselves, how much more severe would the word 'nigger' be? And how much worse might the perceptions of people that are not black youth themselves be?

My friend is not a social scientist, smart as he is he barely finished school, but this exercise was a masterstroke and I often wonder if the youngers in question have continued to ponder the profound insight they stumbled upon that day.

US hip hop has fundamentally shaped the attitudes, tastes, language, fashion, political consciousness and general swag of my generation across racial and economic lines, though this affiliation is clearly most pronounced within the black community. However, today is a unique time to be a UK hip hop artist. Since the birth of hip hop and for decades afterwards, UK industry gatekeepers at radio and TV pretty much ignored domestic MCs – with a few notable exceptions – always preferring to support US artists over and above – rather than as well as – local artists. I think this partly has to do with the simple fact that US hip hop was plainly of better musical and lyrical quality, and it must be honestly acknowledged that the classic

US hip hop albums are still the benchmark, still 'the canon' for anyone entering the field. However, the reasons are also deeper than simple musical quality and stem from the situation of black culture in Britain.

We as black Brits, recent migrants, floating somewhere in the mid-Atlantic, not quite really Caribbean any more with newer arrivals from Africa itself and certainly not American, but not yet confident enough to speak with our own voice, alienated from the nation in which we were born, found ourselves relegated even in our own tastes to a second-class blackness. We preferred 'authentic' Jamaican reggae to the British-Caribbean version, and we preferred 'authentic' US hip hop to UK hip hop, unlike the French, who by the 1990s had developed a thriving domestic hip hop scene with scores of successful rappers, producers and directors. Why did something similar not occur in the UK during the 1990s, despite our much closer connection to the US, being both English speakers and having literal cousins in the States? Ironically, part of the reason is French nationalism. A drive to preserve the French language commands that 40 per cent of music on national radio be in French, which gave a platform to French hip hop in a way that was just not there in the UK. The British music industry, particularly in the area of 'urban' (read black) music, has mostly been happy to just import whatever the American parent corporations of the major labels are selling.

Then, in the early 2000s, things started to change dramatically. It really began with a cable TV station called Channel U that would play pretty much any music video it was sent. While this sometimes meant that the quality was laughably bad, that was part of its appeal and the channel nevertheless gave a regular nationwide platform to UK rappers like myself for the first time. Then the Internet happened and MC-based platforms like Fire in the Booth, SBTV and Grime Daily took UK rappers and grime MCs to a national and then global audience, without the filtration system of the music industry. The results of this both domestically and internationally have been astounding. If you look at the reaction videos on YouTube to mine and other UK rappers' 'Fire in the Booth's, you will find scores of Americans 'reacting' to the lyrics. I also think that, as in France, nationalism is ironically at play in the UK in that I don't think it's a coincidence that part of grime music's recent success has been underpinned by journalists' ability to claim it as an authentically 'British' form of music, even if the 'truly British' status of its dominant practitioners is still in question.

Why is this important to this chapter? Because for the first time in my life black British musicians and rappers in particular are able to communicate across the pond and indeed to the world without the direct interference of corporate media – YouTube and social media notwithstanding – and without the direct control of the apparatus of the UK music industry. The results of this so far have been very interesting. Through artists like Stormzy and Skepta, through dramas like *Topboy* reaching a wide audience, through activist collaboration – mainly via Black Lives Matter – and through social media, black Britain has joined the voices stirring culture and politics into the cauldron that is the black Atlantic in a more sustained way than ever before. While the scholars of yesteryear (Hall, Gilroy etc.) and even our parents' music (lovers rock and rare groove) were arguably of far greater quality than that produced by today's generation they did not, unfortunately, have the Internet. There have been pioneering successful artists before, like Soul2Soul, and Smiley Culture had a number one rapping in Cockney and Jamaican accents way back in 1985, but none of this led to a sustained slew of household names. Scores of rappers who, if born just a decade earlier, would have been told by some dickhead A&R

'we don't know how to market you' and thus relegated to the dustbin, now have viable solo touring careers, with the biggest ones selling out the nation's largest arenas.

That it took the relative consumer freedom of the Internet for this situation to arise is by no means a coincidence. Now that radio has lost a lot of its power, though by no means all, it's clear that audiences of all ethnic backgrounds want authenticity, talent and rawness. And so Stormzy, Skepta, Kano, JME, Giggs, Wretch, Lady Leshurr, Wiley – in short a whole bunch of black artists from 'the hood' – have become the most popular MCs in the country without having to make the corny kind of pop music that an A&R would have told them was necessary to get on the radio back in the day. There has been no need to limit it to one or two 'urban' artists at a time, just as there was never a need to limit the amount of skinny-jeaned white guitar bands. Young artists like Dave are now free to make searing critiques of the prime minister, as he did on his song 'Question Time', and not have to worry about getting on the radio because he can get millions of views and streams on Spotify and YouTube – his first headline tour sold out in a day. Older artists like Lowkey can make critiques of the War on Terror, get millions of views on YouTube and sell thousands of tickets all without a label or radio play.

That the two most successful UK MCs – Stormzy and Skepta – are both of West African rather than Caribbean heritage reflects a demographic shift within the black British population away from Caribbeans being the majority and away from the Caribbean-centric cultural orientation that was the norm when I was growing up. It also speaks to a new-found self confidence in British West Africans.

These musical and cultural sea changes have led to a vastly different perception of Britain in the US. When I first visited New York in 2001 I went to stay with my friend's cousins in the

Bronx. I spent time hanging out on the block there and people noticed my obvious hip hop 'swag' but would then be thoroughly confused when they heard a British accent. It was not unusual to be asked 'Yo, are there black people in England?' or 'Do you know the Queen?' Of course the latter question is just silliness, but the former reflects a genuine ignorance; after all, how would an American in 2001 have possibly known that there were over a million black people living in the UK? Certainly they would not have garnered this from the UK's cultural output. But when I travel to the US these days, New York included, no one asks me such questions any more and people seem aware that there is a hip hop scene, a black population and even 'hoods' over here in the UK.

Even the largest American online hip hop platforms, like The Breakfast Club, Vlad TV and Sway, have recognised this changing trend and have had UK guests on their shows. When I was growing up it seemed that our bigger, cooler American cousins were not even aware we existed, let alone how much we looked up to them; now a transatlantic dialogue facilitated by the web is starting to change the one-way flow of culture and perspective and is producing some interesting currents. Even though we very much admire our black American cousins, we are not punks either, and some signs of natural conflict have started to arise as a result of these transnational black dialogues . . .

In 2012, I was at the Hay Festival of Literature and the Arts, sat among a huge audience watching *Sing Your Song*, the documentary about the life of legendary civil rights activist and singer Harry Belafonte. After the documentary had finished, Harry came on stage to rapturous applause and took his seat next to the Labour MP David Lammy, who would interview him post-screening. I don't recall that much of the interview but I remember Harry's typically charismatic recounting of near-death experiences during the civil rights struggle, his reflections on married life and much more as you would expect to come from such a discussion and such a life. However, when the questions passed to the audience something strange occurred that has really stuck with me.

Harry's discussion with David had touched on mass incarceration and the structural pathologies America is still enforcing so many decades after the days when Harry stood shoulder to shoulder with Dr King. During the questions, the only other black person I could spot in the audience – it is Hay-on-Wye after all – got up to ask a question. She put it to Harry that black Britons were even more disproportionately incarcerated vis-à-vis their white countrymen and women than black Americans, and asked for his thoughts on that fact. To my shock and disappointment, rather than engage with the sister around a critical examination of transatlantic white supremacy – it was British colonists that set in motion America's racial governance after all – Harry told her that she was wrong, that no one was as disproportionately locked up as black Americans, and though I can't recall his exact words he essentially brushed off her point as if it were ridiculous and made no attempt to draw any parallels between the US system of racism and that of the UK, despite their obvious historical connections. I won't go as far as to say that he suggested that there is no racism in the UK but given the time and place that was certainly how it felt. The sister was of course correct; while black Americans are far more likely to be incarcerated than black Brits because America locks up its population in general at far higher rates than Britain, black Britons are seven to nine times more likely – the data fluctuates – to go to prison than their white co-citizens,[5] and they are treated more harshly at every stage of the criminal justice system in the UK.[6] While we are here it's worth noting that indigenous Australians are in absolute terms even more disproportionately incarcerated than black Americans;[7] this is not to negate, contrast or compare, just a statement of fact that should be more known.

Anyway, I was really enraged by Harry's dismissal and felt an urge to stand up and shout out in support of the sister, and in hindsight I am kind of angry that I did not. Here we had a civil rights legend being applauded by an overwhelmingly white British audience for his truly quite remarkable history of anti-racist activism, a man with credibility and stature, a contemporary and friend of some of the giants of American culture, lacking local knowledge and therefore dismissing a valid concern. I'm sure it was just ignorance on Harry's part, but I did feel a little like he had put an 'uppity negro' back in her place. I could tell from how the sister's demeanour shrank at Harry's response that she felt it too. Surely if the audience in question were truly genuine in their anti-racist convictions, they would have been only too thrilled to have a man of Harry's stature offer strategies for tackling the institutional racism of their own society. As it was, this potential exchange was missed. Of course, I cannot speak for nor generalise about that audience but knowing British politics I can make some educated guesses, and it is fascinating to note that it was one of two black people in the crowd that offered the only question that drew those parallels.

As I looked around the room, I thought about how much there was to unpack in this one little event that spoke to the contradictions of race and white supremacy in the US and the UK. On the one hand, you have the long tradition of British liberals showering praise on black American activists, from Martin to Ali to Baldwin and even sometimes Malcolm. British media has consistently made great documentaries on the heroes of the civil rights movement, praising their courage and they were even invited into the hallowed halls of the British academy at a time when black British faces were all but absent from them. You see, for much of Britain, America is where racism happens, and Britain is then by definition not racist because, you know, 'it's not as racist as America'. This is a totally moot and rather idiotic point, as no two countries have the same history and thus no two countries have the same systems of social control, thus no two countries in essence have the same racisms. While British liberals may praise all the Dr Kings in the world, this does not necessarily stop them from reproducing and/or administering the domestic racial hierarchy effectively.

For this reason, most people in Britain, if they know anything about racial injustice at all, are likely to be far more well aware of American issues and history than those on their doorstep, and this includes black people. They are more likely to know of the Alabama church bombing than of New Cross, more likely to know the name Rodney King than Cynthia Jarret, more likely to know Jesse Jackson than Bernie Grant.

It's a shame that Harry was ignorant of the facts, but to me his reluctance to even engage with Britain's racism seems to reflect a larger trend of some successful and well-off black Americans, who conclude based on their privileged experience alone that Europe is some kind of racial paradise. The most famous of these would be other greats like James Baldwin and Richard Wright, who understandably fled to Paris to escape US racism, and the most recent was Samuel L. Jackson, who went on Hot 97 radio in New York in 2016 and ranted about black British actors taking 'American' jobs, during which he suggested that black Brits essentially don't know what racism is because 'over there they been interracial dating for a hundred years'. He also suggested Hollywood was hiring black British actors not because of their talent or the quality but because 'they cheaper than us, man'.

There is no need for me to explain why Samuel clearly knows nothing about black British history – and obviously does not care to – but it is curious that he did not seem to have had a problem with Denzel Washington playing Steve Biko, Danny Glover and Sidney Poitier playing Nelson Mandela, Jill Scott playing a South African, Don Cheadle playing a Rwandan or Forest Whitaker playing Idi Amin. Daniel Kaluuya, the 'black British' actor Samuel was complaining about, was born to Ugandan parents and played a fictional black American in the film *Get Out*. Forest Whitaker played probably the most famous real-life Ugandan, but for Samuel this went unnoticed. Ironically, Daniel Kaluuya had to sue the Metropolitan Police in 2013 for dragging him off of a bus, putting him face down with their boots in his neck and then taking him to the station and strip-searching him because he 'fit the description of a reported criminal'.[8] Daniel was already a fairly successful, award-winning actor at the time this happened, having appeared in the hit teen drama *Skins*. It is utterly inconceivable that a famous white British actor would be treated this way, obviously, so Samuel's comments just reek of American exceptionalism in blackface. According to uncle Samuel, black Americans are apparently qualified to play Africans, Caribbeans or any other black person on the globe, but lord forbid any mere non-American should play a US role – Samuel also had an issue with David Oyelowo playing Martin Luther King. Black South Africans could equally suggest that black Americans don't 'really' understand racism, poverty and violence and therefore Denzel is not qualified to play Steve Biko, because things were 'not as bad' in America as they were in apartheid South Africa, but this would of course be just as idiotic.

Most strangely for an actor of his undeniable quality, Samuel seems to have totally forgotten that acting is literally pretending to be someone you are not; I am sure he has never lived on another planet nor been part of an intergalactic expedition, yet he took up his role in the *Star Wars* franchise without a second thought. The idea that black people and white people 'interracial dating' is evidence of the absence of racism reveals a surprisingly juvenile understanding of how racism works for a man of Samuel's age and brilliance; in Brazil, interracial 'dating' goes back centuries, yet only a total fool could possibly suggest that this has brought Brazil even close to overcoming its racism, in fact it is frequently invoked to avoid dealing with it at all.

Samuel's rant was really not that far off your stereotypical 'white bigot' complaining about foreigners 'coming over here and taking our jobs', and it's really odd that he had not bothered to ask himself why so many black British actors are going to America in the first place. Other than the obvious existence of Hollywood, it's worth looking at the kinds of opportunities available for black British actors domestically. What kind of roles was Idris Elba playing before he went to the states and became Stringer Bell? Could it be that the black British acting exodus is partly reflective of the limited range of opportunities for diverse roles for black talent? And a lack of black directors and writers like Jordan Peele, who made *Get Out*? Or other institutional challenges that you would have thought a black American of Samuel's age would have been able to relate to? He was totally uninterested in these questions, sadly. On the other side of this nationalist nonsense, black British actress Cush Jumbo claimed that black Brits were getting these roles in Hollywood because 'we are better than the Americans': Denzel, Viola and Samuel himself are obvious proof that this is not true, and nor should we be in some paranoid and stupid competition with black Americans.

Another black American great, Maya Angelou, told the *Guardian* in February 2012 that 'black Britons don't have the same spirit as black Americans.'⁹ In all fairness to mama Maya, it was a comment in an article about her – extremely favourable – views on Barack Obama, so who knows how exactly she intended it, but the inference seemed totally clear to me; black Americans are somehow better, braver, stronger, more 'spiritual'. A 'spiritual' comparison between black Britain and America is a ridiculous and ahistorical one; black Americans have four centuries of shared history on American soil, black Brits for the most part migrated from multiple countries across the British Commonwealth and beyond in various periods throughout the past seventy years, and thus the fact that we have managed to meld any sort of coherent black struggle at all given our diverse origins and differing histories is actually remarkable. But if we expand the scope to the 'spirit' of the black people of the British Commonwealth/Empire, we start to find figures like Marcus Garvey, Bob Marley and Kwame Nkrumah and some of the largest slave rebellions in human history – so no lack of spirit at all then.

Another brilliant black American, Ta-Nehisi Coates, followed his idol – the great James Baldwin – in romanticising Paris in his book *Between the World and Me*, which no doubt surprised black and brown Parisians no end. The Paris of the 1960s was no racial paradise, with the 1961 massacre of some forty-plus Parisian-Algerians during Algeria's war for independence and the clear segregation of that era. Nor is the Paris of today anything close to a racial utopia. It's strange that anyone could visit Paris and fail to notice the visible racial segregation of the African and Caribbean 'French' population ghettoised in 'Bronx'-style housing projects. It is even stranger that these obvious things could escape some of the most perceptive and insightful black Americans writing specifically about racial injustice. One could be forgiven if these romantic insights were about London, where on the face of it the segregation is not so visible unless you go to the prisons, but for Paris nothing of the sort could be argued, even at a glance. Middle-class black African diplomats studied at some of America's top universities back in the 1940s and 1950s and, due to their nationality and class location, some of them had a great time in America, but that was hardly a representative black experience for the America of that period.

It's not that these people are uniquely ignorant – far from it, the people I just mentioned are all incredibly smart people – it's that power and prosperity can blind us all and I'm sure that there are insights I have missed or faux pas I have made while travelling that someone operating from a different social location or with more local knowledge might have noticed or been sensitive to.

It really should be unsurprising that wealthy black American artists and writers who travel to Europe for work and are surrounded there by well off, probably well educated, likely liberal-minded white Europeans who are fans of theirs would not experience the sharp end of European racism. The obvious mistake these people made is to universalise the experience of the privileged foreigner. I might conclude from staying in five-star hotels in Manhattan – which I also did on my first trip to NY – that New York is a multicultural and incredibly wealthy paradise; I have, however, spent enough time in the Bronx since to know that's not the case. What's more, upon encountering American police I have literally seen them breathe a sigh of relief when they hear my British accent and realise that I am not one of 'their' negroes.

What is most sad for us is that these black American icons are our icons too. We view their slights in exactly the same way as black Americans would were these comments directed at them, i.e. as one of our own dissing us, quite like Bill Cosby's infamous respectability rants against poor black people in America.

Of course, many black American academics and icons have engaged with 'the struggle' during their time in the UK and Europe. For example, just nine days before he died, Malcolm X visited Smethwick in the West Midlands, where there had been a history of racial segregation and where a Conservative MP had run the election slogan 'if you want a nigger for a neighbour, vote Labour'.[10] In short, I do not want the above to be seen as broad strokes of condemnation, but rather a thread that picks up on some contradictions and tensions that will continue as multiple black voices continue to arise. West Africans have made similarly ignorant generalisations about black Americans, British Caribbeans were very ignorant and mean to newly arriving West Africans when I was young and so on.

I am a pan-Africanist, which means I am for cultivating a proper mutual understanding between the populations of Africa and its various diasporas – given that we face similar and connected historical challenges – to the extent that this is possible without being idealistic. The issues discussed here are some of the misunderstandings of class, location and specific histories that are likely to resurface in our transatlantic dialogues. Black Americans have been and will continue to be the most culturally prominent, visible and, for now, the most prosperous black population in the world, located as they are in the centre of today's only real empire, the richest nation ever. The situation for black Britons mirrors that of our US cousins but in microcosm, in that we are obviously not any smarter than Afro Brazilians or black French people, but the global prominence of the English language and our location in the other imperial power affords us a global audience that Afro Brazilians or black French people simply do not have.

On the surface of things, a direct comparison between the 'black experience' in Britain and America may seem totally superficial because the historical differences are so vast. Black Americans were enslaved in America, in the land where they now reside, so when slavery was reformed – not abolished – in 1865 they were subject to a whole century of overt and essentially state-approved violent and legislative terrorism, both after and during the brief period known as the Reconstruction. This terror reached its apex in the 4000-plus spectacle lynchings that occurred in the early part of the last century, exhibiting some of most fantastical savagery in the annals of history which were often watched by thousands of white people, including children, in a picnic-like atmosphere. Eggs and lemonade were consumed, commemorative postcards were created and the body parts of black people that had been roasted alive, castrated and carved into pieces were kept as souvenirs.[11] Clearly, nothing like this kind of white-supremacist terrorism has occurred in twentieth-century domestic Britain.

There was also no formal segregation in the UK, by which I mean there were no laws officially preventing black people from voting, from renting houses where they chose to and from enrolling in whatever state-funded schools they lived within the catchment area of, though some MPs did openly call for a colour bar. British Caribbeans came to the UK voluntarily, on their own purse and as British citizens exercising the rights inherent in that citizenship. Post-war Britain adopted the principles of social democracy, meaning that the death penalty was abolished by 1947 and that all British citizens, regardless of colour, had access to higher education, healthcare and a degree of social security. This means that the state cannot racialise these institutions – the death penalty, healthcare and education – in the same way and to the same degree as the United States, thus eliminating some of the material basis for the most extreme racism. Black Brits emigrated into a society with an already established white underclass and were mostly dumped in areas where that underclass already lived; black Americans and the indigenous peoples were the foundation of the US underclass.

So a comparison between British and American racism seems ludicrous then, doesn't it? Well, not so fast – yes, domestic Britain's social democratic racism is certainly quite distinct from America's formal and then de facto apartheid. However, once we expand our scope to include the entire British Commonwealth, the situation looks quite different. As you saw in the chapter on empire, during the same years that Americans were enjoying their lynching picnics Britain had put hundreds of thousands of British Kenyans into concentration camps and engaged in brutality every bit as savage as the American south. While South African apartheid has usually been associated with the Afrikaner-led National Party and its rise after 1948, Britain played a key role in originally developing South African apartheid.

Yes, black Brits emigrated from the Commonwealth 'freely', but their free migration cannot be divorced from the neocolonial economics and deliberate underdevelopment in which the British state is implicated. Even within that migratory history we can glean that race was every bit as important to Britain's rulers as it was to those of the USA in the post-war era; British governments were just rather more subtle about it. Yes, there was no formal segregation on British soil, but the post-war governments spent tens of millions of pounds of taxpayers' money to bring European migrant workers and refugees to Britain while working extremely hard to limit the number of non-white British citizens from the Commonwealth that could come to Britain, even though that was their legal right and even though they – unlike the European refugees arriving at the same time – were paying for themselves. Additionally, Westminster encouraged the white dominions to keep their whites only immigration restrictions even though the entire Commonwealth had fought the Nazis together. The reason for this was without a shadow of a doubt about ruling-class racism and nothing else.[12]

Even within domestic Britain there have been some striking parallels between the black British and black American experience, most obviously seen with the aforementioned disproportionate incarceration and suspicious deaths in police custody, though of course the scale of both problems is far, far greater in the US. Within media and among Britain's senior politicians, a social Darwinian racial explanation for crime has taken root, one that was clearly borrowed from American parlance; the issue of so called 'black on black' violence, or excessive melanin syndrome, if you will. As former Prime Minister Tony Blair put it:

> What we are dealing with is not a general social disorder, but specific groups or people who for one reason or another, are deciding not to abide by the same code of conduct as the rest of us . . . The black community – the vast majority of whom in these communities are decent, law-abiding people horrified at what is happening – need to be mobilised in denunciation of this gang culture that is killing innocent young black kids. But we won't stop this by pretending it isn't young black kids doing it.

I'm unsure who these people Mr Blair was referring to are, those that apparently pretend black people don't ever kill, but I am yet to come across them. No one is more familiar with black people's capacity to kill than other black people if by virtue of nothing else but proximity.

This narrative of a uniquely black criminality became so strong in the London of my youth that a special police department was set up to tackle black-on-black violence! A person could take a totally superficial look at America without reference to history, see the horrendous violence in Chicago, and start a simplistic narrative about 'black-on-black crime', but the fact that this narrative has become so deeply embedded in British media, policing and political discourse just looks unbelievably bizarre when viewed nationally.

When I was growing up, part of Britain was a war zone. Until the 1998 Good Friday agreement brought an 'end' to what is known as 'The Troubles', thousands of people had been killed in Northern Ireland as a result of the conflicts there. Even during the 1990s, the Troubles included multiple shootings and bombings that killed scores of people, including the 1998 bombing by the UVF that killed the three Quinn brothers aged nine, ten and eleven. If you asked someone why Northern Ireland – or indeed Glasgow – was so violent they would almost certainly give you a history lesson in both cases, one about the British Empire and its legacies in Ireland in one case, and the resultant conflicts between Catholics and Protestants there, and the other an interlinked story about the legacies of class neglect and deprivation in what was one of the poorest parts of Western Europe, the 'housing schemes'[13] of Glasgow. Neither of these explanations would be 'making excuses' for the violence of either region or the peoples there, but simply be trying to give some context for one of the most complex human phenomena; murder.

Given that the historically most violent regions of the UK had virtually no black population at all and given that working-class youth gangs stabbing and shooting people had existed in Britain for well over a century – who do you think the gangs attacking our grandparents when they arrived were? – you can imagine my shock when I discovered that there was, in the UK, such a thing as 'black-on-black' violence. None of what occurred in Northern Ireland had ever been referred to as 'white-on-white' crime, nor Glasgow, nor either world war, the Seven Years War, the Napoleonic Wars, nor any conflict or incident of murder, however gruesome, between humans racialised as white. Despite hundreds of millions of 'white' people killing each other throughout European history, witch hunts, mass rapes, hangings, torture and sexual abuse, and despite the fact that the two most violent regions of Britain in the 1990s were almost entirely white, there was no such thing as white-on-white violence.

Yet apparently working-class black Londoners had imported from America a rap-induced mystery nigger gene (similar to the slave sprint one?) that caused black people to kill not for all of the complex reasons that other humans kill, but simply because they are 'black', and sometimes because they listened to too much rap, grime or dancehall. This is, after all, what the phrase 'black-on-black crime' is designed to suggest, is it not? That black people are not like the rest of humanity, and that they do not kill as a complex result of political, historical, economic, cultural, religious and psychological factors, they kill simply because of their skin: their excessive melanin syndrome. The fact that yellow-on-yellow crime, mixed race-on-mixed race crime or white-on-white violence just sound like joke terms but black on black violence has 'credibility' speaks very loudly about the perceived relationship between blackness and depravity in this culture.

I could quote dozens and dozens of articles from the 1990s from all sections of the British press carrying this thread of 'blackness and crime', but I won't bore you. What we should note though is that this style of reporting has changed very little in three decades. For example, on 3 September 2016, Rod Liddle from the *Spectator* wrote an article with the headline and subtitle:

WHY DON'T BLACK LIVES MATTER WANT TO BAN THE NOTTING
HILL CARNIVAL?
Protestors would do well to focus on black-on-black crime
– but they don't and they won't[14]

Beneath the headline is a gruesome photo, that presumably was
taken at that year's carnival, of a young man with a bloody
blade in his hand looking directly at the camera and in the
background what appears to be another young man who he has
just stabbed in the leg, with a crowd of scared and shocked
onlookers who have clearly just run away from this conflict
further in the background. What's fascinating is that both the
stabber and the stabbed in this picture are both visibly 'mixed
race', but of course there is no such thing as mixed race-on-
mixed race violence, because these young boys only kill because
of the black half of their genetics, stupid. Presumably only
their black halves go to prison and/or die too – which is great
news for me. The 'writer' goes on to argue that Black Lives
Matter UK should apparently protest Notting Hill Carnival
because it's a greater danger to black people than the police;
that year there were five stabbings, according to the article.

The idiocy of this line of argument is so juvenile I'm not sure
I should even patronise you by bothering to deconstruct it but I
will, despite myself. Black Lives Matter protest a history of
racialised violence in the USA, Britain and elsewhere, where
white vigilantes and police literally get away with killing black
people because in the not so distant past black people were
thought to be and legally classified as subhuman; in the case of
the USA, these killings are often caught on camera. If white
police officers and/or vigilantes went to prison when they killed
black people on camera, there would be no Black Lives Matter
movement. Thus the article destroys its own flimsy 'argument'
by pointing out that there were 400 arrests that year at Carnival,

presumably including that of the young man who is glaring at us with a bloody knife in his hand in the picture. And therein lies the point: the young man will be arrested. If the person he stabbed died, with such convincing photo evidence he will almost certainly go to prison for murder. But no matter how many police in America get caught on camera shooting people or how many police in Britain have verdicts of unlawful killing returned against them, almost none of them will go to prison, or even so much as lose their jobs.

There is an even more sinister suggestion coming from these 'why don't black people protest black-on-black crime?' journalists; the idea that all black people are implicated in the actions of all others, that if a single black human kills another anywhere at any time on the planet then the rest of us lose our right to protest systemic state injustice, or any racist wrong done to us for that matter. Would these white people like us to turn this argument around on them? Somehow I doubt it. But it is notable that displays of transatlantic black solidarity nark so many people.

Where does all this leave us? What are the prospects for any kind of revived black-led justice movements? What new cultures might emerge from the new interactions between Britain's inner cities and those of America? In what ways might the black Atlantic evolve in the coming years? Any practical pan-African-ism to my mind must also recognise difference and diversity; it's no good saying 'anti-black racism exists, so black people must become a simple monolith'. While black America's particular racial history has produced a political tradition that cannot in any honest way avoid centring the black–white dichotomy, it's understandably hard to convince our Igbo homies that fled Biafra or those that fled the civil war in Sierra Leone that mighty whitey is the sole – or even in many cases the primary – issue. It's notable that while black-American political scholarship has been grounded in critiquing race and white supremacy, continental African scholars and activists – who obviously understand the legacies of colonialism and white supremacy just as well as anyone – have chosen, as is proper, to also focus their critiques on the failures, greed, corruption and murder of Africa's own ruling elites.

Can we, the Caribbean and black-American descendants of racist chattel slavery who have been made 'black', tell the Yoruba people, of whom there are almost fifty million, that they must simply forgo their specific ethnic history of over 2000 years in favour of simplified black solidarity, simply because racism exists? Should Jamaican Rastas ignore the history of religious persecution, police brutality and class snobbery they have suffered in Jamaica, simply because 'we are all black'? Or will the approaches and dialogues have to be more subtle and nuanced? As black Britain becomes majority West African, how important is it not to forget the battles that the first generation of post-war Caribbean migrants and their children fought so that later black migrants would not have to? Can black America incorporate the very different political traditions and experiences of the Caribbean and West Africa, and how does this entire conversation relate to the human situation as a whole and the inequalities, conflicts and challenges facing everyone? Only time will tell.

11 – THE DECLINE OF WHITENESS, THE DECLINE OF RACE? (OR THE END OF CAPITALISM?)

'Europe is no longer the center of gravity of the world. This is the significant event, the fundamental experience, of our era.'

– Achille Mbebe[1]

'Certainly, the dominance of the West already appears just another, surprisingly short-lived phase in the long history of empires and civilizations'

– Pankaj Mishra[2]

It was 5 a.m. in Hong Kong, an hour I would normally consider to be the dead of night, but it was my first time in the city and I only had twenty-four hours there so I was eager to get up and about. I looked out of my hotel window to see the slowly rising sun and to my shock I was greeted by a vision of a whole city already coming awake. Scores of people were scurrying about as if it was the middle of the day, but they were clearly not on their way to work. I could see old couples doing Tai Chi on their rooftops, people going for walks, running, playing basketball and meditating. Beyond the skyscrapers and the prosperity, the contrast of the green mountainous beauty with the bustling city, the endless shopping malls and hotels, what stuck with me about Hong Kong was this early morning ritual. I had seen something similar a few weeks before when I visited Hanoi and I thought it was a carnival day, but apparently not, it was just a typical Tuesday morning. It felt very strange to see people doing such 'unusual' exercises – a few people were stick fighting, one guy in Hanoi had been practising with a sword – so publicly and at such an early hour.

Though I myself practise an Asian martial art and grew up watching Kung Fu films, what interested me was not the stereotype of ninja-Kung-Fu Asians being seemingly confirmed, but rather just how average everybody was. These were not Shaolin super-Asians but regular folks, including grandparents, mostly not of a great standard of training but just trying to keep fit, and somehow the early hour combined with the sheer volume of people struck me as politically significant. In my mind, this simple morning ritual spoke of a culture on the ascent, and I saw in it a togetherness that may well have been entirely absent for those that participated in it. This is when I accepted that everything the scholars were saying was true, that unipolar Western dominance was over and that the return to pre-eminence – or at least to parity – of Asia awaited us.[3] A couple of years later, the Beijing Olympics happened and we all saw an opening ceremony that was so spectacularly impressive that you could almost not help but read it as China officially announcing to the world that the century of shame was well and truly over and that the Middle Kingdom was back to business as usual.

There were little signs that the world could see this too: one day I walked into the massive Foyles bookstore on Charing Cross Road and as I was staring at the shelf labelled 'The Classics', I noticed something strange. Up until now the classics had always meant books written within the 'Western' tradition; it did not matter that Africans and Asians had millennia of written literature too.[4] Not any more. On the shelf before me I saw Chinese and Japanese classics, like *The Romance of Three Kingdoms*, *The Tale of Genji* and *The Water Margin*. Times were changing.

Less than a century ago, the Chinese in British-ruled Hong Kong lived in squalid, segregated ghettoes and were governed by racist legislation;[5] today the ethnic Chinese of Hong Kong are on average some of the richest people on the planet. How quick the pace of change in world affairs. When China was militarily and economically weak and politically fragmented by external and internal forces, Chinese people left China as exploited indentured servants and found themselves on the receiving end of many of the same racist assumptions and discriminatory immigration legislation as other 'subject races'. Today you can check into any Park Lane hotel and you are as likely to see a Chinese guest as any other nationality. Over the past few decades, China has pulled at least 500 million people out of poverty (the Communist propagandists at the World Bank actually put the figure at around 800 million), industrialised at a pace faster than any nation before and today stands at the leading edge of many green technologies, and it has managed to do all of this without invading and colonising half the planet.

For these and many other reasons – despite obvious and undeniable injustices in China – you would think China would be universally admired by those who claim to believe industrial capitalism to be the holy grail of human achievement. Yet reading about China in the press, I can't help but feel a tinge of the old 'yellow peril' sentiment still lurking beneath the narratives. And if the brilliant documentary filmmaker John Pilger is correct, the USA is already in the process of waging war on China. Watching *The Coming War On China*, his documentary on the subject, and looking at an image of the American military bases that surround China, and knowing a little history of US foreign policy, it's hard not to fear the worst.

Under Barack Obama, the US government made it official that they were planning a 'pivot to Asia', and while of course the discourse is couched in suitably liberal language for public consumption, anyone with any kind of background in international relations – including the more honest American analysts – knows that ultimately this policy will be about 'containing' China. Translation: America intends to continue dominating the world, regardless of what the majority of the world's people want. Remember that more people in the world see the USA as the greatest threat to world peace than any other country, and this is according to results from American polling companies, before the election of that man that is currently in the White House. For example, a Gallup poll of 2014 asked 66,000 people from sixty-five countries which nation they thought was the greatest threat to world peace, and a quarter thought the United States, with just 6 per cent saying China. This trend is echoed in earlier polls.

While this has obviously not been a book about China, what I have tried to show is how globe-shifting forces, ideas and events well beyond our individual control shape the lives and times of individuals like you and me and consequently determine a certain degree of our experiences, however much we might like to believe that we are in control of our lives. How 'the West' in general and Anglo-America in particular will react to a nascent Asian power and prosperity, how they will contest global trade and military relationships, will be one of the key drivers of questions about race and class in the twenty-first century. Just as the Cold War shaped race and class relations in the mid twentieth century[6] and just as European geopolitical dominance in the nineteenth century made white supremacy a 'credible' way of understanding the world for so many.[7]

Now that Europe is no longer the centre of gravity in world politics or economics, and now that the biggest Western power is pivoting to Asia – no prizes for guessing where that means the US is pivoting away from – how will Western Europeans react to dropping to 'third place' behind Asia and the USA in economic and military terms? How will American politicians and military personnel react when faced with the choice of preserving American power through alliances with Japan and India against China or being loyal to their European cousins? If you've read enough political history, the likely answer to that one seems fairly obvious. It's easy to see how, in the twenty-first century, the very idea of race and even 'Western' society itself could easily come apart at the seams.

Similarly, from a pan-Africanist perspective, how will successful 'black Westerners' react to this changing world? Will we maintain emotional links with the interests of the global south beyond a generation or two or will we fall into the trap of the 'black bourgeoisie' that black American writer Franklin Frazier famously lamented way back in 1957? Will relative comfort and privilege change us for the worse? When all of the Caribbean- and Indian-born post-war generation are dead, as will soon be the case, and we are just British people, how will this affect our political consciousness? I say 'we' because I make no pretensions to super humanity and I wrestle every day with my own doubts, weaknesses, egotism and greed. I often look at the world and just think fuck it, why bother, but I know that's how we are supposed to feel, that's why the corruption is so naked and freely visible – to wear down people who have the conviction that things could be better.

There is a picture of several Indian women in saris I often use in one of my lectures about perception. The women appear to be in their fifties and thus would usually be referred to as 'aunties'. An Indian 'auntie' might conjure images of a wise older woman preparing a delicious biryani with a secret recipe that, despite years of observing auntie at work, her British-born younger relatives just cannot replicate. The image of a Jamaican grandmother is not entirely dissimilar, for if there is anyone that has come to represent love, caring, great cooking and wise familial authority it is the grandmother or 'auntie'.

When I show this picture to an audience, I ask them to add a caption that will tell me what is happening in the picture. Students are invariably aware that some kind of trick is at play but nonetheless a flurry of hands go up with the usual assumptions; 'they are at a wedding', 'auntie has just shared her secret biryani recipe with the family', 'it's Diwali'. After these few guesses, the audience looks more intently at the picture and starts noticing the details; the men in the background wearing glasses, the fact that the women are in what looks like a classroom and not a kitchen, and eventually the small screens in the distance that show faint images of satellites and planets, and the answer dawns on someone. 'It's the Indian satellite mission to Mars,' someone shouts, and a collective pause is followed by laughter as people realise the significance of the trick.

This image may prove to be one of the most important metaphors for the twenty-first century – the picture features Seetha Somasundaram, the Programme Director of the ISRO (Indian Space and Research Organisation) space science programme, Minal Rohit, project manager of the methane sensor for Mars and Nandini Harinath, the Deputy Operations Director for the Mars Orbiter Mission. These 'aunties' in the picture – despite some sexist claims by Internet trolls to the contrary – were some of the most senior scientists on the Indian mission Mangalyaan, a rocket that reached Mars in 2014, a feat which was achieved for around 10 per cent of the cost of NASA's Maven rocket, which was launched just a week later.

If there was one image that I could pick that sums up the stupidity of racism and sexism, the legacies of anti-colonial struggles, and the potential of all people to be brilliant, this might well be it. This image of older brown women leading the world in literal rocket science, an area of work so challenging that it has become the metaphor for intellectual difficulty. The twenty-first century could well turn out to be a shit century in which to be a bigot clinging to old assumptions of gender, race and the eternal supremacy of a particular culture or geographic region, or alternatively old hierarchies might well continue to reassert themselves. But the fact that India has achieved this in less than a century of independence from Britain, and at a time when the country still has more desperately poor people than any other, only makes it all the more fascinating to contemplate what the future holds.

The Ancient Egyptians believed that their pharaoh was sacred, a representation of God on Earth, indeed the very essence of monarchy is rooted in this religious idea of divine kingship. As long as Kemetic (Egyptian) civilisation was strong and stable, technologically unparalleled by its contemporaries and militarily able to defend itself, this illusion of divine kingship may well have felt truly plausible. As someone who has been fascinated since childhood by Ancient Egypt, I've always wondered how the people of that land might have reacted when they realised that their king was not so divine after all; that their land could be conquered by foreign barbarians and that the universe offered them no pre-ordained special treatment as a result of their monarch's relationship with the divine. One could even argue, as the Ghanaian pan-Africanist scholar and novelist Ayi Kweh Armah has, that this belief actually paralysed the Ancient Egyptians and made them unable to cope with the reality check when it came. How else do we explain their ability to build complex structures that still puzzle modern engineers alongside their failure to build a proper defensive fort across the thin strip of land through which the successive invaders that had constantly threatened the kingdom had come?

In a sense, I think whiteness has functioned quite similarly to divine kingship, paralysing those who are intensely invested, trapping them into a resentment of the reality that they are obviously not superior. For several centuries, people racialised as white were often taught – sometimes by some of the best minds in 'their' societies – that they were inherently superior to other human beings, that they could disregard the feelings of their 'negro' slaves, their Indian subjects and their vanquished Mandarins without having to fear consequences because their supremacy was in fact eternal, pre-ordained by god or science or culture.

When major shocks to this system did come, people racialised as white were often unable to process what was occurring. During the Haitian Revolution, for example, the white French came up with all kinds of fantastical theories about the rebels being white people in black face rather than accept the obvious fact that their former slaves had risen against them, as human beings are likely to.[8] This denial was best summed up by one French colonist who said, 'All experienced colonists know that this class of men have neither the energy nor the combination of ideas necessary for the execution of this project, whose realisation they are nevertheless marching towards.' Similar racial reactions can be observed in response to Reconstruction in America and particularly the rise of Imperial Japan, which caused a diplomatic racial crisis in the Western world.[9] The politicians of the time were very careful not to speak too openly about this racial anxiety and historians have generally neglected this factor since, but a few scholars have taken the time to show us just how much impact the Pacific War had on the racial balance of world power.[10]

Despite a seemingly pervasive belief that only people of colour 'play the race card', it does not take anything as dramatic as a slave revolution or Japanese imperialism to evoke white racial anxieties, something as trivial as the casting of non-white people in films or plays in which a character was 'supposed' to be white will do the trick. For example, the casting of Olivier award-winning actress Noma Dumezweni to play the role of

Hermione in the debut West End production of *Harry Potter and the Cursed Child* got bigots so riled up that J. K. Rowling felt the need to respond and give her blessing for a black actress to play the role. A similar but much larger controversy occurred when the character Rue in the film *The Hunger Games* was played by a black girl, Amandla Stenberg. Even though Rue is described as having brown skin in the original novel, 'fans' of the book were shocked and dismayed that the movie version cast a brown girl to play the role, and a Twitter storm of abuse about the ethnic casting of the role ensued. You have to read the responses to truly appreciate how angry and abusive they are.[11] As blogger Dodai Stewart pointed out at the time:

> All these ... people ... read *The Hunger Games*. Clearly, they all fell in love with and cared about Rue. Though what they really fell in love with was an image of Rue that they'd created in their minds. A girl that they knew they could love and adore and mourn at the thought of knowing that she's been brutally killed. And then the casting is revealed (or they go see the movie) and they're shocked to see that Rue is black. Now ... this is so much more than, 'Oh, she's bigger than I thought.' The reactions are all based on feelings of disgust.
>
> These people are MAD that the girl that they cried over while reading the book was 'some black girl' all along. So now they're angry. Wasted tears, wasted emotions. It's sad to think that had they known that she was black all along, there would have been [no] sorrow or sadness over her death.

The film and play examples may seem trivial, and it's easy for most sane people to denounce such idiocy, but the racial reactions to Reconstruction, civil rights, decolonisation and the rise of Japan were anything but trivial and I sincerely doubt that the reactions to the return of China and what that means for world affairs will be trivial either. I believe to some extent we are living through another crisis of whiteness, perhaps the final one, and that this crisis is tied up with several other complicated political and historic threads, such as the looming ecological disaster, domestic class conflict, Islamic fascism, the pivot to Asia and, if the Marxist scholars are correct, the very end of capitalism itself, though I am aware that capitalism's inevitable end has been predicted ever since its beginning![12]

Recent events in Anglo-America cannot but compel us to reflect on all of these threads. I am no fan of Barack Obama and recognise that he was in essence – beyond the Kenyan dad, the beautiful black family, the singing of Al Green and the fist bumps – not substantially different from other US presidents, in that he continued America's wars, arms industry, deportation procedures, drone programme and general global aggression, but we cannot help but reflect on the election of the man that has succeeded him. It is notable that white-supremacist groups cheered the election of Obama in 2008, as they hoped and believed that the racist backlash would support their agendas; they were not mistaken.

The election of Donald Trump, a reality TV star with no previous political experience and a man openly endorsed by Neo-Nazis, white nationalists, the KKK and other beacons of light, has been sold to us even by some notable white 'leftist' and liberal commentators as a rebellion against the status quo, the rage of an apparently forgotten group of Americans. These people seem to know nothing about American history or race politics or worse, they are choosing to cover for white supremacists. In either case, their views are not supported by the data at all.

The idea that 'economic anxiety' was the key driver of Trump's election simply melts into thin air when we recognise that the poorest Americans – black and indigenous – did not support Trump in any great capacity. In fact, the average Trump voter earned twice the median salary of the average black American, yet less than 10 per cent of black Americans voted for Trump. As writer Ta-Nehesi Coates caustically points out:

> Trump won white women (+9) and white men (+31). He won white people with college degrees (+3) and white people without them (+37). He won whites ages 18–29 (+4), 30–44 (+17), 45–64 (+28), and 65 and older (+19). Trump won whites in midwestern Illinois (+11), whites in mid-Atlantic New Jersey (+12), and whites in the Sun Belt's New Mexico (+5). In no state that Edison polled did Trump's white support dip below 40 percent. Hillary Clinton's did, in states as disparate as Florida, Utah, Indiana, and Kentucky. From the beer track to the wine track, from soccer moms to NASCAR dads, Trump's performance among whites was dominant. According to Mother Jones, based on preelection polling data, if you tallied the popular vote of only white America to derive 2016 electoral votes, Trump would have defeated Clinton 389 to 81.[13]

There are multiple studies, including a Gallup one involving a huge sample of 125,000 Americans, that simply dispel the myth that economic hardship was the determinant for Trump's election. A factor, sure; *the* factor, no way. The determining factor was whiteness, and as Coates explains, 'to accept that whiteness brought us Donald Trump is to accept whiteness as an existential danger to the country and the world.'

While I do not accept the logic that Trump is a danger to the world but Obama was not – American foreign policy is a danger to the world full stop – and while I do not buy into the hysteria that sees Trump as a radical break with American history, I must admit I was still surprised by his election. I expected Clinton to win and continue the mundane, run-of-the-mill, 'democratic' white supremacy and classism where unjust deportations, millions of citizens lacking healthcare, chronic homelessness, bombing random brown countries, cheering for the torture and execution of foreign heads of state without even a sham trial, mass incarceration and the disproportionate execution by police of unarmed black civilians continue to be American norms. But Trump won and while not every Trump voter is a card-carrying Nazi, they are totally fine with a president whose white-suprem-acist sympathies were entirely plain long before he took office and have only become clearer in the time since.

The 'good news' to keep in mind is that half of eligible adult Americans did not vote at all, and that had Bernie Sanders won the nomination there is good reason to believe he could have beaten Trump and, ultimately, Mr Trump actually still lost the popular vote. However paradoxical it may seem, Trump's elec-tion, horrendous as its effects will certainly be for millions of Americans, may turn out to have some unintended positive long-term effects. I know you probably think I have gone crazy here, so bear with me. If Trump's White House does not start a nuclear war – something a president certainly cannot do all by himself despite what you may have seen in the movies – the election of a reality TV star that makes spelling mistakes on his Twitter and retweets the likes of Britain First puts white supremacy so obviously and nakedly in the spotlight that people are simply forced to confront it. At the time of writing this, Trump has not yet had his state visit to the UK, yet by the time you read this he will have, and I bet the protest against his presence, to the most odious side of America and to at least a certain aspect of the 'special relationship', was huge, wasn't it?

I detest the policies of Bill Clinton and Barack Obama but I cannot deny they were both brilliant men; incredibly intelligent, charismatic, competent and confident. Even someone that sees

Anglo-American foreign policy as the greatest threat to world peace – as I do, along with a quarter of humanity – could easily be taken in by men of their quality. Trump's election, on the other hand, may well have woken up Western liberals to the dangers posed to the future of humanity by unchecked white supremacist grumblings, dangers the rest of the world have long since known. But maybe I'm just trying to see the best. Maybe the next three years will bring us ever closer to the brink of nuclear war, maybe Trump pulling the country out of even limited frameworks of international peace and cooperation such as UNESCO, the Paris climate accords and the UN compact on migration will do irreparable damage to the world and make Obama and Clinton look wonderful in hindsight. But as I watched the Trump inauguration on a TV screen in Addis Ababa, it all looked so satirical that I could not help but see the signs of an empire in decline. The question, then, is how painful might the fall be? America's great contradiction is that it is in some respects a successful multi-racial polity, one that has produced inspirational cultures of critical scholarship and art, often in resistance to the very white supremacist underpinnings of American ruling class ideology. But the most visible, celebrated and prosperous black people in the world also come from a country that has bombed multiple black and brown countries since 1945 (and even its own citizens) and is home to a network of racialised prison labour camps unparalleled in human history. It's easy for people in Europe to look to America as 'the racist country', especially at the moment, but how will people in Europe react if and when their nations undergo similar demographic changes to those that the US has? My guess is not very well. It is America's biggest contradiction that the country is perhaps the best example of a successful multi-racial polity in the world today, and also a brutal white-supremacist empire at the same time. Which of these trends shall win?

Which brings us back to the UK.

It's understandable given the timing of two campaigns, the central focus of both on demonising immigrants, the close political relationships of Britain and America and the particularly close relationship between Nigel Farage and the Trump administration that so many people have conceptually linked Trump and Brexit, codenamed Trexit. Before we look at Brexit, I would like to make some obvious observations. By analysing the role that xenophobia and racism played in Brexit – a role much more ambiguous than in the election of Trump – I am not suggesting that everyone that voted leave is akin to the Grand Wizard of the KKK, nor that remain voters are a homogeneous group of revolutionary anti-racists. This should be so obvious it should hardly need stating, but given our national immaturity around discussions of race it perhaps does. I have met black socialists that voted leave, I have met absolute xenophobes that voted remain, and everything in between. The ruling class was itself massively divided on the issue, with the Murdoch press and Tony Blair – usually in such sublime agreement when it comes to waging war – occupying opposite camps. I myself am neither remain nor leave per se, as I wrote at the time; I think there are valid reasons to leave the EU but I was driven to a remain position by a) the xenophobic tone of the leave campaign – though both sides were of shockingly poor intellectual quality – and b) an assessment of Britain's current political landscape. So while there were obviously multiple motivations around such a complex issue what I do wish to emphasise, as a few others also have, is the role that race, xenophobia, anti-intellectualism and ahistorical analyses played in the Brexit campaign, popular perceptions of it and ultimately its outcome. We've heard it said repeatedly that leaving the EU will allow Britain to stop neglecting the Commonwealth, but those of us that actually come from Commonwealth countries tend to shudder when we hear this. Why?

Well, apart from the imperial history you read earlier, it's because what have we seen to reflect this new-found love for the Commonwealth in recent years? 'Immigrants go home' vans trawling the streets of Tower Hamlets; I wonder who they were looking for? Anyone who has been to Tower Hamlets knows that they certainly were not looking for Swedish people or white New Zealanders. In 2015, David Cameron announced that the UK would be building a £25 million prison in Jamaica to rehouse Jamaican nationals currently in Britain's prisons. The problems with this were multi-faceted; first, there are more Irish and Polish nationals in Britain's prisons, so why the focus on Jamaica? Second, there were only 700 Jamaican nationals in the UK's prisons anyway, so one may also question if the project is worth £25 million of taxpayers' money in a country that is already the most heavily incarcerated in Western Europe by quite some distance. Third, and perhaps worst of all, the Jamaican government responded to what was being reported and said that it was inaccurate and that no such deal had been signed, rather that discussions had just been opened. More recently we have seen deaths at immigration detention centres and charter planes full of Jamaican nationals, Kenyans, Nigerians, Ghanaians and other Commonwealth nationalities, many of whom had spent decades here and had British children and British partners, being sent 'back' to countries that some of them had not visited since childhood. As you saw from the last chapter, Commonwealth migration policy has historically been defined much more by race than anything else.[14]

If the British government were serious about wanting to engage for the first time in a mutually beneficial relationship with the non-white parts of the Commonwealth, this is a strange way to go about it. Furthermore, there are now millions of Indian, Ghanaian and Jamaican Brits who could and would serve as natural mediators, trade partners and facilitators with their countries of origin. But to my knowledge our expertise, insight and ties to our nations of origin have not been sought out by these would-be Commonwealth lovers. If the British state's intentions for Africa and Asia are what they say they are – democracy, prosperity, peace and stability – it would surely welcome the input of those of us who obviously desire these things for our family and friends 'back home'.

When one examines the data around Brexit voting patterns and how they relate to geographic locations, age, ethnicity and party allegiance, it seems even harder to sell the idea that Commonwealth love was any kind of a motivating factor at all. According to the Lord Ashcroft exit poll data:

- 96 per cent of UKIP voters voted leave (hardly surprising)
- Control over immigration was cited as the second most important reason for voting leave
- Of the people who thought multiculturalism was an ill, 81 per cent voted leave
- Of the people who thought immigration was an ill, 80 per cent voted leave
- Of those who thought feminism was a force for ill, 71 per cent voted leave
- Of the thirty areas with the most old people, twenty-seven voted leave
- Of the thirty areas with the least university-educated people, twenty-eight voted leave
- Of the thirty areas with the most people identifying as English not British, all voted leave

The remain voter stats were almost an exact inverse and concluded that:

- 71 per cent of the people that thought immigration was a net good voted remain
- 71 per cent of those that thought multiculturalism was a force for good voted remain
- 75 per cent of 18–24 year olds voted remain (61 per cent of over 65s voted leave)
- The regions of England that are multicultural skewed remain, those that are not skewed leave[15]

Despite all of the claims that economic hardship determined the result, as scholars Satnam Virdee and Brendan McGeever point out:

> While exit polls confirmed that around two-thirds of those who voted in social classes D and E chose to leave the EU we should also note that the proportion of Leave voters who were of the lowest two social classes was just 24 per cent. Leave voters among the elite and middle classes were crucial to the final outcome, with almost three in five votes coming from those in social classes A, B and C1.[16]

Among black Brits 74 per cent voted remain, the highest of any ethnic group, so what could explain this? Do black Britons – who are overwhelmingly working class – just love the EU? I would suggest not. Many black Britons are well aware that European unity, if not of course the EU itself, was fostered in no small part by the pan-European project of racialised enslavement and the joint Scramble for Africa of the European powers. So it seems rather unlikely that an undying commitment to European unity is what drove this group. My suspicion is that a lifetime of being treated like immigrants in their own country generally makes black Brits quite sensitive to anti-immigrant rhetoric.

Which brings us on to a question of nationalism: why did

the Northern Irish and Scots behave so differently to the English, even though their nations are much less ethnically diverse? How come the anti-immigrant fervour did not register in the same way in the lilywhite parts of Scotland and Northern Ireland as it did in England? Clearly in Northern Ireland concern over the potential return of a hard border between Northern Ireland and the Republic was a factor, but you can't say the same for Scotland.

That England, a country not properly invaded since 1066 but which has invaded almost every nation on the planet, can have a party named the UK Independence Party win 13 per cent of the national vote in 2015 speaks volumes about collective amnesia and ability to distort the facts. The ability of Britain to invade almost the entire planet and then for a significant portion of the country to proclaim themselves victims of some kind of invasion or colonisation may well not seem directly 'racial', but it certainly echoes quite clearly the way white America, with its long-term history of racist pogroms, lynching, slavery and segregation, has somehow emerged believing itself to be the victim of racial discrimination.[17] Britain entered the EU freely, it has voted leave freely, the only blood that was shed around this issue was when a white-supremacist ultra-nationalist lunatic assassinated an MP perceived to be too kind to 'immigrants' during the campaign – hardly a country under siege like so many of those on the receiving end of Britain's imperial conquests.

Which brings us onto the final point about Brexit; immigration was central to the campaign and such an important issue for voters, but as Dr Nadine El-Enany, Senior Lecturer in Law at Birkbeck University, pointed out at the time, Britain had never 'lost control' of its borders:

Britain never joined Schengen, and not only continues to exercise border controls in relation to EU nationals, but also has a flexible opt-out from EU law on immigration and asylum – which it has consistently exercised to opt into restrictive measures that further strengthen its capacity to exclude, and out of those aimed at enhancing protection standards. In view of this, Britain's decision to depart from the EU primarily over the question of immigration and border control demands scrutiny. The Leave campaign argued that exiting the EU would allow Britain to 'take back control of its borders' and would 'make Britain great again'. The referendum debate was eclipsed by the topic of migration, and not exclusively that of European citizens. The epitome of the Leave campaign's scaremongering about migration was perhaps the moment Nigel Farage unveiled a poster depicting non-white refugees crossing the Croatia-Slovenia border in 2015 along with the slogan 'Breaking Point'.[18]

We can look at the above demographics, remember that picture and claim racial fear-mongering was not a central factor if we wish, but I sincerely doubt that if Farage had used a queue of scantily clad Russian models running across the border that the 'breaking point' line would have hit home in quite the same way.

Perhaps the worst part about this whole debacle is that by now it should be abundantly clear to all that Brexit will pave the way for an even more extreme version of the Thatcherite sell-off of UK assets and services, and the domination of the UK economy by US and transnational capital. It was not, to my mind at least, a choice between the EU and 'independence', but a choice between staying part of a flawed union or choosing to deepen ties with the American Empire and continue the 'Americanisation' of the British economy. If Britons wish to learn what a US-style healthcare service looks like, they are free to talk to any poor American.

Many scholars, particularly those of colour, have made a

similar analysis of the whiteness of Brexit, and no doubt persons racialised as white will accuse them of reading race into everything, but every so often Britain's obsession with whiteness comes to the fore all by itself. The 2011 census revealed that people identifying as 'white British' are now a minority in London. Almost every major newspaper ran an article on this revelation, asking what this meant for the future of the capital, though obviously in as racially muted language as possible. I remember hearing radio debates on the 'issue', and in all of the kerfuffle no one mentioned something obvious: lamenting this apparent decline in the 'white British' population obviously asserts just how clearly we see whiteness and Britishness as being synonymous, which is usually something we deny. A decline in British Indians living in London would hardly be deemed newsworthy by every major paper. I take this moment to remind you that most immigrants that came to Britain even before Britain joined the EU came from Europe and were thus 'white'.

The good news is that, despite what all the doomsday white nationalists are saying, the 'mixing of the races' has consistently worked not to reinforce interpersonal racism but to undermine it, my home city being one of the best examples of this in the world. There are racists and bigots in London, for sure, and the power structures in London are racialised, without a doubt, but nonetheless Londoners on the whole have clearly gotten used to people that are supposedly different. An attempt to recruit for a far-right party in Ladbroke Grove, Camden or Lambeth would be a funny experiment to watch. The other funny thing about these doomsday reports of white decline is that while the papers in question would probably baulk at the idea that white people are uniquely racist, this is what their narrative implicitly implies. We so-called ethnic minorities are just expected to live with difference and accept it. I never went to school with any other people who were Caribbean-Scots-English, but it did not kill me.

These articles imply that, or at least ask if, white people are incapable of doing what British Indians, Ghanaians and Cypriots have had to do in London, which is to get used to 'different' peoples and cultures.

Similar 'white decline' demographic time bomb articles have been circling in US and European media for some years now, and this demographic shift is what white extremists are laughably labelling 'white genocide'. In reality, it is only the threat of a continued reduction in white privilege – a potential sharing of global power and the spread of equality before the law and the institutions of the state to people not racialised as white. In America, people racialised as white, whether they become a minority or not, will still hold virtually all of the key levers of economic, military and political power. There are no groups I know of with a history of barbecuing white people in front of thousands and collecting their body parts as souvenirs, there are no black police officers refusing to treat white people as victims as they lie dying in the street, and then putting their families under surveillance when they campaign for justice, and there are no torture camps in the third world to which white citizens are deported to stay in for years without trial or due process.

Though the threat from Islamic fascist terrorists is real enough, they are equally willing to kill black and brown people as white people – in fact, the vast majority of people killed by Isis, Boko Haram and Al Shabaab have been in Africa and the Middle East, obviously. Thus there is no reason for white populations to be any more afraid of or more willing to entertain a flat cultural essentialism about almost 1.8 billion Muslims than the rest of us. Though it's entirely understandable and human that a portion of the people racialised as white fear that, if they become a 'minority' (which means seeing whiteness as a defining factor, obviously), others will do to them as they have done to others, the idea of white racial victimhood – at this point at least – is laughable. So laughable that when you ask for specific examples of ways in which white people are victimised for being white, if you get any answer at all it is likely to be 'People just assume I'm a racist.'

However, the narrative of white racial victimhood is very useful in class terms for the white ruling classes. By demonising the undeserving ethnic other with whom poor whites have more materially in common, the upper classes can use a racial solidarity rooted in the history of dominating the other to mask a history and reality of exploitation. Those that instrumentalise race in this way generally could not give two shits about the 'chavs' in Liverpool or the 'rednecks' in Alabama.

There is nothing even remotely resembling genocide happening to white people.

If white people choose to have fewer children because they are more prosperous — a pattern we see repeated in other rich non-white nations like Japan — that is totally their free choice. Similarly, white and 'non-white' people voluntarily having sex with each other now that they are free of state-imposed apartheid laws or widely acceptable moral scorn, thus producing little mongrels like me, is hardly in the same conceptual universe as physical extermination, but that is how warped the white nationalist worldview is.

As we watched the Neo-Nazis march through Charlottesville chanting 'The Jews will not replace us' on their way to defend a statue of a man that fought a war to keep slavery, we are confronted by the lunatic contradictions of white-supremacist identity. While claiming to be supreme, these people clearly do not believe what they are selling, for if Aryans are inherently superior there would be no need at all to worry about Jews or niggers 'replacing' them. Surely an innate Aryan supremacy should make them by definition irreplaceable? This constant articulation of supremacy and victimhood has long been a cornerstone of white-supremacist discourse.

Today, life in Western Europe, Australia and North America is, by the material standards of the world and human history, really quite spectacularly wonderful – even for those of us that grew up poor. Europe has enjoyed an unprecedented level of peace and prosperity for the past seven decades, free from the kinds of major conflicts that have defined so much of its history.

You would think that today would be a time that Europeans, particularly those on the political right, would be celebrating the spectacular domestic success of their model of capitalism, for never before in European history has healthcare, education, peace and prosperity been so widespread as it has in the era since 1945. Yet strangely we find not optimism and dynamism coming from the European right, but rather a lament for the supposedly dying continent and the inevitable 'decline of the West' and even, at the extreme end of now-acceptable paranoia, fear of an apparently imminent takeover by the Muslims.[19]

These thinkers are not particularly original but rather are echoing an old refrain that goes back at least a century to writers like Oswald Spengler, Maddison Grant and Lothrop Stoddard, who bemoaned the decline of the West and/or the white race at the very time when white supremacy and Western pre-eminence were at the peak of their global power. But even the threat of Muslim terrorists starts to look far less daunting when viewed against the long and very recent history of violence in Europe such as the British in Ireland, the IRA, ETA, GRAPO, post-Franco right wing militias in Spain and during Italy's Years of Lead, and certainly not like an existential threat to the continent's survival. The fact that the terrorism of Islamic fascists has been characterised as a failure of multiculturalism but the equally murderous terrorism of the above groups was not is in itself quite fascinating.

In some ways, though, the 'decline of the West' lot are correct that the Europe they imagine is indeed doomed, because it never really existed in the first place. This lilywhite Europe where everyone knew their place, things were peaceful and everyone got along simply melts into thin air against the historical record of land clearances, the violence of nation-state formations, religious purges, anti-Jewish pogroms, the Hapsburgs, Napoleon, a couple of world wars and the inquisition.

But just because the supposed golden age never existed does not mean that people will not strive after it. On 21 January 2017 the far-right parties of several major European countries met for the first time in the German city of Koblenz to outline their 'vision for a Europe of freedom' – I am entirely unsure who it is Europe is colonised by and needs to be free of, but again we see a clear articulation of a sense of victimhood. Very few, if any, of these parties espouse an easily recognisable 'old school' white-supremacist discourse for now, but when regional leaders in the German ADF party are talking openly about how Holocaust guilt has 'strangled' Germany we are already in the territory of Nazi apologia being acceptable in public discourse. These far-right groups were extremely explicit about the inspiration they took from the Brexit vote and Trump's victory in the US, with the French far-right politician Marine Le Pen calling 2016 'the year the Anglo-Saxon world woke up' (in reference to Trump's election) and the Dutch far-right leader Geert Wilders paraphrasing Trump's slogan after the Koblenz meeting by tweeting #WeWillMakeOurCountriesGreatAgain.

Most of the animosity of these groups has so far gone towards Muslim immigrants, but black people who are not Muslims watch carefully, as we are certain that people willing to accept flat generalisations about 1.8 billion Muslims or wild theories about global Jewish conspiracies will invariably not be crying over a few dead black people. These groups and their ideas are not fringe, as liberals seem to wish they were, and liberalism seems to be entirely ill-equipped to meet and challenge them. It seems to me ridiculous to believe that there will not be major conflicts in the coming decades in Europe between the Muslim populations, far-right groups and the state that will inevitably also have consequences for black and brown non-Muslims and for anyone else who just wants to live in peace. Burying our heads in the sand or pretending that Europe is now so enlightened and democratic that the pogroms against outsiders that have characterised so much of its history prior to 1945 cannot return is pure delusion.

Think about it like this; whilst people in Europe like to feel as if they/we are so much more racially enlightened than the Americans in almost all European countries the percentage of the population that is not racialised as white is less than 5 per cent of the total – though this is projected to increase sharply over the next generation – and yet we have all the racial fear-mongering, immigration detention, barely disguised racially motivated migration legislation and, in the case of France, visible and clear segregation. It's easy to point to America as the racist state, but how will Europe react to its changing demographics coupled with a relative loss of global power? We will soon see.

On the other side of the world, how will Australians and New Zealanders adapt to the reality of their geographic location? Will they accept the inevitable reality that China, India and Japan are likely to be their most practical business partners in the twenty-first century, or will they cling to the notion that they are part of Britain's white dominions? Having visited both countries, I must confess it's a little unfair to simply lump them together on this question; New Zealand seems to be further ahead than Australia in adapting to this rapidly changing world in terms of domestic 'race relations', yet Australia seems to understand its 'Asian' location very well in business terms.[20] The long-term 'demographic' effects of business and trade relations with industrialized Asian economies are obvious enough.

The key question therefore becomes this: what happens once money no longer whitens? When whiteness is no longer a metaphor for power? When whiteness is no longer default? When Chinese or Indian actors can be 'universal' sex symbols in the way that Brad Pitt and George Clooney are thought to be? When the world's leading economies are decidedly in Asia? Whiteness will have to find a totally new meaning. This process is already well underway, and some of the problems we are seeing in the West discussed above are the pangs of people racialised as white getting used to this new world. It is one of the central arguments of this book that some of the major political currents in the Western world today must be understood through the racial reframing of the world. A reframing that has been taking place since 1945, and only looks like accelerating in the years to come.

The boundaries where 'race' ends and class, geopolitics or ethnic, national and regional conflicts begin are of course blurred. There are literally billions of people alive today who've had far more extreme experiences of poverty, brutal law enforcement and exploitation than I have simply because of where they were born. So while I critique imperialism, I also acknowledge the contradiction of my own 'Western' privileges, brought about in part – ironically – by my proximity to whiteness. If the Brazilian police had shot me that day it would certainly have made some level of news. If they shot me now, my being better known would perhaps shine an international light – in the UK at least – on Brazilian police brutality far brighter than the deaths of tens of thousands of Afro Brazilians.

In closing, it is worth asking what the formative race and

class experiences of a child born in 2018 into a similar family to mine might be. If current trends continue, for the most part the answers don't look very positive. They will be even more likely to go to prison than I was, as Britain's incarceration state has expanded greatly during the course of my lifetime. They will probably be far less likely to receive adequate healthcare, as the NHS continues to shrink and/or be privatised. The banana skins will almost certainly not return and the small black middle class is probably now permanent, but the 2018 child will likely have far less chance of 'lifting themselves out of poverty' than I did, as the mechanisms that helped make that possible for me continue to be deliberately eroded.

On a global level, what might the definitive political struggles that inform the political consciousness of my 2018 equivalent be? Formal apartheid almost certainly cannot return to South Africa, though a civil war that will have racial and ethnic complications still seems entirely possible, and I sincerely doubt that the white farmers newly returned to Zimbabwe will attempt to restore the old pre-1980 undisguised racial order (having been to Zimbabwe many times myself, I can guarantee black Zimbabweans simply would not stand for it anyhow). But America could quite feasibly be split into ethno-states by extreme violence, as empowered white nationalists wish for it to be. Similarly, pogroms against European Muslims and, by ethnic extension, Sikhs and random brown people who 'look Muslim', as well as continued terrorist attacks by white nationalists and Islamic extremists and the wider reprisals and discrimination those attacks will be used to justify, seem to me quite likely to be common features of twenty-first-century continental Europe, but unlike in previous centuries Europe is unlikely to be able to spill its domestic conflicts out onto Africa, Asia and the Americas.

As you may be able to tell, I am not particularly optimistic about the future and I hope to be proved spectacularly wrong. I fear the only question for the life of someone like me born in 2018 is how extreme the tragedies and carnage they will surely live through will be. With that said, as you have surely noticed by now many victories have been won before and they will be won again. Formal Apartheid fell when it did because of black South African resistance, international pressure and material assistance from Cuba. The National Front were run out of London by black Caribbeans, South Asians and an important set of 'white British' allies. British law firms have brought cases against the state on behalf of Kenyans tortured in British concentration camps during the 1950s, and while the scale of the payouts they received was meagre in comparison to the horrors inflicted, the enormity of the British government's lies and deception regarding empire was placed under a critical spotlight by these cases like never before. So my apparent lack of hope is more a recognition that tragedies will inevitably occur, that many of these coming tragedies will be racially charged and stratified by class but that real people will react in all of the myriad of ways they have done before – which includes reacting by giving birth to new traditions of resistance and creativity and working to create new futures. For children born in 2018 into relative poverty and racialised as non-white, the future seems filled with massive potential for change for the better brought about by a relative democratisation of global and local power, but equally the possibility of a reassertion and legitimation of extreme forms of bigotry combined with the increased inequality that is affecting everyone.

The answers to these questions, and the shape of the world children born now will inhabit, will be determined not just by politicians and billionaires, but by millions of supposedly ordinary people like you and me who choose whether or not to engage with difficult issues, to try and grasp history, to find their place in it, and who choose whether to act or to do nothing when faced with the mundane and mammoth conflicts of everyday life.

CHAPTER 1 – Born in the 1980s

1. La Rose, John, *The New Cross Massacre Story* (London: New Beacon, 2011)
2. The Moonshot youth club and the Albany theatre, both popular with black youth and sites of anti-racist organising, had been gutted by fire in the previous years before New Cross as well as an earlier racist petrol bomb attack on a party in nearby Ladywell back in 1971.
3. Kushner, Tony, *The Battle of Britishness: Migrant Journeys, 1685 to the Present* (Manchester: Palgrave Macmillan, 2012); Panayi, Panikos, *An Immigration History of Britain: Multicultural Racism Since 1800* (London: Routledge, 2010)
4. Panayi estimates that 700,000 Irish migrants have come to Britain since 1945 (in addition to the 1.5 million that came between 1800–1945). Total migration from the whole of south Asia since 1945 he estimates to be around 1 million; total migration from Africa, Asia and the Caribbean since 1945 he estimates to make up 2.4 million of the 6.2 million total.
5. Paul, Kathleen, *Whitewashing Britain: Race and Citizenship in the Postwar Era* (Ithaca: Cornell University Press, 1997)
6. Gilroy, Paul, *After Empire: Melancholia or convivial culture?* (London: Routledge, 2004)
7. Williams, Elizabeth, *The Politics of Race in Britain and South Africa: Black British Solidarity and the Anti-apartheid* (London: I.B. Tauris, 2017)

8. Britain engineered a coup against the democratically elected, Cheddi Jagan in 1953 in British Guiana and, even though Iran was never a British colony, Britain and the US that same year engineered a coup against the democratically elected Mohamad Mosaddeq.

9. Linebaugh, Peter, *The London Hanged: Crime and Civil Society in the Eighteenth Century* (London: Verso, 2006)

10. A June 2017 report by the Resolution Foundation found that Brits born between 1981–85 had on average just half the net wealth of those born just five years earlier. D'Arcy, Connor and Gardiner, Laura, *The Generation of Wealth: Asset Accumulation Across and Within Cohorts* (June 2017). Retrieved from URL www.resolutionfoundation.org/app/uploads/2017/06/wealthpdf

11. Prison Reform Trust Bromley Briefings 2017. Retrieved from URL www.prisonreformtrust.org.uk/Portals/0/Documents/Bromley%20Briefings/Summer%202017%20factfile.pdf

12. Eastwood, Niamh, Shiner, Michael and Bear, Daniel, *The Numbers in Black and White: Ethnic Disparities in the Policing and Prosecution of Drug Offences in England and Wales* (London: Release Drugs, the Law and Human Rights, 2013)

Interlude: A Guide to Denial

1. During a 2005 interview on *60 Minutes* with Mike Wallace, Freeman literally said that the way to end racism was to stop talking about it. He has repeated similar sentiments about the race and class work in multiple interviews since.

2. Draper, Nicholas, *The Price of Emancipation: Slave-Ownership, Compensation and British Society at the End of Slavery*

(Cambridge: Cambridge University Press, 2013); Hall, Catherine, *Legacies of British Slave Ownership* (Cambridge: Cambridge University Press, 2016)

CHAPTER 2 – The Day I Realised My Mum Was White

1. Humphreys, Margaret, *Empty Cradles* (London: Corgi, 2011)
2. You can read a good portion of the original text online on at the encyclopaedia of Virginia. Retrieved from URL https://www.encyclopediavirginia.org/_An_act_concerning_Servants_and_Slaves_1705
3. Allen, Theodore W., *The Invention of the White Race: Vol I: Racial Oppression and Social Control* (London: Verso, 2012)
4. Ignatiev, Noel, *How the Irish Became White* (London: Routledge, 2008)
5. Wolfe, Patrick, *Traces of History: Elementary Structures of Race* (London: Verso, 2016) p. 77
6. Garner, Steve, *Whiteness: An Introduction* (Oxford: Routledge, 2007) p. 70
7. Wolfe, Patrick, *Traces of History,* p. 73
8. Eze, Emmanuel Chukwudi, ed., *Race and the Enlightenment: A Reader* (London: Blackwell, 1997)
9. Wolfe, Patrick, *Traces of History*
10. Nascimento, Abidias Do, *Brazil Mixture or Massacre?: Essays in the Genocide of a Black People* (Massachusetts: The Majority Press, 1979)
11. The most notorious of these child massacres occurred on 22 July 1993, when eight street children were killed by members of the police outside the Candelaria church in Rio de Janeiro. One of the survivors of the massacre, Sandro Rosa do Nascimento, went on to hijack a bus and hold several people hostage for hours,

while he voiced outrage at social injustice in Brazil. This incident is portrayed in the critically acclaimed documentary *Bus 174*.

12. Linebaugh, Peter, and Rediker, Marcus, *The Many-Headed Hydra: The Hidden History of the Revolutionary Atlantic* (London: Verso, 2012)

13. Dubois, Laurent, *Avengers of the New World: The Story of the Haitian Revolution* (Cambridge, Massachusetts: Harvard University Press, 2004)

14. Blackmon, Douglas A., *Slavery By Another Name* (New York: Anchor Books, 2008)

15. Horne, Gerald, *Race War: White Supremacy and the Japanese Attack on the British Empire* (New York: New York University Press, 2004) pp. 17–18

16. In 1937, Churchill told the Palestine Royal Commission: 'I do not admit for instance, that a great wrong has been done to the Red Indians of America or the black people of Australia. I do not admit that a wrong has been done to these people by the fact that a stronger race, a higher-grade race, a more worldly wise race to put it that way, has come in and taken their place.' Heyden, Tom, "The Greatest Controversies of Winston Churchill's Career" *BBC News* (26 January 2015). Retrieved from URL www.bbc.co.uk/news/magazine-29701767

17. For an examination of how much the conflict in the Pacific was considered to be racial by the Japanese as well as the Europeans, see: Dower, John W., *War Without Mercy: Race and Power in the Pacific War* (New York: Pantheon, 1986)

18. Davies, Barbara, "Cocktail Party" *Daily Mail* (8 December 2016). Retrieved from URL www.dailymail.co.uk/news/article-4011866/cocktail-party-Brits-faced-evil-decadent-expat-lives-Hong-Kong-ended-overnight-Japan-s-unspeakably-savage-invasion-75-years-survivors-relive-horror-html

19. Mills, Charles, *The Racial Contract* (Ithaca: Cornell University Press, 2017)

CHAPTER 3 - Special Needs?

1. Cobain, Ian, *The History Thieves: Secrets, Lies and the Shaping of a Modern Nation* (London: Portobello Books, 2016)

2. Ken Robinson's brilliant TedTalk – literally entitled "Do Schools Kill Creativity?" – has fourteen million views. Retrieved from URL www.youtube.com/watch?v=iG9CE55wbtY

3. Hart, John, "The Big Lesson From the World's Best School System? Trust Your Teachers" *The Guardian* (9 August 2017). Retrieved from URL www.theguardian.com/teachers-network/2017/aug/09/worlds-best-school-system-trust-teachers-education-finland

4. For good histories of racism and educational policy see: Tomlinson, Sally, *Race and Education: Policy and Politics in Britain* (London: Open University Press, 2008) or Tierney, John, *Race Migration and Schooling* (London: Holt, Rinehart and Winston Ltd., 1982)

5. Coard's original book is hard to come by but the full text can be found in Richardson, Brian, *Tell it Like it is: How Our Schools Fail Black Children* (Staffordshire: Bookmarks Publications, Trentham Books, 2005)

6. Coard, Bernard, "Why I Wrote the 'ESN Book'" (5 February 2005). Retrieved from URL www.theguardian.com/education/2005/feb/05/schools.uk

7. See Gillborn, David, *Racism and Education: Coincidence or Conspiracy? White Success, Black Failure* (London: Routledge, 2008)

8. Burgess, Simon, and Greaves, Ellen, "Test Scores, Subjective Assessment and Stereotyping of Ethnic Minorities" (2009)

CHAPTER 4 – Linford's Lunchbox

1. Carrington, Ben, *Race, Sport and British Politics* (California: Sage, 2010)

2. Taylor, Daniel "Graham Rix and Gwyn Williams accused of racism and bullying while at Chelsea" *The Guardian* (18 January 2018). Retrieved from URL https://www.theguardian.com/football/2018/jan/12/graham-rix-gwyn-williams-accused-racism-bullying-chelsea

3. Taylor, Daniel "Liverpool's Rhian Brewster: 'When I'm racially abused, I just want to be left alone'" *The Guardian* (28 December 2017). Retrieved from URL www.theguardian.com/football/2017/dec/28/liverpool-rhian-brewster-racial-abuse-england-uefa

4. Bring them home report. Retrieved from URL www.humanrights.gov.au/sites/default/files/content/pdf/social_justice/bringing_them_home_report.pdf

5. Earle, T. F., and Lowe, K. P., *Black Africans In Renaissance Europe* (Cambridge: Cambridge University Press, 2010)

6. Walker, Robin, *When We Ruled: The Ancient and Mediaeval History of Black Civilisations* (London: Generation Media, 2006) pp. 46–54

7. Davidson, Basil, *The African Slave Trade: A Revised and Expanded Edition* (London: Back Bay Books, 1980), p. 63

8. Beckert, Sven, *Empire of Cotton: A New History of Global Capitalism* (London: Penguin Random House, 2014)

9. Curtin, Philip D., *The Image of Africa: British Ideas and Action, 1780–1850* (London: Macmillan, 1964)

10. Long, Edward, *The History of Jamaica* (Cambridge: Cambridge University Press, 2010)

11. For examinations of Enlightenment thinking about race see: Eze, Emmanuel Chukwudi, ed., *Race and the Enlightenment: A Reader* (London: Blackwell, 1997) and especially Smith,

Justin E. H., *Nature, Human Nature, & Human Difference: Race in Early Modern Philosophy* (Princeton and Oxford: Princeton University Press, 2015)

12. Jordan, Michael, *The Great Abolition Sham: The True Story of the End of the British Slave Trade* (Gloucestershire: The History Press, 2005) p. 93

13. Richardson, David, ed., *Abolition and Its Aftermath: The Historical Context, 1790–1916* (London and New York: Routledge, 1985)

14. Davidson, Basil, *The African Slave Trade: A Revised and Expanded Edition* (London: Back Bay Books, 1980)

15. I am aware that Bernard Lewis has a reputation for being extremely orientalist, nonetheless the primary sources he amasses to make the point seem undeniable to me and also there is a palpable lack of widely available texts on race and slavery in the Arab world. See Lewis, Bernard, *Race and Slavery in the Middle East: An Historical Enquiry* (New York: Oxford University Press, 1990); Gordon, Murray, *Slavery in the Arab World* (New York: New Amsterdam Books, 1987)

16. Jahn, Janheinz, *Neo African Literature: A History of Black Writing* (New York: Grove Press, 1968); Kwei Armah, Ayi, *The Eloquence Of The Scribes: A memoir on the sources and resources of African literature* (Dakar, Senegal: Per Ankh, 2006)

17. Mbembe, Achille, *Critique of Black Reason* (Durham and London: Duke University Press, 2017)

18. Article 13 of the Haitian constitution of 1805 explicitly excludes the 'Polanders and Germans' from the category white and article 14 reads 'All acception [sic] of colour among the children of one and the same family, of whom the chief magistrate is the father, being necessarily to cease, the Haytians shall hence forward be known only by the generic appellation of Blacks.'

CHAPTER 5 – Empire and Slavery in the British Memory

1. The hymn 'Amazing Grace' was written by British slave trader John Newton.

2. The 2007 documentary is called *Maafa Truth*.

3. Thomas, Hugh, *The Slave Trade: The History of the Atlantic Slave Trade 1440–1870* (New York: Simon & Schuster, 1997) p. 793

4. Turner, Camilla "Outcry after grammar schools pupils asked to buy slaves with 'good breeding potential' in history class" *Daily Telegraph* (13 July 2017) Retrieved from URL www.telegraph.co.uk/education/2017/07/13/grammar-school-criticised-asking-pupils-buy-slaveswith-good/; Alleyne, Richard "Head apologises for lesson in 'slave trading' at school" *Daily Telegraph* (28 November 2012) Retrieved from URL www.telegraph.co.uk/news/uknews/9710013/Head-apologises-for-lesson-in-slave-trading-at-school.html; Davis, Anna "East London school apologises after pupils told to dress as slaves for black history month" *Evening Standard* (17 October 2017). Retrieved from URL www.standard.co.uk/news/london/east-london-head-apologises-after-pupils-told-to-dress-as-slaves-for-black-history-month-a3660606.html

5. Lusher, Adam "How Britain imprisoned some of the first black fighters against slavery" *Independent* (17 July 2017) Retrieved from URL www.independent.co.uk/news/uk/home-news/slavery-black-prisoners-of-war-race-racism-portchester-castle-english-heritage-exhibition-britain-a7846051.html

6. Dubois, Laurent, *Avengers of the New World: The Story of the Haitian Revolution* (Massachusetts: Harvard University Press, 2004) p. 21

7. Jordan, Michael, *The Great Abolition Sham: The True Story of the End of the British Slave Trade* (Gloucestershire: The History Press, 2005) p. 69

8. Dubois, Laurent, *Avengers of the New World*, p. 256

9. Ibid. pp. 290–91

10. For a look at how post-revolutionary Haiti was dealt with by the major world powers of the time see: Horne, Gerald, *Confronting Black Jacobins: The United States, The Haitian Revolution, and the Origins of the Dominican Republic* (New York: Monthly Review Press, 2015)

11. For a study of post-revolutionary Haiti and class/colour conflict see: Nicholls, David, *From Dessalines to Duvalier* (London: Macmillan Caribbean, 1984). For the US-backed overthrow of Jean Bertrand Aristide see Hallward, Peter, *Damming the Flood: Haiti, Aristide, and the Politics of Containment* (London: Verso, 2007)

12. Draper, Nicolas, *The Price of Emancipation: Slave-Ownership, Compensation and British Society at the End of Slavery* (Cambridge: Cambridge University Press, 2013); Hall, Catherine, *Legacies Of British Slave Ownership* (Cambridge: Cambridge University Press, 2016)

13. Ramdin, Ron, *The Other Middle Passage: Journal Of A Voyage From Calcutta To Trinidad 1858* (Hertford: Hansib Publications, 1994)

14. For the story of the remarkable man that let this revolt see: Kennedy, Fred, *Daddy Sharpe: A Narrative of the Life and Adventures of Samuel Sharpe, A West Indian Slave Written by Himself, 1832* (Jamaica: Ian Randle Publishers, 2008)

15. Newsinger, John, *The Blood Never Dried: A People's History of the British Empire* (London: Bookmarks Publication, 2006) p. 30

16. Sherwood, Marika, *After Abolition: Britain and the Slave Trade since 1807* (London: I. B. Tauris, 2007)

17. Diouf, Sylviane A., ed., *Fighting the Slave Trade: West African Strategies* (Athens: Ohio University Press, 2003)

18. Ibid., p. 183

19. Newsinger, John, *The Blood Never Dried*

20. For a meticulous comparative study of slavery across societies and cultures and throughout history see Patterson, Orlando, *Slavery and Social Death: A Comparative Study* (Massachusetts: Harvard University Press, 1982)

21. Diouf, Sylviane A., ed., *Fighting the Slave Trade*, p. 211

22. Newsinger, John, *The Blood Never Dried*

23. Mishra, Pankaj, *From the Ruins of Empire: The Revolt Against the West and the Remaking of Asia* (London: Allen Lane, 2012)

24. Mackenzie, John M., *Propaganda and Empire: The Manipulation of British Public Opinion, 1880–1960* (Manchester: Manchester University Press, 1984)

25. Cobain, Ian, *The History Thieves: Secrets, Lies and the Shaping of a Modern Nation* (London: Portobello Books, 2016)

26. Kushner, Tony, *The Battle of Britishness: Migrant Journeys, 1685 to the Present* (Manchester: Palgrave Macmillan, 2012) p. 67

27. Gott, Richard, *Britain's Empire: Resistance, Repression and Revolt* (London: Verso, 2011)

28. Newsinger, John, *The Blood Never Dried*, p. 10

CHAPTER 6 – Scotland and Jamaica

1. Gane-Mcalla, Casey, *Inside the CIA's Secret War In Jamaica* (Los Angeles: Over The Edge Books, 2016)

2. For a quick overview of Jamaica's neocolonial challenges see: Prashad, Vijay, *The Darker Nations: A People's History of the Third World* (New York: The New Press, 2007) pp. 224–45, and the 2001 documentary *Life and Debt* directed by Stephanie Black.

3. Isaac, Benjamin, *The Invention of Racism in Classical Antiquity* (Princeton and Oxford: Princeton University Press, 2004)

4. Eliav-Feldon, Miriam, Isaac, Benjamin, and Ziegler, Joseph, *The Origins of Racism in the West* (New York: Cambridge University Press, 2009) p. 5

5. Whitman, James Q., *Hitler's American Model: The United States and the Making of Nazi Race Law* (Princeton: Princeton University Press, 2017)

6. For a study specifically looking at the evolution of anti-black and anti-Jewish racism see Frederickson, George M., *Racism: A Short History* (Princeton: Princeton University Press, 2015)

7. Eliav-Feldon, Miriam, Isaac, Benjamin, and Ziegler, Joseph, *The Origins of Racism in the West* p. 26

8. Frederickson, George M., *Racism: A Short History* (Princeton: Princeton University Press, 2015)

9. Paul, Kathleen, *Whitewashing Britain: Race and Citizenship in the Postwar Era* (Ithaca: Cornell University Press, 1997)

10. Frederickson, George M., *Racism: A Short History*

CHAPTER 7 – Police, Peers and Teenage Years

1. Humphries, Stephen, *Hooligans or Rebels? An Oral History of Working-Class Childhood and Youth 1889–1939* (London: Blackwood, 1997) p. 174

2. Hall, Stuart, Critcher, Chas, Jefferson, Tony, Clarke, John and Roberts, Brian, *Policing the Crisis: Mugging, the State, and Law and Order* (Basingstoke: Macmillan, 1978)

3. For a history of Glasgow's gangs see: Davies, Andrew, *City Of Gangs: Glasgow and The Rise Of The British Gangster* (London: Hodder & Stoughton, 2014)

4. McKenna, Kevin, "Glasgow's dark legacy returns as gangland feuds erupt in public killings" *The Guardian* (22 July 2017).

Retrieved from URL www.theguardian.com/uk-news/2017/jul/22/glasgow-gangland-feuds-erupt-in-public-killings

5. FitzGerald, Marian, Hale, Chris and Stockdale, Jan, *Young People & Street Crime: Research into young people's involvement in street crime* (Youth Justice Board for England and Wales, January 2003)

6. Hirsch, Donald and Valadez, Laura, *Local indicators of child poverty – developing a new technique for estimation* (Loughborough University: Centre for Research in Social Policy, July 2014)

7. Douglas, Mary, *Purity and Danger: An Analysis of Concepts of Pollution and Taboo* (London: Routledge, 2002)

8. Onibada, Ade, "Brothers Who Distribute Empowering Black Books Arrested" *Voice* (9 September 2016). Retrieved from URLwww.voice-online.co.uk/article/brothers-who-distribute-empowering-black-books-arrested

9. Scottish Violence Reduction Unit, *Violence is Preventable – Not Inevitable* (January 2005). Retrieved from URL www.actiononviolence.org.uk/

10. Prison Reform Trust Bromley Briefings 2017. Retrieved from URL www.prisonreformtrust.org.uk/portals/o/Documents/Bromley%20Briefings/summer%202017%20factfile.pdf

11. Dreisenger, Baz, *Incarceration Nations: A Journey to Justice in Prisons around the World* (New York: Other Press, 2017); Davis, Angela, *Are Prisons Obsolete?* (New York: Seven Stories Press, 2003)

12. Khomami, Nadia "Most London knife crime no longer gang related, police say" *The Guardian* (13 October 2016). Retrieved from URL www.theguardian.com/uk-news/2016/oct/13/most-london-knife-no-longer-gang-related-police-say

13. *Memorandum submitted by The Metropolitan Police Authority: The Colour Of Justice.* Retrieved from URL https://publications.parliament.uk/pa/cm200607/cmselect/cmhaff/181/181we44.htm

14. Macpherson, William, *The Stephen Lawrence Inquiry Report Of An Inquiry by Sir William Of Cluny*. Retrieved from URL https://www.gov.uk/government/uploads/system/uploads/attachment_data/file/277111/4262.pdf

15. For good books on general police corruption in the UK see: Gillard, Michael and Flynn, Laurie, *Untouchables: Dirty Cops, Bent Justice and Racism in Scotland Yard* (London: Bloomsbury, 2012); Hayes, Stephen, *The Biggest Gang: Shining a Light on the Culture of Police Corruption in Britain* (London: Grosvenor House Publishing, 2013). For the specific use of spy cops in Britain see Evans, Rob and Lewis, Paul, *Undercover: The True Story of Britain's Secret Police* (London: Faber & Faber, 2013). For a political history of British policing see Bunyan, Tony, *The History and Practice of the Political Police in Britain* (London: Quartet Books, 1977)

16. Watch the 2001 documentary *Injustice*, directed by Ken Faro, for a look at some of the worst cases of police brutality in British history.

CHAPTER 8 – Why Do White People Love Mandela? Why Do Conservatives Hate Castro?

1. Mandela, Nelson and Castro, Fidel, *How Far We Slaves Have Come: South Africa and Cuba in Today's World* (New York: Pathfinder, 1991)

2. Williams, Elizabeth M., *The Politics of Race in Britain and South Africa: Black British Solidarity and the Anti-apartheid Struggle* (London: I.B. Tauris, 2017)

3. Mandela, Nelson and Castro, Fidel, *How Far We Slaves Have Come* p. 27

4. Dewey, Caitlin, "Why Nelson Mandela was on a Terrorism Watch List in 2008" *Washington Post* (7 December 2013).

Retrieved from URL www.washingtonpost.com/news/the-fix/wp/2013/12/07/why-nelson-mandela-was-on-a-terrorism-watch-list-in-2008/?utm-term.c13ad289887e

5. Mandela, Nelson and Castro, Fidel, *How Far We Slaves Have Come* p. 20

6. For the saga of Cuba in Africa see: Gleijeses, Piero, *Conflicting Missions: Havana, Washington And Africa 1959–1976* (Chapel Hill: University of North Carolina Press, 2003); Gleijeses, Piero, *Visions of Freedom: Havana, Washington, Pretoria, and the Struggle for Southern Africa 1976–1991* (Chapel Hill: University of North Carolina Press, 2013); and Villegas, Harry, *Cuba & Angola: The War for Freedom* (Atlanta: Pathfinder, 2017). Villegas is one of the Cuban guerrillas that fought in Angola and several other key campaigns of the era.

7. Gleijeses, Piero, *Visions of Freedom* p. 30

8. *Apartheid Did Not Die* is the title of a brilliant film by John Pilger exploring how the basic economic structures of apartheid remained in place.

9. Hallward, Peter, *Damming the Flood: Haiti, Aristide, and the Politics of Containment* (London: Verso, 2007)

10. Miller, Phil, "The British Army's Secret Plan to Keep South Africa's Ruling Party in Power" *Vice* (16 May 2016). Retrieved fromURLwww.vice.com/en_us/article/kwke4n/exclusive-the-british-armys-secret-plan-to-prop-up-south-africas-ruling-party

11. Branson, Richard, "Visiting Cuba and Scientific Achievements" (14 November 2017). Retrieved from URL www.virgin.com/richard-branson/visiting-cuba-and-scientific-achievements

12. Walker, Chris, "From Cooperation to Capacitation: Cuban Medical Internationalism in the South Pacific" *International Journal of Cuban Studies* (Spring 2013, 5.1); Huish, Robert "Why does Cuba 'Care' so much? Understanding the Epistemology of Solidarity in Global Health Outreach" *Public Health Ethics (Vol. 7 No 3, 2014)* pp. 261–276

13. Kirk, John M. and Walker, Chris "Cuban Medical Internationalism: The Ebola Campaign of 2014–15" *International Journal of Cuban Studies 8.1* (Spring 2016)

14. See: Curtis, Mark, *Web of Deceit: Britain's Real Role in the World* (London: Vintage, 2003); Cobain, Ian, *Cruel Britannia: A Secret History of Torture* (London: Portobello Books, 2012)

15. Colhoun, Jack, *Gangsterismo: The United States, Cuba and the Mafia 1933–1966* (New York: Or Books, 2013)

16. For a look at how racist ideas evolved in step with real world power relations see Furedi, Frank, *The Silent War: Imperialism and the Changing Perception of Race* (London: Pluto Press, 1988)

17. Prashad, Vijay, *The Darker Nations: A People's History of the Third World* (New York: The New Press, 2007); Jansen, Jan C. and Osterhammel, Jurgen, *Decolonisation: A Short History* (Princeton and Oxford: Princeton University Press, 2017)

CHAPTER 9 – The Ku Klux Klan Stopped Crime by Killing Black People

1. Department for Education and Skills, *Priority Review: Exclusion of Black Pupils "Getting it. Getting it Right"* (Spring 2006)

2. Strand, Dr Steve "Minority Ethnic Pupils in the Longitudinal Study of Young People in England: Extension Report on Performance in Public Examinations at Age 16" *Research Report DCSF-RR029* (University of Warwick: Institute of Education, University of Warwick, 2007)

3. Wigmore, Tim "The lost boys: how the white working class got left behind" *New Statesman* (20 September 2016) Retrieved from URL www.newstatesman.com/politics/education/2016/09/lost-boys-how-white-working-class-got- left-behind

4. Lott, Tim "It's no surprise that working class white boys do badly at school" *The Guardian* (18 November 2016) Retrieved from URL www.theguardian.com/lifeandstyle/2016/nov/18/its-no-surprise-that-white-working-class-boys-do-badly-at-school

5. Paton, Graeme "White Boys Let Down By Education System" *Telegraph* (22 June 2007). Retrieved from URL www.telegraph.co.uk/news/uknews/1555322/White-boys-let-down-by-education-system.html

6. "White Boys 'Are Being Left Behind' by Education System" *Mail Online* (22 June 2007). Retrieved from URL www.dailymail.co.uk/news/article-463614/white-boys-left-education-system

7. Gillborn, David, *Racism and Education: Coincidence or Conspiracy? White Success, Black Failure* (London: Routledge, 2008)

CHAPTER 10 – Britain and America

1. Rothstein, Richard, *The Color of Law: A Forgotten History of How Our Government Segregated America* (New York: Liveright, 2017)

2. Washington, Harriet A., *Medical Apartheid: The Dark History of Medical Experimentation on Black Americans from Colonial Times to the Present* (New York: Anchor Books, 2006)

3. In 1921 the prosperous black neighbourhood of Greenwood, Tulsa, Oklahoma known locally as Black Wall Street was burned to the ground by jealous white supremacists; at least 300 people were killed. Many other black towns were sacked during this time such as East St Louis in 1917. In 1985 the back-to-nature black-led movement known as MOVE was bombed from the sky in Philadelphia.

4. For a discussion of the politics of hip hop see Rose, Tricia, *The Hip Hop Wars: What We Talk About When We Talk About Hip Hop – And Why It Matters* (New York: Basic Books, 2008)

5. Ranesh, Randeep "More black people jailed in England and Wales proportionally than in US" *The Guardian* (11 October 2010). Retrieved from URL www.theguardian.com/society/2010/oct/11/black-prison-population-increase-england

6. With regards to sentencing for non-violent drug offences see: Eastwood, Niamh, Shiner, Michael, and Bear, Daniel "The Numbers in Black and White: Ethnic Disparities in the Policing and Prosecution of Drug Offences in England and Wales" (London: Release Drugs, the Law and Human Rights, 2013). For racialised applications of joint enterprise law see: Williams, Patrick and Clarke, Becky, *Dangerous Associations: Joint Enterprise, Gangs and Racism. An Analysis of the Processes of Criminalisation of Black, Asian and Minority Ethnic Individuals* (London: Centre for Crime and Justice Studies, 2016)

7. FactCheck Q&A: *Are Indigenous Australians the most incarcerated people on Earth?* (6 June 2017). Retrieved from URL https://theconversation.com/factcheck-qanda-are-indigenous-australians-the-most-incarcerated-people-on-earth-78528

8. "EXCLUSIVE: Skins actor Daniel Kaluuya sues Met over mistaken arrest on bus claiming they picked on him because of his race" *Evening Standard online* (10 October 2013). Retrieved from URL www.standard.co.uk/news/london/exclusive-skins-actor-daniel-kaluuya-sues-met-over-mistaken-arrest-on-bus-claiming-they-picked-on-8871075.html

9. Muir, Hugh "Maya Angelou: 'Barack Obama has done a remarkable job'" *The Guardian* (15 February 2012). Retrieved from URL www.theguardian.com/books/2012/feb/15/maya-angelou-barack-obama-remarkable-job

10. Jefferies, Stuart "Britain's most racist election: the story of Smethwick 50 years on" *The Guardian* (15 October 2014). Retrieved from URL www.theguardian.com/world/2014/oct/15/britains-most-racist-election-smethwick-50-years-on

11. You can read an incredibly thorough breakdown of the history of white supremacist lynching's in America at: "Lynching in America: Confronting the Legacy of Racial Terror" *Equal Justice Initiative, Third Edition*. Retrieved from URL https://lynchinginamerica.eji.org/report – but be warned, it is truly stomach curdling stuff.

12. Of the 1962 Commonwealth Immigration Act, Home Secretary Rab Butler said that its 'great merit' was that it could be presented as non-discriminatory even though in practice 'its restrictive effect is intended to, and would in fact, operate on coloured people almost exclusively.' See: Paul, Kathleen, *Whitewashing Britain: Race and Citizenship in the Postwar Era* (Ithaca and London: Cornell University Press, 1997) p. 166. Paul's book is probably the best systematic examination of just how much race and white supremacy guided Britain's post-war policies on migration, but also see: Panayi, Panikos, *An Immigration History of Britain: Multicultural Racism since 1800* (London: Routledge, 2010); Kushner, Tony, *The Battle of Britishness: Migrant Journeys, 1685 to the Present* (Manchester: Palgrave Macmillan, 2012); Tierney, John, *Race Migration and Schooling* (London: Holt, Rinehart and Winston Ltd, 1982)

13. From the phrase housing schemes is derived the Scottish pejorative 'schemie' for people that live in the hood.

14. Liddle, Rod "Why don't Black Lives Matter want to ban Notting Hill Carnival?" *Spectator* (3 September 2016). Retrieved from URL www.spectator.co.uk/2016/09/why-dont-black-lives-matter-want-to-ban-the-notting-hill-carnival/

CHAPTER 11 – The Decline of Whiteness, the Decline of Race? (Or the End of Capitalism?)

1. Mbembe, Achille, *Critique of Black Reason* (Durham and London: Duke University Press, 2017)

2. Mishra, Pankaj, *From the Ruins of Empire: The Revolt Against the West and the Remaking of Asia* (London: Penguin Books, 2012)

3. See: Jacques, Martin, *When China Rules the World* (London: Penguin, 2012); Frank, Andre Gunder, *ReOrient: Global Economy in the Asian Age* (Los Angeles: University of California Press, 1998). For a better understanding of how similar levels of (or at least experiments with) 'development' had been made across civilisations before the age of imperialism, and an understanding of Eurocentric distortions of history, see any of the following: Blaut, J. M., *Eight Eurocentric Historians* (New York: Guildford Press, 2000); Goody, Jack, *Renaissances: The One or the Many?* (New York: Cambridge University Press, 2010); Goody, Jack, *Capitalism and Modernity: The Great Debate* (Cambridge: Polity, 2004); Abu-Lughod, Janet L., *Before European Hegemony: The World System A.D. 1250–1350* (New York: Oxford University Press, 1991); Amin, Samir, *Eurocentrism: Modernity, Religion, and Democracy: A Critique of Eurocentrism and Culturalism* (New York: Monthly Review Press, 2009)

4. For a look at how recently and fleetingly the West was constructed, see the essay 'There Never Was a West' by David Graeber in *Possibilities: Essays on Hierarchy, Rebellion and Desire* (Chicago: AK Press, 2007)

5. Horne, Gerald, *Race War: White Supremacy and the Japanese Attack on the British Empire* (New York and London: New York University Press, 2004) p. 18

6. Klinker, Philip A., and Smith, Rogers M., *The Unsteady*

March: The Rise and Decline of Racial Equality in America (Chicago: University of Chicago Press, 2002)

7. Furedi, Frank, *The Silent War: Imperialism and the Changing Perception of Race* (London: Pluto Press, 1988)

8. See Popkin, Jeremy D., *Facing Racial Revolution: Eyewitness Accounts of the Haitian Insurrection* (Chicago and London: University of Chicago Press, 2007)

9. See Foner, Eric, *Reconstruction: America's Unfinished Revolution 1863–1877* (New York: Harper & Row, 1988) and Horne, Gerald, *Race War: White Supremacy and the Japanese Attack on the British Empire* (New York and London: New York University Press, 2004

10. See Furedi, Frank, *The Silent War: Imperialism and the Changing Perception of Race* (London: Pluto Press, 1988)

11. Stewart, Dodai "Racist Hunger Games Fans Are Very Disappointed" *Jezebel* (26 March 2012). Retrieved from URL https://www.jezebel.com/5896408/racist-hunger-games-fans-dont-care-how-much-money-the-movie-made; Holmes, Anna, "White Until Proven Black: Imagining Race In Hunger Games" *New Yorker* (30 March 2012). Retrieved from URL www.newyorker.com/books/page-turner/white-until-proven-black-imagining-race-in-hunger-games

12. Streeck, Wolfgang, *How Will Capitalism End: Essays on a Failing System* (London: Verso, 2017)

13. Coates, Ta-Nehisi, *We Were Eight Years In Power: An American Tragedy* (London: Hamish Hamilton, 2017)

14. See: Paul, Kathleen, *Whitewashing Britain: Race and Citizenship in the Postwar Era* (Ithaca: Cornell University Press, 1997)

15. Lord Ashcroft "How the United Kingdom Voted on Thursday . . . and why" (24 June 2016). Retrieved from URL http://lordaschcroftpolls.com/2016/06/how-the-united-kingdom-voted-and-why/

16. Virdee, Satnam and McGeever, Brendan, *Racism, Crisis, Brexit: Ethnic and Racial Studies* (21 August 2007). Retrieved from URL https://eprints.gla.ac.uk/144467/7/144467.pdf

17. Gonyea, Don, *Majority of White Americans say they believe whites face discrimination* (24 October 2017). Retrieved from URL www.npr.org/2017/10/24/559604836/majority-of-white-americans-think-they-are-discriminated-against;

18. Perez, Maria, "White Americans Feel They Are Victims Of Discrimination, A New Poll Shows" *Newsweek* (24 October 2017). Retrieved from URL www.newsweek.com/white-americans-feel-they-are-victims-discrimination-new-poll-shows-691753

19. IPR Blog, *Things Fall Apart: From Empire to Brexit Britain* (2 May 2017). Retrieved from URL http://blogs.bath.ac.uk/iprblog/2017/05/02/things-fall-apart-from-empire-to-brexit-britain/

20. See for example: Murray, Douglass, *The Strange Death of Europe: Immigration, Identity, Islam* (London: Bloomsbury, 2017)

21. Hiro, Dilip, *After Empire: The Birth of a Multipolar World* (New York: Nation Books, 2010) p. 175

Every reasonable effort has been made to trace copyright holders, but if there are any errors or omissions, John Murray Press will be pleased to insert the appropriate acknowledgement in any subsequent printings or editions.

SELECT BIBLIOGRAPHY

Abu-Lughod, Janet L., *Before European Hegemony: The World System A.D. 1250–1350* (New York: Oxford University Press, 1991)

Allen, Theodore W., *The Invention of the White Race: Vol I: Racial Oppression and Social Control* (London: Verso, 2012)

Ani, Marimba, *Yurugu: An African-Centred Critique of European Cultural Thought and Behaviour* (Washington DC: Nkonimfo Publications, 1994)

Baldwin, James, *The Fire Next Time* (London: Penguin, 1963)

——, *I Am Not Your Negro* (New York: Vintage International, 2017)

Ballantyne, Tony, *Orientalism and Race: Aryanism in the British Empire* (Basingstoke: Palgrave Macmillan, 2002)

Baptist, Edward E., *The Half Has Never Been Told: Slavery and the Making of American Capitalism* (New York: Basic Books, 2014)

Bayly, C.A., *The Birth of the Modern World 1780–1914* (Malden: Blackwell Publishing, 2004)

Beckert, Sven, *Empire of Cotton: A New History of Global Capitalism* (London: Vintage, 2014)

Bellagamba, Alice, Greene, Sandra E., and Klein, Martin A., *African Voices on Slavery and the Slave Trade* (New York: Cambridge University Press, 2013)

Bernasconi, Robert and Lott, Tommy L., ed, *The Idea of Race* (Cambridge: Hacket Publishing Company, 2000)

Black, Edwin, *War Against the Weak: Eugenics and America's Campaign to Create a Master Race* (Washington DC: Dialog Press, 2012)

Blackburn, Robin, *The Overthrow of Colonial Slavery 1776–1848* (London: Verso, 1988)

Blackmon, Douglas A., *Slavery By Another Name* (New York: Anchor Books, 2008)

Blaut, J.M., *Eight Eurocentric Historians* (New York: Guilford Press, 2000)

Blum, William, *Killing Hope: US Military and CIA Interventions since World War II* (London: Zed Books, 2014)

Bressey, Caroline, *Empire, Race and the Politics of Anti-Caste* (London: Bloomsbury, 2015)

Burbank, Jane and Cooper, Frederick, *Empires in World History: Power and the Politics of Difference* (Princeton and Oxford: Princeton University Press, 2010)

Burgis, Tom, *The Looting Machine: Warlords, Tycoons, Smugglers, and the Systemic Theft of Africa's Wealth* (London: William Collins, 2015)

Campbell, Horace, *Rasta and Resistance: From Marcus Garvey to Walter Rodney* (London: Hansib, 2007)

Carrington, Ben, *Race, Sport and Politics: The Sporting Black Diaspora* (California: Sage Publications, 2010)

Cashmore, Ernest, *Out of Order?: Policing Black People* (London: Routledge, 1991)

Centre for Contemporary Studies, *The Empire Strikes Back: Race and Racism in 70s Britain* (London: Routledge, 1982)

Chang, Ha-Joon, *Bad Samaritans: The Guilty Secrets of Rich Nations & the Threat to Global Prosperity* (London: Random House, 2007)

Chinweizu, *The West and the Rest of Us: White Predators,*

Black Slavers, and the African Elite (Nigeria: Pero Press, 1987)

Claeys, Gregory, *Imperial Sceptics: British Critics of Empire 1850–1920* (New York: Cambridge University Press, 2010)

Coates, Ta-Nehisi, *Between the World and Me* (New York: Spiegel & Grau, 2015)

Cobain, Ian, *The History Thieves: Secrets, Lies and the Shaping of a Modern Nation* (London: Portobello Books, 2016)

——, *Cruel Britannia: A Secret History of Torture* (London: Portobello Books, 2012)

Cohen, Stanley, *Folk Devils and Moral Panics: The Creation of the Mods and Rockers* (London: Routledge, 2011)

Curtin, Philip D., *The Image of Africa: British Ideas and Action, 1780–1850* (London: Palgrave Macmillan, 1964)

Curtis, Mark, *Secret Affairs: Britain's Collusion with Radical Islam* (London: Serpent's Tail, 2012)

——, *Web of Deceit: Britain's Real Role in the World* (London: Vintage, 2003)

Davidson, Basil, *The African Slave Trade: A Revised and Expanded Edition* (London: Back Bay Books, 1988)

Davis, Angela Y., *Women, Race and Class* (New York: Vintage, 1983)

Davis, David Brion, *The Problem of Slavery in Western Culture* (New York: Oxford University Press, 1966)

Dawson, Raymond, *The Chinese Chameleon: An Analysis of European Conceptions of Chinese Civilization* (London: Oxford University Press, 1967)

Devine, T. M., ed., *Recovering Scotland's Slavery Past: The Caribbean Connection* (Edinburgh: Edinburgh University Press, 2015)

Diouf, Sylviane A., ed., *Fighting the Slave Trade: West African Strategies* (Athens: Ohio University Press, 2003)

Dower, John W., *War Without Mercy: Race and Power in the Pacific War* (New York: Pantheon, 1987)

Draper, Nicolas, *The Price of Emancipation: Slave-Ownership, Compensation And British Society At The End Of Slavery* (New York: Cambridge University Press, 2010)

Dubois, Laurent, *Avengers of the New World: The Story of the Haitian Revolution* (Massachusetts: Harvard University Press, 2004)

Earle, T. F. and Lowe, K. P., *Black Africans in Renaissance Europe* (Cambridge: Cambridge University Press, 2010)

Eddo-Lodge, Reni, *Why I'm no Longer talking to White People About Race* (London: Bloomsbury Circus, 2017)

Eliav-Feldon, Miriam, Isaac, Benjamin, and Ziegler, Joseph, *The Origins of Racism in the West* (New York: Cambridge University Press, 2009)

Elkins, Caroline, *Britain's Gulag: The Brutal End of Empire in Kenya* (London: Pimlico, 2005)

Eze, Emmanuel Chukwudi, ed., *Race and the Enlightenment: A Reader* (London: Blackwell, 1997)

Fanon, Frantz, *The Wretched of the Earth* (London: Penguin, 1963)

Floyd, Jr., Samuel A., *The Power of Black Music: Interpreting its History from Africa to the United States* (New York: Oxford University Press, 1995)

Frank, Andre Gunder, *ReOrient: Global Economy in the Asian Age* (Los Angeles: University of California Press, 1998)

Frank, Andre Gunder and Gills, Barry K., *The World System: Five Hundred Years or Five Thousand?* (London: Routledge, 1996)

Franklin, Jane, *Cuba and the U.S. Empire: A Chronological History* (New York: Monthly Review Press, 2016)

Frasier, Franklin Edward, *Black Bourgeoisie: The Book that Brought the Shock of Self-Revelation to Middle-Class Blacks in America* (New York: Free Press Paperbacks, 1997)

Frederickson, George M., *Racism: A Short History* (New Jersey: Princeton University Press, 2015)

Furedi, Frank, *The Silent War: Imperialism and the Changing Perception of Race* (London: Pluto Press, 1988)

Garner, Steve, *Whiteness: An Introduction* (New York: Routledge, 2007)

Garvey, Amy Jacques, *The Philosophy & Opinions of Marcus Garvey: Or Africa for the Africans* (Massachusetts: The Majority Press, 1986)

George, Susan, *How the Other Half Dies: The Real Reasons for World Hunger* (London: Penguin, 1986)

Gillard, Michael and Flynn, Laurie, *Untouchables: Dirty Cops, Bent Justice and Racism in Scotland Yard* (London: Bloomsbury Reader, 2012)

Gillborn, David, *Racism and Education: Coincidence or Conspiracy?: White Success Black Failure* (London: Routledge, 2008)

Gilroy, Paul, *After Empire: Melancholia or Convivial Culture?* (London: Routledge, 2004)

——, *The Black Atlantic: Modernity and Double Consciousness* (Verso: London 1999)

——, *There Ain't No Black in the Union Jack* (Oxfordshire: Routledge, 1992)

Gleijeses, Piero, *Visions of Freedom: Havana, Washington, Pretoria, and the Struggle for Southern Africa 1976–1991* (Chapel Hill: University of North Carolina Press, 2013)

Goldenberg, David M., *The Curse of Ham: Race and Slavery in Early Judaism, Christianity, and Islam* (Princeton: Princeton University Press, 2003)

Goody, Jack, *Renaissances: The One or the Many?* (Cambridge: Cambridge University Press, 2010)

Gordon, Murray, *Slavery in the Arab World* (New York: New Amsterdam Books, 1987)

Gott, Richard, *Cuba: A New History* (New Haven and London: Yale University Press, 2005)

Hall, Stuart, Critcher, Chas, Jefferson, Tony, Clarke, John, and Roberts, Brian, *Policing the Crisis: Mugging, the State, and Law and Order* (Basingstoke: Macmillan, 1978)

Hiro, Dilip, *After Empire: The Birth of a Multipolar World* (New York: Nation Books, 2010)

Hobson, J. A., *Imperialism: A Study* (New York: Cosimo Classics, 2005)

Hobson, John M, *The Eurocentric Conception of World Politics: Western International Theory, 1760–2010* (Cambridge: Cambridge University Press, 2012)

Hoggart, Richard, *The Uses of Literacy: Aspects of Working-Class Life* (London: Penguin, 1990)

Horne, Gerald, *Race War!: White Supremacy and the Japanese Attack on the British Empire* (New York and London: New York University Press, 2004)

Humphries, Stephen, *Hooligans or Rebels?: An Oral History of Working-Class Childhood and Youth 1889–1939* (London: Wiley, 1997)

Inikori, Joseph E., and Engerman, Stanley L, ed, *The Atlantic Slave Trade: Effects on Economies, Societies, and Peoples in Africa, the Americas, and Europe* (Durham: Duke University Press, 1992)

Isaac, Benjamin, *The Invention of Racism in Classical Antiquity* (Princeton: Princeton University Press, 2004)

Jacques, Martin, *When China Rules the World: The End of the Western World and the Birth of a New Global Order* (London: Penguin, 2012)

Jansen, Jan C., and Osterhammel, Jürgen, trans. Riemer, Jeremiah, *Decolonization: A Short History* (Princeton: Princeton University Press, 2017)

John, Gus, *Moss Side 1981: More Than Just a Riot* (London: Gus John Books, 2011)

Jordan, Michael, *The Great Abolition Sham: The True Story of the End of the British Slave Trade* (Gloucestershire: The History Press, 2005)

Jordan, Winthrop D., *White over Black: American Attitudes Toward the Negro 1550–1812* (Chapel Hill: University of North Carolina Press, 1968)

Kendi, Ibram X., *Stamped From The Beginning: The Definitive History of Racist Ideas in America* (New York: Nation Books, 2016)

Kennedy, Fred, *Daddy Sharpe: A Narrative of the Life and Adventures of Samuel Sharpe, A West Indian Slave Written by Himself, 1832* (Jamaica: Ian Randle Publishers, 2008)

Khaldun, Ibn, *The Muqaddimah: An Introduction to History, The Classic Islamic History of the World* (Princeton: Princeton University Press, 2005)

Kiernan, V. G., *The Lords of Humankind: European Attitudes to Other Cultures in the Imperial Age* (London: The Cresset Library, 1969)

Klinkner, Philip A. and Smith, Rogers M., *The Unsteady March: The Rise and Decline of Racial Equality in America* (Chicago: University of Chicago Press, 2002)

Kovel, Joel, *White Racism: A Psychohistory* (London: Free Association Books, 1988)

Kushner, Tony, *The Battle of Britishness: Migrant Journeys, 1685 to the Present* (Manchester: Palgrave Macmillan, 2012)

La Rose, John, *The New Cross Massacre Story* (London: New Beacon, 2011)

Lindqvist, Sven, *The Dead Do Not Die: "Exterminate all the Brutes" and Terra Nullius* (New York: The New Press, 2014)

Linebaugh, Peter and Rediker, Marcus, *The Many-Headed Hydra: The Hidden History of the Revolutionary Atlantic* (London: Verso, 2012)

Mandela, Nelson and Castro, Fidel, *How Far We Slaves Have Come!: South Africa and Cuba in Today's World* (New York: Pathfinder, 1991)

Mbembe, Achille, *Critique of Black Reason*) (Durham and London: Duke University Press, 2017)

Mesquita, Bruce de and Smith, Alastair, *The Dictator's Handbook: Why Bad Behavior is Almost Always Good Politics* (New York: Public Affairs, 2011)

Mills, Charles, *The Racial Contract* (Ithaca: Cornell University Press, 2017)

Mishra, Pankaj, *From the Ruins of Empire: The Revolt Against the West and the Remaking of Asia* (London: Allen Lane, 2012)

Morefield, Jeanne, *Empires Without Imperialism: Anglo-American Decline and the Politics of Deflection* (New York: Oxford University Press, 2014)

Morton, A. L., *A People's History of England* (London: Lawrence & Wishart, 2003)

Nascimento, Abdias, *Brazil: Mixture or Massacre?: Essays in the Genocide of a Black People* (Massachusetts: The Majority Press, 1989)

Newsinger, John, *The Blood Never Dried: A People's History of the British Empire* (London: Bookmarks, 2006)

Newton, Huey P., *Revolutionary Suicide: Founder of the Black Panther Party* (London: Wildwood House, 1974)

Painter, Nell Irvin, *The History of White People* (New York: W. W. Norton and Company, 2010)

Panayi, Panikos, *An Immigration History of Britain: Multicultural Racism since 1800* (London: Routledge, 2010)

Parenti, Michael, *Against Empire* (San Francisco: City Light Books, 1995)

Patterson, Orlando, *Slavery and Social Death: A Comparative Study* (Massachusetts: Harvard University Press, 1982)

Paul, Kathleen, *Whitewashing Britain: Race and Citizenship in the Postwar Era* (Ithaca: Cornell University Press, 1997)

Paxton, Robert O., *The Anatomy of Fascism* (New York: Random House, 2005)

Poliakov, Leon, *The Aryan Myth: A History of Racist and Nationalist Ideas in Europe* (New York: Basic Books, 1974)

Prashad, Vijay, *The Darker Nations: A People's History of the Third World* (New York: The New Press, 2007)

Ramey, Lynn T., *Black Legacies: Race and the European Middle Ages* (Florida: University Press of Florida, 2016)

Rich, Paul B., *Race and Empire in British Politics* (Cambridge: Cambridge University Press, 2009)

Roediger, David R., *The Wages of Whiteness: Race and the Making of the American Working Class* (London: Verso, 2007)

Rose, Tricia, *The Hip Hop Wars: What We Talk About When We Talk About Hip Hop – and why it matters* (New York: Basic Books, 2008)

Sherwood, Marika, *After Abolition: Britain and the Slave Trade since 1807* (London: I. B. Tauris, 2007)

Smith, John, *Imperialism in the Twenty-First Century: Globalization, Super-Exploitation, and Capitalism's Final Crisis* (New York: Monthly Review Press, 2016)

Smith, Justin E. H., *Nature, Human Nature, & Human Difference: Race in Early Modern Philosophy* (Princeton: Princeton University Press, 2015)

Stepan, Nancy, *The Idea of Race in Science: Great Britain 1800–1960* (Basingstoke: Macmillan, 1982)

Streeck, Wolfgang, *How Will Capitalism End?: Essays On A Failing System* (London: Verso, 2016)

Tharoor, Shashi, *Inglorious Empire: What the British Did to India* (Delhi: Aleph Book Company, 2016)

Thompson, E. P, *The Making of the English Working Class* (London: Penguin, 1991)

Thompson, Leonard, *The Political Mythology of Apartheid* (New Haven: Yale University Press, 1985)

Whitman, James Q., *Hitler's American Model: The United States and the Making of Nazi Race Law* (Princeton: Princeton University Press, 2017)

Williams, Elizabeth M., *The Politics of Race in Britain and South Africa: Black British Solidarity and the Anti-Apartheid Struggle* (London: I. B. Tauris, 2017)

Wolfe, Patrick, *Traces of History: Elementary Structures of Race* (London: Verso, 2016)

ACKNOWLEDGEMENTS

I would like to thank my manager Chanelle Newman for everything, Adam Elliot Cooper for all of his insightful criticism and feedback on the manuscript of this book, my editor Kate Hewson for the same reason and my mum for reasons that should be obvious once you've read the book. I'd like to big up Professor Gus John, Dr Lez Henry, Andrew Muhammad, Toyin Agbetu, Stafford Scott, Mark and Charmaine Simpson and Paul Reid and Monique from the Black Cultural archives in Brixton. I'd like to thank all of the pioneers of the British Pan-African supplementary school/self-education movement. I'd like to especially thank the staff at the – now defunct – Winnie Mandela School. I'd like to thank Uncle Emmanuel from Centerprise bookstore in Hackney, Maarifa books, New Beacon Bookstore and all of the independent African-Caribbean bookshops up and down the country, most of which are now sadly closed. I'd like to thank my school teachers Anne Taylor, Basil Muhammad and Peter Djurovski and all of the inspiring teachers out there trying to push their students and helping them to find their way in the world. I'd like to thank everyone at the Hip-Hop Shakespeare company and all of the teachers, educators and youth workers who we have had the pleasure of engaging with. I'd like to thank my more recent teachers Esther Standford-Xosei and Robin Walker from whom I have learned so much. Thank you to Steve Strand, David Gilborn, Helen Yaffe and Liam Hogan who all sent me their work to use and answered my annoying barrage of emails! Also a big shout out to Andrew Philipou, Lavar Bullard, Niles Hailstones, Paul Gladstone-Reid, Crystal Mahey-Morgan and Anne Marie-Springer.

Special thanks to all of the scholars, writers, activists and artists whose work has inspired mine and shaped this book and my life.

ABOUT THE AUTHOR

Akala is a BAFTA and MOBO award-winning hip-hop artist, writer and social entrepreneur, as well as the co-founder of The Hip-Hop Shakespeare Company. With an extensive global touring history, Akala has appeared at numerous festivals both in the UK and internationally, and has led innovative projects in the arts, education and music across South East Asia, Africa, India, Australia and New Zealand. Akala has also appeared on Channel 4, ITV, MTV, Sky Arts and the BBC promoting his music and poetry, and speaking on wide-ranging subjects from music, race, youth engagement, British/African-Caribbean culture and the arts, with numerous online lectures and performances that have millions of views on YouTube. In 2018 he was awarded an honorary degree from Oxford Brookes University and the University of Brighton. Widely celebrated for his compelling lectures and journalism – he has written for the *Guardian*, *Huffington Post* and the *Independent*, and spoken for the Oxford Union and TEDx – Akala has gained a reputation as one of the most dynamic and articulate talents in the UK.